MW01641261

It's the *Principal* of the Thing!

Arthur E. Woznicki

ISBN 0-7414-3769-4

Editor: Joseph A. Mercier

Published by:

INFINITY
PUBLISHING.COM

1094 New DeHaven Street, Suite 100
West Conshohocken, PA 19428-2713
Info@buybooksontheweb.com
www.buybooksontheweb.com
Toll-free (877) BUY BOOK
Local Phone (610) 941-9999
Fax (610) 941-9959

Printed in the United States of America

Printed on Recycled Paper

Published February 2007

Dedication

It's the Principal of the Thing is dedicated to the industrious, tireless, expert and courageous principals who are making a positive impact on teachers AND learners in their schools. America desperately needs every one of you.

Further this book is dedicated to my wife, who has raised two teachers, and to my entire family.

Contents

It's the *Principal* of the Thing

Introduction

Where are our school principals? Why are principals rarely held accountable when our public schools are disparaged while our teachers, whom our principals theoretically supervise, are broadly criticized for our schools' failings? As we know, these failings are widespread. Yet the boss is left out when solutions are sought to resolve our schools' dilemma.

This book's intent is to rouse you, the general public, to realize that the school principal is either the key to a school's success or its failure. Too many schools are deficient. Too many inept, unskilled and ineffectual principals head those schools. This condition must be changed. We must teach our principals, convince them, pressure them, encourage and motivate them to help teachers to grow. They must show teachers how to improve their craft and inspire them to do their job better. It can be done. Our children will be the better for it.

Discounting the principal's importance by school critics, I submit, is an omission of grave consequence, for it is the principal's responsibility to ensure that our schools are productive, that teachers are competent, and constantly and continually improving. This book makes clear and stresses that the principal plays the crucial role in determining the quality of America's public schools. I contend, that only when competent principals lead our schools, will our nation's schools thrive.

My aim is to communicate clearly the urgent and desperate need for our nation to hold its principals accountable for the delivery of the best education possible to our youth. I assert that the principal is the nerve center of the school; the conductor of the teaching orchestra without whom the education offered by teachers will be disjointed and discordant.

The principal remains the focal point throughout this work. The chapters validate for the reader that the salvation of our schools can only be gained with the expertise of instructional leaders at their helms.

One widely held and valid assumption regarding our public schools is that they will improve when teachers improve *and only then*. However, that improvement will only be achieved with the guidance and help of a capable principal. With instructional assistance provided by an expert principal, teachers will refine their skills and improve their teaching. Are our schools in the hands of that kind of accomplished leadership?

Further, my intent is to sound the alarm. The days of managing schools by principals who are not *instructional leaders* must end. Boards of education, with the help of their superintendents, throughout this nation must track down its principals in the nooks, crannies and shadows of the buildings they manage and retrain and assign them to their vital and fundamental task of supervision; a task that too many principals don't do, don't care to do or can't do. It is time to require our principals to provide instructional assistance in the classrooms of America. Unless this instructional prerequisite is underscored and etched into every principal's job description, our schools are destined to fall into an abyss of ineffectiveness.

The public needs to be awakened to the existing crisis in our schools and require their school boards to hold principals accountable. The book shines a light into the dark and dusty corners of the principalship. What are the principals doing; what *aren't* they doing?

The theme of this book is the principal as a coach. Its purpose is to introduce the lay public to the concept of *coaching teachers* as the essential and primary supervisory technique for improving instruction. In a coaching relationship the principal and teacher work as a team seeking ways to improve teaching and learning. In a traditional supervisory relationship the boss (principal) opines about the subordinate's work without seeking input from the *underling* and usually without data to support the boss's opinions. The latter, unlike a teaming relationship, is a superior/subordinate affiliation. Sadly, even traditional classroom supervision is neglected in many schools. An excessive proportion of teachers in our nation's schools would be surprised to find their principal sitting in their classrooms for the purpose of supervising them.

We must shake the dust off unproductive principals, retrain them and require them to become their teachers' teachers. They must trade their lumbering hammer and nails management style for the finesse tools of brush, oil and canvas and illustrate for their teachers how they can grow and become better at their craft. If principals can't meet the standards set for them, there must be a collective resolve to terminate their services.

In addition to presenting the need for skilled and expert principals, the book addresses the other responsibilities the principal bears daily. These everyday tasks are integral and necessary elements of a job whose primary mission is to ensure that students are armed with the basic skills they will employ throughout their lives.

All aspects of the principalship are laid out in this book. The book's focus is on the *elementary* principal. The supervision model can, however, be replicated at the middle and high schools and in urban and rural schools as well.

The chapters offer insight into the everyday world of the principal. They attempt to persuade all who read the dialog and the anecdotes with a convincing argument that *It's the Principal of the Thing* can help resuscitate education in America

If our schools are to succeed the principal is the vital cog to make that happen. *It's the Principal of the Thing* portrays two principals: one an outstanding educator, the other, an uninvolved school manager. The book contrasts the two principals and their effect on the teachers and children in their schools. It describes what happens when a principal is not prepared to supervise as opposed to what happens when a principal, with instructional expertise, coaches teachers in a collegial fashion.

The narrative depicts a teacher in trouble, his inept principal, an unaware superintendent and an uninformed school board. The scene shifts to a converse school setting where competent professionals flourish with guidance from a proficient coach.

Tenure's effect and how the teachers' union influence teaching are presented for the reader's information.

The skilled school principal, in addition to providing instructional guidance, oversees the school curriculum, communicates effectively, selectively recommends the hiring of new staff and creates a budget that reflects school needs. Money is requested judiciously.

Pouring more money into schools is NOT the answer to school improvement. In this book I recount that staggering amounts of dollars have been spent on schools since the federal efforts of the 60's and the distribution of federal money through the Elementary and Secondary Education Act of 1965. The goal of that act was to close the gap between deprived students and their more privileged counterparts.

The squandered billions of dollars spread over the course of forty-plus years have failed to bridge that gap and have had minimum impact on classroom instruction. By reviewing and judging the status of education beginning with the Great Society efforts, one can conclude that the problems of the past remain the problems of the present. Those excessive tax dollars have had little effect on teacher or school improvement. The political and fallacious assumption continues to be that more federal dollars, in the form of large-scale amendments to the 1965 act and its 1994 revisions and *The No Child Left Behind Act*, will bring a newer and better answer to our schools' deficiencies.

Year after year, decade after decade, those who analyze public education continue to believe that by throwing money at the states, cities and towns, schools will improve. We have been inundated by chicanery crafted by politicians who strive to become identified with tax-supported programs that carry their name. Invariably, politicos seek solutions with dollars. But the dollars are, and have been since the inception of entitlements in the 60's, continuously doled out in flawed ways and too often placed in the wrong tills and the wrong hands.

Money, as it is dispensed now, will *never* make our schools what we want them to be! Give all teachers a $5,000 bonus to improve and, unless there is a principal who is coaching those teachers, it's safe to assume that the teachers will continue to teach as they have been teaching for years. Give every student a computer and, unless the teachers are trained to use the computer as an instructional tool, the technology will be of little value. This book suggests some new, though difficult, options for the redistribution of dollars for education.

This book has been itching and struggling, for a very long time, to free itself from deep within my soul. It has finally surfaced following years of frustration. I have written about the critical need to address the principals' role in our schools. The principals must change from their managerial function to that of instructional leaders. Our schools are burdened with scores of principals who are untrained as classroom supervisors and, therefore, unable to improve teaching and learning in our nation's schools. Unless our leaders recognize this need and make major adjustments to the job, our schools are doomed to fail this generation's needs.

The work is not a scholarly tome. It is not a sophisticated research paper developed in an ivory tower for professional educators. There are no graphs, Venn Diagrams, percentages and few footnotes. The account is founded on logical assumptions made over a period of years regarding teaching and learning. It is based on my own experiences as a teacher and administrator in public schools for twenty-nine years.

The seed for this work was planted in the mid-sixties when I was teaching morning classes in the West Hartford Connecticut Public Schools summer school. We teachers were shown a brand new way to observe and analyze teaching. Our superintendent, Dr. Charles O. Richter, had recently hired Dr. James J. Moore as the district's new director of K-12 instruction and assigned him to conduct afternoon workshops for us summer school teachers. Dr. Moore had completed his own workshop at the renown Harvard-Lexington Summer Program where he had been trained using the latest methods for overseeing instruction designed specifically for principals and supervisors. It was a model of supervision produced, following intensive study and research into the science of teaching and learning, by Robert Goldhammer and Morris Cogan. Their findings have come to be known as Clinical Supervision.

Dr. Moore inspired us with this thought-provoking and fascinating approach to supervision. His presentations were instructive, enlightening, sequential, logical and motivating. I immediately became a student of this so-called clinical approach to supervision and applied its theories at the school where I subsequently served as principal.

Following four years of practicing my craft at the school level, I moved to the central office where I joined Dr. Moore as the district's second director of instruction replacing Dr. Leon Pierce who left the district to become a superintendent of schools elsewhere. I learned to conduct my own supervision workshops for principals and supervisors from my two colleagues, James J. Moore and Leon R. Pierce.

Subsequent to my own training, I was contracted to run summer workshops for the principals in Montgomery County, Maryland for two consecutive summers. I organized and led workshops and made presentations for administrators regarding clinical supervision in a number of school districts in Connecticut, New York, Massachusetts, Maryland and Kentucky.

My administration experiences cover twenty-one years of subscribing to and honing my own supervision skills as principal and, later, as evaluator of principals while director of K-12 instruction in the district.

It was my good fortune to have worked with first-rate principals. The nationally recognized West Hartford Public School System is testimony to their talent. As I traveled and observed other districts, I found, to my dismay that supervision skills were clearly lacking among a shockingly large number of principals. It would be a rare teacher, I lamented, who would significantly improve without appropriate instructional supervision. Where will they get it?

Throughout this book I assert that the principal is critical to improved teaching. The principal is the conductor of the teaching orchestra without whom the teaching act will be disjointed and discordant. The principal remains the focal point. It validates for the reader that the salvation of our schools can only be gained through the expertise of instructional leaders.

The Old River Schools are fictional but the events described are real. In the narrative Old River borders an inner city. The problems facing rural, suburban and city schools, while different, can be improved but only when instructional leaders are appointed to lead all schools. Though schools are impacted by cultural forces brought upon them by today's society over which the schools have little control, educators must work with what they can and do control: the instruction they bring to their students whether inner city or not.

This work recognizes the outside forces that daily intrude on the principal's agenda. Events are described to give the reader a sense of what a public school principal is confronted with on a regular basis making the coaching responsibility more difficult to fulfill. Each anecdote depicted in the book was experienced or witnessed by the author.

Dear readers, *It's the Principal of the Thing!*

Chapter 1:
Does Certification = Qualification?

Harry Latter, an elementary school teacher, slowly and reluctantly rises from bed. Somewhat groggy, he clears the sleep from his brain and focuses on the day ahead. Ugh, it's only Wednesday, three more days 'til the weekend, he laments. His thoughts slowly turn to his fifth-grade classroom as he flicks on a light in the kitchen and shakes cereal into a small bowl, slices a banana, empties the last of a quart of milk over the mixture and pours a cup of coffee. Harry remains gloomy about the prospect of another day at work. He retrieves the morning paper, opens the blinds and turns to the sports page blocking all thoughts of the task ahead.

Following a shave and shower, Harry dresses indifferently. He steps into a casual pair of chinos spotted with a few faint but unmistakable coffee stains. He slips on an open-collared and somewhat wrinkled polo shirt; unlike the tedious clothes *his* teachers wore when Harry was a student. He's thankful for the informality of today's teachers' attire. At least that's an improvement, Harry reasons. He does not consider that his choice of slovenly dress sends a subliminal message to his students that this *learning business* can't be very serious. The drive to school takes about 45 minutes; Harry has to get on the road. His wife and two kids are stirring upstairs. He bids them good-bye and leaves for work. This, his fourth year of teaching, has been nothing but bad.

Driving to school, Harry Latter briefly reflects on classroom issues that lay ahead. But, he doesn't have to face those until he has coffee with colleagues in the faculty room. Entering the teachers' lounge, Harry gladly joins the morning sports conversation with a few colleagues. He is filled with information about yesterday's games. As yet, he has given little thought to beginning the formal school day.

The opening bell rings and students rush in from the playground and the cafeteria where deprived kids are provided with free and nutritious breakfasts. Before leaving the faculty lounge, Harry refills his mug and heads down the hall to begin another dreadful day *in the cell*, as he calls his room: a warden in his own little prison.

Most of Harry Latter's class arrive in the classroom before their teacher and are already milling, chatting and jostling when he arrives. His 5th graders are a very active group.

"How many times do I have to remind you to sit down and be quiet when you're in this classroom?" bellows Mr. Latter entering the room. "And, Warren, what do I need to do to calm you down?"

Janie is hollering to a friend across the room paying no heed to Mr. Latter. "Janie, come here." Janie slowly sashays up to Latter's desk.

"Yeah?"

"I've told you a hundred times if I've told you once to stop your nonsense, your attitude is getting worse. In fact, it's lousy."

"Yeah?" she sasses again.

"That does it. I'm through with your impertinence and your insolence. I'm going to call your mother and tell her what an impudent young lady you're becoming."

"Uh-uh," Janie replies indifferently.

And so it goes. Mr. Harry Latter's classroom has behaved this way for much of the school year. He is unable to connect, not only with the few minority and immigrant kids, but with the rest of the class as well. His approach to this daily chaos is to intimidate by hollering and berating. Each day, his outcry becomes more strident and less effective. His threats to call parents are ignored. Harry never follows through with these warnings and the class knows it. He is too intimidated by the parents to call any of them since his humiliation at a board of education meeting earlier in the year regarding vandalism in his room.

Several parents, who have children in Mr. Latter's class, complained bitterly at that board meeting concerning the deplorable condition of the brand new student furniture in Mr. Latter's room. They were shocked, they said, when they visited at Open House and saw the furniture. Some students had somehow managed to scratch their initials into the desktops almost as soon as the furniture was unboxed. Even the chairs were marred with indelible pen marks. The negative attention that Latter got from this incident unsettled Harry to the extent that he avoids contact with the parents as much as possible. The defacements are reflexions of Harry's mismanagement. Principal Bill Higgins' course of action was to have a custodian repair and scrub the furniture until it was at least, acceptable.

As a result of that episode, the children have become more emboldened as Harry's yelling, bullying and threatening have become more meaningless. Many in the class pay little attention to him. He shares his dislike for these youngsters with other teachers and blames the lack of discipline in his room on unruly kids, uncaring parents and the absence of parental control. He is convinced that power is his right to wield as a teacher. Caring, kindness, support and respect for his students are not ever considered as possible solutions for his inability to manage the class. Who can advise him that he must take a very different approach with his class? Where is his principal? Why isn't he supervising Harry?

Harry Latter best typifies the dilemma facing the recruitment of qualified teachers for America's schools. There are basically two types of individuals who select teaching for their life's work: those who are devoted and dedicated to making a difference in the lives of young people and those who opt for teaching as their occupation of choice because they assume it's an easy job and they will have oodles of time off. *No one* chooses a teaching career for the money.

Harry's surname ironically identifies him with the latter group. As a high school senior with average grades he lacked ambition and chose to pursue a teaching career in college. He chose it for its regular pay, medical insurance and lots of time off. He found his way into the school of education at the state university.

Unlike applicants to prestigious universities where the competition is so keen that applicants must have, at minimum, a notable high school transcript sprinkled with extra-curricula accomplishments, schools of education usually accept high school seniors from a candidate pool that matches the two kinds of teacher aspirants described above. There are too few of caring and dedicated applicants seeking entrance to schools of education, which makes it difficult to enroll only those with a principled commitment to teaching. The result is that schools of education, to survive, regularly take in applicants who are mediocre high school students and even a few who can prove they have a pulse. Harry Latter's pulse was beating when he was accepted into the school of education.

Unchallenging, for the most part, mundane certification courses continue to be the norm for preparing teachers and administrators; too often taught by uninspired faculties. Harry finished four years at State where he majored in elementary education. He was a middling and undistinguished student; bright but not motivated. He graduated with mostly B's, a few C's and fewer A's. According to all accounts, he did acceptable work during his two student teaching assignments. Therein lies another of education's problems.

His college supervisor, Dr. Erwin Geslo, observed Harry several times during his two separate student teaching stints. He sat with Harry following each observation and gave him general feedback regarding his teaching, offering minor suggestions for improvement. The college's two grading options were pass/fail. He passed Harry.

Dr. Geslo, a retired school of education professor, remained active as a supervisor of student teachers following his official departure from his lengthy professorship. Erwin Geslo had lost his passion for college teaching as he approached retirement. Supervising students on a part-time basis was the perfect occupation for his post-retirement years. Because of his fading enthusiasm he had lost interest in emerging theories concerning learning and teaching, yet was content with his part-time work observing student teachers. Unfortunately for his young charges he was *an old soldier fading away.*

Geslo first observed Harry during his junior year of student teaching in a third grade where he was paired with a veteran classroom teacher who was appointed to be Harry's onsite mentor at Lincoln School not far from the college. Dr. Geslo was also his supervisor for Harry's senior student teaching assignment in a fifth grade with another experienced teacher. Neither classroom teacher was of significant help to Harry. Both avoided any methodical work with him. Neither offered much in the way of useful suggestions for improvement, choosing instead to simply take over the class when Harry ran into a problem, which was frequent enough to cause some concern. However, each of Harry's elementary school mentors went along with Erwin Geslo's "pass" grade.

When Harry applied to the Champlain School District following graduation he brought with him a very ordinary transcript. Champlain, as were most school districts, was seeking male elementary teachers, a dying breed, and was willing to overlook some deficiencies in male resumés. Harry was glib, attractive and made a good first impression. The district hired him and placed Harry in a 5th Grade at Whitewood School under the supervision of Principal William, "Call me Bill," Williams.

Harry and *Bill* became fast friends. Both were sports enthusiasts, loved golf and bridge. Bill was pleased to know that Dorothy, Harry's wife, enjoyed bridge as did Bill's wife, Marge. The two couples made their card game a weekly Friday evening event. Bill confided to Harry that, at long last, the superintendent had the good sense to send him a real man. Other than showing Harry where his classroom was and where the supplies were located, Bill did little to prepare Harry for his assignment. Oh, he gave him the curriculum guides, a class list and led him to a rolling table to cart the necessary textbooks and supplies to his classroom and encouraged Harry to seek him out for any reason at all.

"If you need anything, Harry, my door is always open."

Macho Harry didn't wish to appear needy in any way so he asked for nothing and certainly not for assistance in his classroom. The two new colleagues, Harry and Bill, spent more time together playing one hole of golf than they would spend together in the classroom for an entire school year. Each Friday afternoon as soon as the bell rang for dismissal they'd meet on the first tee at the Champlain Public Golf Course.

Fortunately for Harry he had two successive classes of well-behaved and respectful kids for his first two years of teaching at Whitewood. Initially, Harry was enthusiastic about his new job. The fifth-graders sat passively and politely through long stretches of Harry's lecturing. Mostly, he talked using textbooks to guide his lessons while the children listened. Bill Higgins occasionally peeked into the classroom with a wave to Harry and a "hi" to the kids. Things were going smoothly for Harry because of the nature of the children and the absence of any pressure from his principal. It was atypical for ten-year-old children to be as receptive as his first two classes were at Whitewood.

He began to run into some problems toward mid-November of his third year. He had a different mix of kids. They were easily distracted and several became difficult to control. Harry often raised his voice to quiet a couple of unruly youngsters. He began to lose some interest in his job, fluffing off a few of his responsibilities. He didn't put much time into planning and he took every shortcut that he could with his preparation.

A few parents complained but Harry was able to get through the year without too much trouble. Many parents who had children in his class heard rumors from other parents and tales from their children about some kids' bad manners in the class and of Harry's hollering at them. Once, it was alleged, he broke a yardstick slamming it down on a student's desk. But, most parents reasoned, his anger was probably the result of a couple of disruptive kids acting up. After all, there were few complaints during Harry's previous two years at Whitewood. But Harry was having difficulty controlling a number of children. He had very little help from anyone especially his principal. The year ended without any *major* incidents. Superintendent Alecea Morea placed Mr. Harry Latter on tenure following Bill Higgins' recommendation.

Harry's fourth year begins poorly and turns progressively worse. The classroom ship has sprung several leaks and is slowly sinking. As his woes pile up he becomes more disenchanted. He dislikes, not only the children, but his job as well. He awakens each day tired and ornery. By the time he carries his coffee from the staff room to his class, he is in an ugly mood.

Yet, his colleagues are fond of Harry. They find him to be a far different person from the one his students know. Though several teachers realize that Harry has trouble controlling his young charges, not one of them finds it curious that the principal doesn't help Harry. In fact, Bill Higgins only observes the teachers who, by state law, must be supervised such as non-tenure teachers or teachers who are assigned to the district evaluation cycle every third year. However, even those visits prove to be unproductive for the teachers whom Higgins oversees. The supervision is minimal, halfhearted, ineffective and fruitless. Principals in Champlain use check-lists to evaluate their staff. Teachers, not assigned for evaluation, would be taken aback to find the principal in their classroom to supervise their teaching.

Mister William Higgins has been the Whitewood School principal for six years. Higgins is an impressive man. He is lean and athletic and has a confidence that can intimidate. He is impressed with his appearance and his title.

He and Harry remain good buddies. They continue to play cards, bowl and golf together. They and their wives socialize frequently.

Higgins is proud of his role as principal in his comfortable suburban school. It has given him stature in the community and has opened several social doors för him. In fact, William Higgins was named principal of Whitewood School because of his connection with two school board members with whom he golfed. Though he took the required courses to become certified as a principal, he found a great deal of what was presented in his course work to be useless, irrelevant and dull. Sadly, much of it was. Courses required for certification had little relevance to the job he was hired to do. So, like too many others in education, Higgins received his administrative certificate but his qualification was questionable.

A number of professors, who taught administrative certification courses where Higgins matriculated never taught in public schools. Most lectured from texts which offer few applicable "how-to's" for the modern schoolmaster. Nor did the professors of administration generally offer much insight into how children learn or how teachers teach. It followed that supervision offerings had many voids. Certified under such conditions, one would be hard-pressed to suggest that William Higgins was qualified for an instructional role in a contemporary and progressive education system. Bill Higgins had been a good teacher ergo the assumption was that he would be a good principal.

With his preparation, there was little hope that Higgins would or could affect Latter's teaching in a way that would help *him* to become proficient. Classroom discipline is the first step in developing an atmosphere for learning. Learning cannot occur in a disorderly classroom any more than a ship can successfully sail with mutinous sailors aboard. Until Mr. Latter can bring order to his room, the first step he must take to create a learning environment, no meaningful learning will result. BUT, who is going to confront Harry with his futile approach to discipline?

It is painfully obvious that pouring more dollars into a school such as Whitewood, whether those dollars come from federal, state or local taxes, is tantamount to pouring water on dead flowers. To improve the poor learning environment that exists at Whitewood, Bill Higgins needs to be replaced by a principal who is an instructional expert. Such a leader would meet with Harry Latter and deal with his fundamental problem then work with him to overcome his ineffective approach to discipline. Can Harry be saved? Can he become a productive teacher? If Harry can learn to manage his classroom, what other skills must he develop to become successful at his craft? Higgins knows next to nothing about instruction nor how to supervise teachers. He is a manager and just fair at that.

Replacing Mr. Higgins would not be an easy task. Bill Higgins belongs to the administrative union in town and the union would fight his removal with every legal force it could muster to defend Higgins.

The other all-too familiar problems at Whitewood are obvious. The school has at least one struggling teacher in Harry Latter and an ineffectual principal unable to recognize the mess in Harry's or the needs in other teachers' classrooms. This situation will remain unchanged until the school district and school board refuse to tolerate poor instructional leadership. This holds true for rural, suburban, urban and state boards of education across the nation.

Sadly, Harry Latter's inability to control his students is only the first of many concerns that logically follow his mismanagement. Quality instruction and quality learning cannot be addressed until Harry establishes control. He has personal traits that could serve him well were he able to manage his classroom and be motivated enough to become a competent professional.

Though adults find Harry considerate, friendly and interesting as do his friends and acquaintances, his students do not see *that* Mr. Latter. Harry is paralyzed in the classroom. He lacks a plan and lacks a principal with the ability to lead him out of his classroom hell. Harry is unable to project his personal qualities to his students with the provoking and ineffective practices he has adopted *to control* them.

While Harry struggles with his students, other teachers are plugging along in other classrooms with daily routines that have become ordinary and boring to students and staff alike. Teachers who drone on in front of young children are not motivating them. Teachers who don't know how to inspire children; teachers who don't know the art of questioning; teachers who don't know how to bring closure to a lesson or teachers who drift far from the assigned curriculum are all in need of assistance from an expert in instruction. Many of the aforementioned teachers do fine work with pieces of instruction but are unaware of their deficiencies in other areas.

Unfortunately, a preponderance of teachers across this nation lack appropriate and effective supervision. Professionals in a host of other fields regard expert input into their work as critical to their development and progress. Do teachers?

Bill Higgins is not providing instructional leadership to his staff. He is unable to supervise effectively. Supervision is an interesting word repeated so often that it has lost its simple message. *Super*: great, excellent, superior. *Vision*: foresight, forethought, farsightedness. *Supervision*: guidance, direction, management. It is apparent that Mr. Higgins is overmatched in his job. He plainly does not have the insight and skills to assist his teachers. He lacks *Super Vision*! Sadly, he too, is unaware of his deficiencies.

And what is Superintendent Alicia Morea doing to resolve Whitewood's troubles? Is she aware that fundamental difficulties exist at the school? What is her responsibility? Does she evaluate and assess the principals under her aegis? How does she ensure that the principals and department heads are helping teachers to improve their skills? Is she an instructional leader or a budget manager and board of education puppet? What should her role be? Are other schools in her district faced with similar crises as

Whitewood's? Who, in the communities across America, knows enough about the value of improving teacher effectiveness through meaningful supervision by principals to put pressure where it will best serve the students?

Boards of education must wake up. They must require a supervisory plan from their superintendents assuring the public that qualified principals are supervising competent teachers, thus ensuring teacher growth in the art of teaching. Do lay board members across this nation have any insight into instructional development? What wisdom and guidance affecting teacher growth do board members offer the community they represent?

Our national problem with education begins with a basic lack of understanding of the real cause of failure in many of our public schools. Where one finds principals who supervise teachers in the art of teaching and learning and who ensure the application of that knowledge in the classroom, those schools succeed! Identify any outstanding urban, suburban or rural school and you will find outstanding educational leaders serving in every one of those institutions.

Far too many school districts across this nation are in similar straits to those in the Champlain School District. How are we to save schools like Whitewood and teachers like Harry Latter?

Symbolic tools: bulldozers and demolition balls must raze old and failing practices. Concrete and steel girders supporting new theories of learning, framed by strong principles and *principals* must become the new foundation on which the nation's schools are restructured from bottom to top. These resources must be used to renovate, reconstruct and erect an education system that relies and holds responsible the instructional leadership in its schools: the superintendent and the building principals, the captains of the school ships for the success of their schools. That is where our national efforts, including spending programs, must be re-focused and re-distributed. Is Harry Latter failing? Is Bill Higgins failing? Is Alicia Morea failing? Is the Champlain School Board failing? Is Champlain representative of school districts across America?

Harry Latter is in quicksand. The situation in which he finds himself offers no way out. No help is forthcoming. The school year inches along until, finally, it comes to a merciful end for Harry. Summer brings a brief but welcome respite. Harry is freed, for the moment, yet senses no freedom. Harry frets about the next school year. He is tenured and has medical coverage for himself, his wife and two young children. He needs the job but the job is choking him. It represents security and it represents insecurity. He worries. There is no escape from his personal quagmire.

The upper echelons of control, the superintendents commanding the armada of school ships within their districts, bear the responsibility for staffing their ships with skilled captains who can identify weaknesses such as Harry's and provide appropriate assistance for all teachers. To accomplish such a lofty goal will demand superintendents who hold instruction sacred and make it their highest priority. It is obvious that the feet of district superintendents must be held to the fire by local boards of education for it is they who must assure our nation, through their boards of education, that our principals are doing their jobs.

Are the boards of education in the hands of citizens who comprehend the need to ensure that their superintendents hire and train only principals who possess instructional expertise? Board members must understand that *only* proficient instructional leaders can ensure the success of their schools. Boards of education, once committed to the concept of expert instructional leadership, shall direct their CEO, the district superintendent, to make certain that principals have the skills to right listing school ships.

A national effort to accomplish this aim is not solely the responsibility of the school districts. A critical accountability for our nation is to certify AND qualify future teachers and to prepare principals to become instructional leaders: *teachers of teachers.* Such responsibility lies within the states that create certification requirements and the colleges and universities that prepare professional educators. The teacher and principal training programs must not only bear witness to certification but also offer programs that *qualify* aspiring professionals. The onus of preparing instructional leaders, in addition to preparing managers, falls collectively to them.

Bill Higgins had no such preparation. Too often graduate schools are mired in certification practices of the past. Too many college staffs have few direct connections with the schools and classrooms of today and the difficulties facing the supervisors at those sites. Too many who teach in the ivory towers of education have no current hands-on knowledge of the social and corresponding instructional issues being dropped into the classrooms of our public schools. Too many have lost touch with the existing world of instruction regarding today's student needs and the related supervision skills required to meet them. They are akin to our Congress, which has little understanding of the everyday world which their constituents face daily.

Yet, these preparing institutions, in partnership with state boards of education, testify to the readiness of principals by certifying them for a school responsibility that doesn't groom them for the world they are about to enter. Poorly trained principals are handed the keys to enter the school leadership door with certification in hand. Qualification, they soon learn, is indeed quite a different animal.

Fortunately, a silver lining is edging the dark clouds of some administrative certification programs as more cutting edge colleges and universities are addressing qualification, an essential dimension in the overall restructuring of the role of the principal. Several states are demanding a more rigorous certification process with a strong emphasis on classroom supervision. A number of colleges and universities are now employing adjunct personnel that currently hold leadership roles in public school districts. Coupled with up-to-date professors who recognize today's classroom issues and today's student needs there is renewed hope emerging for our public schools. These professionals are up-to-speed regarding the latest research concerning instruction, learning, teaching and supervising.

But improving circumstances such as these are uncommon in far too many districts, states and universities. More is required. The Harry Latter's should never slip between the cracks only to begin a free-fall from which there is no return. Who is going to intervene? Harry faces students who bring diversity to his schoolroom. He is facing children with cultural and social differences. They are foreign to Harry's world. He is unprepared and unable to cope.

Only an instructional leader can save the likes of Harry Latter, not only with classroom management techniques, but also with up-graded instruction and sensitivity to children's needs. Harry's principal must assist him to develop teaching skills, compassion and understanding for the youngsters he is assigned to teach.

Mr. Harry Latter was prepared poorly from the day he first entered college. Schools of education's primary responsibility is to graduate only qualified student teachers. That obligation must begin with entrance prerequisites that lead to both, certification and qualification. Those were missing from Harry's preparation.

Harry Latter has no idea how to reach his pupils. His continued failures cause him to resent the students and blame their culture and parents for his inability to work with them. Though he will have the approaching summer vacation to reflect on his ineffectiveness, Harry will put thoughts of his job on the back burner and involve himself in more pleasurable activities during his time off. The end of the school year, for Harry and for Harry's students, could not have come soon enough.

Chapter 2:
Change of Scenery

School has been closed for a week when Bill Higgins invites Harry to be his guest and golf partner at the Raging Hills Country Club. Higgins arranged an 18-hole match with two teachers from the Old River School District. Harry is a profitable partner on a golf course and is often sought out by others when matches are played for a few bucks or a few beers. Bill and Harry arrive a few minutes before their scheduled match. When Jack Deane and Alan Bowles pull in, Bill makes the introductions.

The foursome tees off at 8:00 AM. As usual, Harry plays well. The morning sun is pleasant but ominous-looking clouds loom in the western sky. Socially, Harry wins over his new acquaintances with his wit and his skill. On the seventh hole the four golfers who had been watching the sky feel the first few drops of rain from the steel gray clouds now above them. Soon it's pouring. Lightning and loud thunder chase the four men into the clubhouse. While waiting out the rain, they order sandwiches and beer. Bill Higgins elects to table-hop when he recognizes a couple of local bigwigs. The remaining three golfers are left to chat about the end of the school year. Alan, Jack and Harry have begun to establish a comfortable relationship as they exchange classroom anecdotes.

Harry says, "I had a rough class this year and I'm expecting one just as bad in September. There are days when I just think I'd like to pack it in and do something else with my life."

Jack and Alan tell Harry that the schools in Old River, where they teach, are pretty good schools and express satisfaction with their jobs.

"We both have principals who roll up their sleeves and dig in whenever we need a hand," says Jack.

Harry is puzzled by Jack's comment. He hardly ever sees Bill in his classroom. For him to come into Harry's class to offer help is beyond his comprehension. The rain continues for more than an hour. The match is postponed to another day.

Early that evening, the phone rings; Dorothy answers. "It's for you."

"Harry? This is Jack Deane."

"Hey Jack, nice to hear from you so soon. What's up?"

"You know, Harry, I was thinking about our conversation this morning and it struck me that you live about twenty minutes closer to Old River than you do to Champlain. I was also thinking about your dissatisfaction with your situation there. Our school has 3rd, 4th and 5th grade vacancies and we're short of male teachers. Any chance I could persuade you to apply here?" Harry is surprised but flattered by Jack's call.

"Geez, Jack, I've never considered moving from Chamberlain to teach elsewhere. It never occurred to me. I don't know; I've kind of had it with the whole idea of teaching, yet there are so many plusses for my family and me that I hate to think of quitting. Do you think your school would be interested?"

"All I can say is there are vacancies at Clarksdale where I teach. We have a supportive community, most of the kids are pretty good and our principal, Jennifer Meyers, is terrific. She's on top of everything and is always available to help. I could mention your name to her if you think you might be interested."

"Wow, Jack, you really hit me over the head. Let me think about it overnight and discuss it with my wife. Can I get back to you tomorrow?"

"Sure. Call me. I'd be happy to get in touch with Dr. Myers on your behalf."

Harry's ability to shine in social situations with adults never fails to impress. He is likable and fun loving. One would never believe how he struggles with pre-adolescents in a classroom. With the unexpected call from Jack, Harry senses an escape. Of course, he believes he can teach because he has convinced himself that *he* was the victim of some impertinent and disrespectful kids in his classroom. This could be his way out! Suddenly the summer looks a little brighter. Dorothy is supportive of his pursuing the possibility. She knows the misery he has put them all through this past year and is not looking forward to another year of the same.

What will Bill Higgins think? Harry's not concerned about Superintendent Morea; he's not sure she even knows who he is. Harry calls Bill and meets him for coffee. Bill is shocked by the thought that Harry is considering a change. He lists for Harry the many reasons for him to stay and points to the pitfalls of new situations in unknown places. He makes a strong effort to keep Harry at Whitewood but realizes that Harry has made up his mind to check out the prospect of making a change. He tells Bill that he wants out if he can get out.

"Obviously, I'd hate to leave you but Old River is so much closer and you know how those parents affected me."

"Well, ol' buddy, if you think you want to change, I won't stand in your way though I wish you'd stick around. I know you'll be saving lots of commuting time and Old River is a damned good system. I know Jennifer Meyers and will, of course, give her my strongest recommendation. We'd miss you around here, but whatever is best for you and Dorothy has my approval."

"Thanks for understanding, Bill. Who knows, I may not even get a job there."

Harry calls Jack to inform him of his interest. Jack, in turn, contacts Dr. Myers and sings Harry's praises to her. Jennifer Myers is enthused over the possibility of gaining another man on her staff; a much needed male role model for the students at her school. She urges Jack to have Mr. Latter fill out an application a.s.a.p. Excited by Jack's information, Harry drives to the Old River Human Resources office to pick up an application and the process is underway.

Bill Higgins extols Harry's virtues to Jennifer Myers and writes a glowing recommendation.

To Whom It May Concern:
Reference for Mr. Harry Latter

Harry Latter is an outstanding teacher who has taught at Whitewood School for the past four years. As Harry's principal I can tell you that Mr. Latter is charming, friendly, bright and experienced. He works hard on behalf of his students. He is able to capture their interests and elevate their skills.

Harry is a raconteur and holds his children's interest with his ability to share his extensive outside experiences with his class. He is willing to take on committee responsibilities, extra-curricular work and his attendance is good.

I support Harry's candidacy for a teaching position in your district without reservation. I will hate to lose him.

William P. Higgins, Principal
Whitewood School

Jennifer notes the lack of specific information regarding Harry's teaching strengths OR weaknesses. The reference offers no insights into his teaching ability. Though Jennifer doesn't realize it, Higgins doesn't really know much about Harry's teaching skills. It's like so many references written by those who have poor observation or supervisory ability. The reference, as Jennifer Meyers reads it, strikes her as being sketchy and general at best. However, Dr. Myers has become accustomed to reading hollow references. For now she is satisfied with Jack's assessment of Harry as a very likeable, bright and sociable person, surely traits not to be overlooked. She likes the sound of, "He is able to capture their interests and elevate their skills."

Bill Higgins' phone comments to her put her more at ease. She scheduled an interview with Harry Latter for the next day.

Dr. Jennifer Myers is deeply committed to her profession as she is to everything she does. She is single and proudly admits to being a career woman. Jennifer Myers' appeal evolves from her enthusiasm for everything she does. Her warm, infectious smile imbues her with an attractiveness that bursts forth from an affectionate personality. She maintains a vigorous exercise program, eats healthful foods and is tireless. She is markedly slender and always fashionably clothed on the conservative side. Every strand of her wavy and prematurely graying hair is in place and trimmed precisely to shoulder length. She embodies a gentle but resolute confidence.

Harry can be described as Jennifer's opposite. He is ESPN: she is PBS. He is slovenly, wrinkled and lax with his clothing: *but not today*. She is neat and particular with hers *as always*.

Harry is tense. He is an arresting man. One is immediately impressed with his piercing, deeply set eyes, square jaw and Michael Douglas-like cleft chin. For his interview, he is dressed in a navy blue serge suit, a lighter blue Van Heusen shirt and a complementary red and blue tie. His black shoes are spit-shined. The last time he dressed like this was two years ago for his aunt's funeral. He looks quite refined entering Dr. Myers' reception room. Her secretary announces Harry's arrival and Jennifer Myers promptly and warmly greets him and shows him to her private office.

Soon into the interview Dr. Myers deduces that Harry has had no effective supervision at Whitewood School. She recognizes that Harry is bright and affable but lacks instructional knowledge. His few responses reveal his deficiency in understanding how children learn. He has persuaded her that he would welcome her supervision. Jennifer Myers decides that Harry could become a good teacher with proper coaching and opts to take on the challenge. She considers him as a sculptor considers a piece of clay: pliant and moldable. Harry has been disingenuous with his part of the interview. He has little desire for direct supervision but has decided not to worry about that until the time comes.

Jennifer recommends hiring Harry to Director of Human Services, Dennis Willingham. Willingham discusses Harry with Jennifer. He has learned that she is seldom without a strong rationale for her recommendations though he wonders about Harry Latter's scanty application, his so-so transcript and the one reference he has attached to it. He chats with Jennifer who speaks to her need and expresses confidence that she sees Harry Latter as a diamond in the rough.

Willingham reluctantly takes Harry's papers with his and Jennifer's recommendation to Superintendent Bernard Green for his scrutiny and signature. Green is a heavy balding man, nearly obese, but with energy to burn who is also charismatic. But he is intimidating when it comes to approving new hires. He examines each and every application brought to him by Willingham who is always required to remain while Green reads.

Dennis Willingham approaches Dr. Green's desk cautiously; he's been in this situation before. He knows he is bringing papers to Bernard Green that are ordinary at best. Dennis Willingham hands the application to his superintendent. Bernard Green immediately senses Dennis' unease.

He scans the application and asks Willingham, "What the hell have you brought me? Are you serious? You know what I want to see in the applications that you bring me. Why should we hire this guy? I don't see anything extraordinary in this application. What's he accomplished? Did he work his way through college? Did he show any leadership in school? Did he belong to any clubs? There is no indication of any kind of extra-curricula activity or accomplishment except that he plays golf and bridge. His undergraduate record is unimpressive. Does he write well? Is he up to Old River standards? What kind of teacher is he? Why in hell, Dennis, are you bringing this application to me?

Are you losing it?" This line of questioning is Superintendent Green's standard pressure tactic for ensuring that his director will scrutinize each candidate's application before daring to seek his signature and reject the kind he has brought him today.

There were several more pointed questions all of which made Willingham squirm. His only response was, "Jennifer has interviewed him and strongly recommends him for her school. She referred to him as a diamond in the rough. She desperately needs another male on her staff and believes she can mold Mr. Latter into a fine teacher."

Warily, Green says, "You two have got to be kidding. You mean to tell me Jennifer wants this guy after reading this barren piece of paper and interviewing him?" Following an unusually long pause, Superintendent Green warily concedes.

"Okay, if Jennifer sees something in this applicant, she must have her reasons though I haven't a clue as to what they could be. I'll sign this but I'm telling you and Jennifer that I'd better not hear that this guy isn't cutting it."

What most notice about Bernard Green are his analytic mind and his logic. He was a Latin scholar and a skilled debater in college and has honed his skills to a very sharp edge that can slice cleanly. Along with his steel-trap mind he has vision and is immediately alert to anything askew such as Harry Latter's application. Yet Bernard Green's charisma and sensitivity seep through a harder countenance. He is an intuitive leader with inherent qualities that only natural leaders have. Dr. Green is also an innovator and strategist, traits the Board of Education detected at the outset of their interviews with him. "Leading," he affirmed at one of his interviews, "is not the same as managing."

Jennifer calls Harry to congratulate him following notification from Willingham who tells her that he took some heavy heat from Bernard.

"Harry, this is Jennifer Myers. I am delighted to notify you that you will be offered a contract to join our staff at Clarksdale School. As soon as you sign the contract that I am mailing this afternoon and return it, we'll send you a packet from the superintendent's office and one from me with helpful information about the district, the school and the orientation program we host for new staff in Old River. Your assignment will be a fifth grade. I'll meet with you within the next couple of weeks to share some important information about your new school and your new class.

"Following our meeting you will meet with Jackie Elton, one of our fourth grade teachers, who will serve as kind of a big sister until you become acclimated to the school. She'll be of great help. Jackie taught many of the youngsters who will be in your class. You and she can examine each student's class folder and discuss some strategies for the opening of school. I'm sure Jackie will share useful information with you. And, Harry, please know that I'm in your corner to assist in any way I can. Never consider me to be a threat. If that day should ever come, it would not come as a surprise. I anticipate a good beginning and a successful career for you at our school. Welcome to Clarksdale, Harry!"

Harry is surprised at how quickly this call came. He is comforted by the way Dr. Myers has greeted him and with her request to have him come in to review the children's personnel folders. Bill Higgins hadn't ever done that with Harry.

"Thank-you, Dr. Myers. I don't know what else to say except that I will sign the contract and I'm very grateful for this opportunity."

Jennifer Myers graciously concludes the conversation, "Again, Harry, welcome and please, now that we're partners, I'm Jennifer."

Summer passes and Harry has met with Jennifer and Jackie Elton. Jennifer's meeting with Harry was to clarify Clarksdale's operating procedures and provide him with class schedules and curriculum guides for the fifth grade. She helped with the little things that mean so much to new staff: where to park, how to obtain classroom supplies, how and when to contact parents, how to handle emergencies including fire drill procedures and how to reach her at any given time. She provided Harry with names, addresses and phone numbers of parents and legal guardians of the children in his class.

As promised, Jackie spent extended time with Harry reviewing each student's education file. She too was an obliging resource. Harry was overwhelmed but grateful for the information and the help. He felt more prepared to begin school than he had in four years of teaching at Whitewood. Summer vacation was nearly over and school would soon begin.

Old River is a mid-sized suburban community. Trapper River separates it from Johnson City, a city in turmoil. Johnson City was, for many years, a stable white, conservative community. Many who now reside in Old River came from Johnson City families. Like so many cities around the country there was an exodus to suburban towns like Old River following World War II. Many of the younger families and returning veterans who came from long-established Johnson City families chose to move to the less crowded and more attractive suburbs while still others simply left their roots for other places.

The baby boom required new schools and new teachers in Old River. The mass departure from Johnson City left a void that was slowly plugged by poor blacks and Hispanics. They inherited the old abandoned two and three-story brick school buildings and moved into old tenements and renovated low cost housing. Scores of suburbanites kept good-paying jobs in the city while commuting from Old River, Champlain and other communities that ring the inner city.

In the 60's and 70's federal housing programs (HUD) and massive amounts of federal dollars encouraged a number of underprivileged minority residents to gain a toehold in communities like Champlain and Old River. Welfare assistance and a number of federal programs helped many in need, including single mothers, to obtain entrée into these neighborhoods. Not all succeeded in suburbia but they relocated from the inner city and their children were enrolled in school districts like Old River. The Elementary and Secondary Education Act (ESEA) with its Title 1 funding was enacted to help needy minority children with their schooling. An influx of new cultures impacted a few Old River schools in a new and challenging way while the community continued to hold the schools to its long established high standards.

The Old River population was proud of its schools. Their school district was celebrated as a lighthouse school system known throughout the country as a public school system worthy of national acclaim and emulation. Standards were high and involvement by the public was often passionate. Community leaders, parents and retirees were part of a strong support group that prided itself on its schools. Harry Latter would enter this prestigious district and would again be teaching a somewhat diverse student population like those with whom he so miserably failed in Champlain.

Since the 60's and through the 70's, 80's and 90's minority enrollment has increasingly become a challenge for white suburban educators. Also, immigrants from many nations have been knocking at Old River's school doors. Asians, Eastern Europeans and Middle Easterners have migrated into the district. Cultural and language differences have provided major tests for this suburban system. In Jefferson School, where Alan Bowles teaches, there are kids from families representing 19 different languages. Those languages are the primary languages spoken in the children's homes. Also challenging teachers are the increasing number of minority students and youngsters coming to school from single parent homes. There are neglected children who may have a parent addicted to drugs or alcohol or on the streets prostituting. Though Clarksdale, like most suburban schools, is not inundated with these changes, it is moderately affected by them.

Jennifer will have to be certain that Harry is prepared to handle his differentiated student population. There will be sure-to-come related issues in addition to his teaching challenges in his new position at Clarksdale; a tall order, indeed!

Chapter 3:
The Maestro

It's the third week of August and Superintendent Dr. Bernard Green has convened his annual *Opening of Schools Meeting* with his principals in the district's administration building. The meeting room is spacious. Photographs of each school and each school principal adorn the east wall giving the room a focal point that Bernard Green believes instills pride in Old River's principals.

Tanned and rested, the principals having returned from three weeks of vacation share anecdotes about summer activities and travels. Their eagerness to begin a new school year resonates throughout their lively chatter. Their anticipation is infectious. Following a half-hour of refreshments and social conversation Superintendent Green calls the principals to order and officially welcomes his administrative leaders.

Bernard Green is a dynamic leader. He challenges Old River's principals to reach ever higher. He's a strategist. He believes in collaboration to a point. The responsibility and pressure of maintaining the superior school district that Old River is comes from his belief that his office is where the buck stops. His is a self-imposed pressure. He leaves nothing to chance. And he expects as much from his school captains as he refers to his principals. He keeps them on their toes and will chide them privately for foolish mistakes but is first to praise them publicly.

He begins this particular meeting each year by delivering an upbeat message much like a football coach giving a pep talk just prior to the opening of a new season. The principals are inspired by his words and anxious to usher in the new school year.

First on the agenda are the principals' annual objectives. Dr. Green begins by addressing that item.

"Our most important task today is to review our established procedures for developing our annual objectives and refresh our recollection concerning the difference between a goal and an objective.

"A goal as we define it is general and timeless. To seek peace is a goal. An objective, on the other hand, must have an intended result that is achievable within a specific time frame and can be measured to determine its success or failure. If achieved, an objective moves an individual or a group toward a goal.

"The following analogy should simplify and clarify the difference. Let's say Mary is unhappy because she is overweight and unhealthy. She decides to improve her health. Her goal, to improve her health, is general and timeless. To move her toward that goal Mary decides on an objective. Her objective is to lose five pounds in six weeks. Next, Mary adopts an action plan that includes a diet and an exercise regimen. She'll eat healthy foods, eliminate snacks and desserts and limit her daily caloric intake. Her exercise routine will begin with a two-mile daily walk at a leisurely pace. She will increase that distance to three miles and her pace to 15 minutes a mile. To monitor her progress Mary will step on a scale each morning and evening. She'll time her daily walks. If she doesn't lose five pounds in a month, she'll adjust her program.

"Our goal is to improve instruction. Your objectives will move us toward that goal. For us, the time frame for meeting our objective is usually a school year. Your objective for improving instruction in your school will clearly state the result you intend to achieve by the end of the coming school year.

"I expect an action plan that shows how you will go about reaching your objective. Please include target dates for completing each item of your action plan. That will help monitor your progress throughout the year. Also include the method(s) you intend to use to measure your results. It's possible that your action plans will need adjusting and fine-tuning. It's logical to make changes to any plan as it unfolds as long as your adopted objective is not altered without my prior approval.

"In laying out this item I realize how autocratic it sounds. Yet, to assure continuity within a common supervision framework for all our schools, the guidelines must be specific and followed. If I've omitted something important please call it to the group's attention so we can address any oversight." Bernard Green waited and asked for feedback that might improve the process. Being this was a review of what the superintendent has been requiring since his arrival in Old River there wasn't anything the group could suggest that had been omitted.

"Are we in agreement, then?" The group nodded.

Green continued, "In addition to your coaching/supervision objective, each of you will write, as you have, at least one objective designed to meet a need that, if successfully carried out, will improve *your* school. Based on last year's evaluation you will write the objective for your school that we agreed to in June."

Some principals need to improve communications with their school community, some need to become more familiar with the curriculum, some are instituting a new program at their school while others will design a professional growth objective.

"Our annual supervision objective," Green emphasized, "is intended to aid you and your teachers to improve together, as professionals and mainly to find ways to assist students to become active and involved learners. This objective will move our schools toward one of the Board's primary goals. Any questions?"

The superintendent wants his principals to live in the classrooms to the extent possible and to *coach* teachers in the art of teaching.

Bernard Green's reputation as an educational leader has been borne out by the fact that he has become known nationally in education circles as a giant among superintendents, a lion among cubs, a maestro and is frequently asked to address national superintendent and principal conferences further enhancing his reputation as a respected leader. His topic is usually, *The Principal as a Coach.* Green emphasizes the importance of the coaching dimension at every opportunity.

His speeches to principal and superintendent groups are similar to the one he's delivering to Old River's principals today.

"Folks, we continue to remind ourselves that our enterprise is children; they are our valued product. I need not repeat that it is the children whom we serve. Each job in this school district has been established for one purpose only: to assist our children in the best way possible to ensure that the learning environment where they are schooled is optimal. From the board of education to the custodian, cook, bus driver, aide, nurse, secretary, teacher, principal, central staff and the superintendent: all must be responsible for that enterprise and that product.

"And your job is the most critical of all in moving us toward our goal of educating our youth. To help this school district meet its hopes and aspirations each of you must contribute by successfully completing your supervision/coaching work. You must labor to make certain that your teachers improve during the coming school year. The best must improve, the good must get better and the weak must progress noticeably and you and I must ensure that result. You are the coaches of the most critically important people in our business, the teachers who deliver instruction to our children." He reminds them of the similarity between principals and coaches.

"As in the past, I expect you to succeed with your coaching objective and to show evidence of that success. This coaching/supervision objective I'm handing out is open for questions and clarification but not for debate."

Superintendent Green distributes the format for the supervision objective to each principal. One can only fantasize how America's public schools would succeed with superintendents of Bernard Green's ilk at their helm.

Harry Latter and two brand new teachers tiptoe into Jennifer Myers' thoughts as Superintendent Green hands out the objective:

DISTRICT-WIDE COACHING OBJECTIVE
(for all Old River principals)

To observe, coach, cause to improve and evaluate (each school's name goes here) teachers' skills as instructors throughout the school year. Evidence of progress will be provided to the superintendent upon request and verification of success will be presented, in writing, at the principal's June evaluation conference.

ACTION PLAN:

- To determine by September 1 the order in which teachers will be coached.

- To have each teacher submit to the principal his/her objectives to meet children's learning needs by September 15.

- To meet with each teacher in September to review their objectives.

- To record and include the date of each formal and informal classroom observation throughout the school year.

- To hold a pre-observation conference with the teacher to be observed for the purpose of mutually understanding the lesson objective(s).

- To determine the methodology and materials to be used for each lesson to be observed.

- To observe the instruction and record the classroom activities as objectively and completely as possible. (coach is a camera).

- To meet with the teacher following the observation for the purpose of reviewing the data collected during the observation and, together with the teacher, determine which lesson objective(s) were met and establish areas for improvement.

- To summarize, in writing, the substance of the post-observation conference and to provide the teacher with a personal copy. That summary will be the focus for the subsequent pre-observation conference between the teacher and the principal.

- To place a copy of the teacher's coaching cycle in a file designated for classroom observations.

- To walk through classrooms as often as time permits for informal five-minute observations and to make note of teacher talk, learning activities, teacher support.

- To make available all classroom observation documents for the superintendent at the spring principal evaluation conference and as requested.

END OF YEAR EVALUATION: PROCEDURES

- To list areas of teacher's growth and to draft, with the teacher, a follow-up plan for the following school year.

- To list specific skills that have been improved and to identify areas for continued growth with the teacher.

"Any need for further discussion? Any questions?" Dr. Green will assess the principals' objectives at their June evaluation conference. He'll check their progress anytime during the year. Assistant Superintendent for Instruction, Al Antonelli, will accompany Bernard or visit schools on his own to help evaluate the progress being made by the principals.

The district-wide objective reflects a program for growth that, with talented and expert principals and department heads, will ensure continuous improved teaching. It implies that the superintendent and the principals are highly skilled in the analysis of what comprises expert instruction and learning. What is not obvious is the inordinate amount of time required of the principals to accomplish this objective in addition to his/her other administrative responsibilities. This problem is addressed in a subsequent chapter.

Dr. Bernard Green concludes this agenda item, "Again, be reminded that your local objective(s), over and above this one, shall address a need(s) distinctly identified with your school." The principals know their job is to produce individual school objectives based on the previous school year's work. The local school objectives are for the purpose of addressing each school's needs whether academic, cultural, social, parental, other identified issues or a combination of some of these.

Will Harry Latter make it in Old River? Does he have a chance? During Green's meeting Jennifer Myers pondered her supervision objective and continued to muse about the three new teachers coming to Clarksdale, one of whom, is Harry Latter her much-needed male teacher.

She is aware that his knowledge of instruction is weak. She has concluded, from her interview with him, that Harry is pleasant and articulate but uninformed regarding the essentials of instruction. Dr. Myers, unfortunately, finds this ignorance to be fairly common among new teachers assigned to her school. However, she is confident of her instructional expertise and believes she can help her new teachers, including Harry, to become good teachers. What she doesn't know is that Harry's problem begins at the classroom door. No one has warned her; no one in Champlain addressed the trouble he had with classroom control. Harry Latter, on the other hand, approaches the new school year with some trepidation and fear of failure.

Regrettably, too many of our nation's school systems are like Champlain and too few like Old River. The restructuring of our schools can only succeed when the nation's boards of education, the states' departments of education, the training institutions and the United States Department of Education are jolted into reality. The nation is desperate for a national leader who can compel the above bureaucracies to work together to address the principalship and upgrade principal certification. Principal candidates must study the psychology of learning and how to assist teachers to effectively instruct youngsters in the learning process before being judged to be qualified.

Boards of education need to understand that teaching will improve ONLY through a systematic coaching program managed by expert instructional leadership delivered by school principals. Boards of education must be accountable to the community they serve by requiring their chief executive officers, the superintendents, to organize training programs for principals in the ever emerging knowledge of supervision and instructional theory. Principals must learn to become effective coaches of their teachers. *There is no other option for improving our schools!* Providing money on the backs of taxpayers to make schools better without holding schools accountable for teacher improvement is stealing from our citizens. It's akin to taxation without representation.

Coaches in many professional fields scrutinize and study the data they assemble from observing their charges; look for patterns and suggest modifications to correct weaker habits and to build on better ones. Is it not logical to assume that teachers would benefit from the same kind of coaching by experts in the field of education?

Chapter 4:
Harry's New Year

Familiar yellow busses cross and crisscross the streets of Old River. Students of several ages, shapes, colors and sizes are shiny and polished as they cluster in small groups along sidewalks waiting for their carriers. When the bus doors open they will take their first hopeful strides into their new school year. It's the last Wednesday in August.

Town traffic is slowed and stopped by the return of the blinking red lights and *stop sign* gates swinging open from the yellow vehicles as young people embark and disembark. Bus drivers, though having taken dry runs, are still familiarizing themselves with their routes. Some take wrong turns, some are late and a few miss pickups. School phones ring and minor transportation confusion disrupts opening ceremonies. No matter how well organized and prepared the schools are for their new beginning, busses rule for a few days while the wrinkles of new routes are ironed out. Adding to the disorder are parents who drive their children to school occasionally blocking bus accesses. Though forewarned by late summer letters that busses will need room to maneuver some ignore the plea.

In addition to the 4 busloads of youngsters being dropped off at Clarksdale School, throngs of young people expectations high, skip, run and stroll along sidewalks leading to their neighborhood school. As requested by Dr. Myers in her welcoming letter to parents, children seek out their teachers who are posted around the flagpole in front of the school. Teachers are holding signs with their names in large block letters. Children fly around like buzzing bees hunting for their hives. Mr. Harold Latter is the object of 24 of these excited youngsters.

Jennifer Myers, nattily clad in a light blue suit, is hostess, greeter and bullhorn wielder. Once certain that most children have arrived, she calls for students to line up with their teachers to sing *God Bless America* followed by *The Pledge of Allegiance*. A recent high school graduate leads the singing as the flag is raised. She is accompanied by background music from a Boston Pops CD wafting through speakers from the school's stereo system, a gift from the PTA.

Subsequent to the flag-raising ceremony, the student body marches, single-file into the school's auditorium where Principal Meyers officially welcomes the young people back to school.

"Your teachers, the entire school staff and I are so happy to be with you again as you take another stride on your journey through Clarksdale School. We all hope that your summer was a good one and that you're ready for the challenge of this new school year. We, the faculty at Clarksdale, are in your corner. We will cheer your accomplishments and play our part to assure that each and every one of you has every opportunity to gain a profitable school experience. We are your home away from home. We will be friends with your families to ensure that, together, we can help you to succeed at Clarksdale.

"Each year at our opening assembly, I choose to close with the same message in hopes that, by the time you leave Clarksdale, you will remember how very important it is to do your best while in school and to be respectful of others. Children, keep in mind that you only go through your school years once. These years will not come again. You have this yearly opportunity to make the most of your education. The better educated you are, the more successful you will be and the more successful you are the more fun and adventure you will experience throughout your life. Make the most of your schooldays. Your schooling will soon pass, never to be recaptured. There will be no second chance to do it all over again."

Dr. Myers paused to let her words sink in.

"With that said, I want to take this opportunity to introduce our teachers to you.

"This year we are privileged and pleased to have three new teachers at Clarksdale. I ask you to give them our warmest Clarksdale welcome." The children applaud and cheer. "These teachers will stand as I call their names.

"Ms. Beverly Gillette is brand new to teaching. She comes to us from nearby Corbin and was an outstanding student teacher at Jefferson, right here in Old River. Ms. Gillette will be in the third-grade. Please stand Ms. Gillette.

"Next is our new fourth-grade teacher. Mrs. Wilma Jackson has taught in Virginia for the past six years. Her husband was transferred to Old River and, of course, Mrs. Jackson came with him. We are fortunate to have this experienced teacher with you lucky fourth-graders.

"Finally, Mr. Harold Latter has joined the Clarksdale faculty from Whitewood School in Champlain. Mr. Latter will teach a fifth-grade class. He is an experienced teacher whom we are pleased to welcome here today."

The students applaud each name with an enthusiasm that is displayed on the first and last days of school only.

"When I call your teacher's name, she or he will stand at the rear of the auditorium. Those of you assigned to that teacher will go to your classroom with him or her." Several names are called and then……….

"Mr. Harold Latter." A cold shiver runs through Harry as he hears his name echo through the auditorium speakers.

The fifth-graders hurry behind Harry's long strides to their classroom. Harry is armed with his lesson plan and has the school's *do's and don'ts* to help him begin his new voyage. Harry, like so many who are beginning a new job, has prepared dutifully for this day. He has a carefully structured lesson plan and is intent on starting out on the right foot. His black shoes are new. He is wearing a white shirt, gray trousers and a new tie. The children like the man who steps before them.

Harry taped the children's names to the front of their desks, something he has always done for the opening of school. He begins by sharing basic school information, which he listed on the white board with a felt tip pen the day before. He is pleased not to have to write on an old dusty chalkboard, the kind he used at Whitewood. Harry will go down the list one item-at-a-time. The school emphasis, he learned from Jennifer and Jackie Elton, is about RESPECT. The word is posted in large block letters at each entrance to the school, in every classroom, in the cafeteria, on the gymnasium door and on the door to the office. Harry will lead a discussion on the meaning of the word in a variety of situations: student-to-student, adult and student, in the halls, the cafeteria, in a school assembly, on the playground and on the school bus.

The children learn that no electronic devices are allowed, that bringing a bicycle to school is a privilege and that roller blades are forbidden on school grounds. Mr. Latter informs his class of guidelines used for emergencies such as fire or unidentified intruders. He explains how to contact the school nurse if ill or injured. They are advised how bussed children will be dismissed. Next he informs them of their scheduled time with specialized teachers of art, music, foreign language and physical education. Harry is very comfortable with and grateful for this *icebreaker* to begin his new school year.

The day goes smoothly by Harry's standards. Jennifer takes time from her busy opening day to walk through the school where she will welcome the children back on a more informal and personal basis. She gets to Harry's class by mid-morning. Her trained eyes sweep the room. She takes mental notes during this brief informal *drop-by.*

Harry is on top of his first day. By the time the dismissal bell rings he is exhausted. Should he do tomorrow's lesson plans here or take a break and do them at home he muses. He is not yet comfortable with the fifth-grade curriculum guides though he received them three weeks before the start of school. He knows he can stay a couple of days ahead of the class by scanning the guides in advance of writing his daily lesson plans; not a good idea.

Dorothy is delighted with Harry's account of his first day. Maybe life will take a turn for the better. Harry and Dorothy enjoy a glass of Merlot and relax with the TV news before dinner. In celebration of his *first day's* success, Harry and Dorothy have a second glass of wine. Their children are too young for school. Their world is with their mommy and daddy so they want to play after the meal. Daddy accommodates them and rolls around with them outside. As cool evening shadows fall across the lawn, Harry and the children call it an evening.

"Daddy has to do some work," he tells them.

With his full day of pressure, two glasses of wine, a filling dinner, the daily news and playtime behind him, Harry is dog-tired. His throat is dry from talking all day. He wishes he didn't have to do his lesson plans. But, he takes out the curriculum guides and begins to write plans for the following day: reading, math, social studies, science and current events. Science and current events get short shrift. After all he just watched the news and fifth-grade science begins with a study of weather. Harry can surely handle that having taught that topic for four years. I'll get right on top of everything tomorrow he rationalizes. This is a day to rejoice.

Unknown to Harry is a call made to Jennifer the week before school opened that informed her of Harry's board of education problem in Champlain when the children in his class ruined their spanking new furniture. A Clarksdale parent's sister lives in Champlain. When she learned that her sister's daughter was to be in Mr. Latter's class, she immediately informed her of the uproar he had caused in Champlain. That juicy item was brought to Dr. Meyers' attention in the name of, "caring for our school."

Dr. Myers filed it along with her mild disappointment in Harry that a schedule of the first day's learning activities for the children to follow was nowhere in the classroom to guide the students on opening day. Nor was there a list of individual student responsibilities posted in the room as she had suggested. The list of rules was all that was observable when she walked through his classroom.

Jennifer had specifically mentioned to Harry in their summer meetings that children need direction and guidance.

"It's important that youngsters know their day's schedule," she had told him. Also, she had advised him that it is the teachers' task to ensure that children understand their job responsibilities for the week. Who is going to be the class messenger, who will clean the boards, who will empty the basket, who will put the desks in order, who will make certain that all papers are picked up, who will lead the lines?

"A major thrust at Clarksdale is teaching students responsibility as well as respect. Going to school," she had clearly told Harry, "is the students' work day. It's their job and they should know what is expected of them." Obviously, her summer remarks missed their target.

Harry begins his second day at Clarksdale in the faculty lounge, as has been his custom throughout his four years at Whitewood. He always got along with his colleagues in settings such as the faculty room. It's the kind of place where he shines and feels most comfortable. It's where Harry expects to get acquainted with his new colleagues. He had been introduced along with Beverly Gillette and Wilma Jackson to the staff but that was at the more formal faculty meeting. He already considers Jack Deane his buddy and feels comfortable with Jackie Elton with whom he spent some time during the summer. But he hasn't informally met any other colleagues. He is caught unawares by an empty room. He checks his watch to be sure of the time.

Did I miss a meeting, he wonders. Classes begin at 8:40; it's now 8:30 and not a teacher in the room!

There is a steaming coffee pot with styrofoam cups by its side. He pours a cup and waits five minutes. Still no one. He is becoming edgy. The door opens and Gail Davis steps into the room.

"Hi Harry," she says nonchalantly.

"Hi, er,"

"Gail Davis," she rescues him, waving her hand.

"Where is everybody? I thought I was in the wrong room."

Gail chuckles, "I assume most of the staff is in class. I'll see you later." Gail heads for her room. Harry is puzzled.

He walks down the hall and into his room and is standing at his desk with coffee in hand as a few children come in chatting and laughing; many are already there. They settle down with Harry's call for the recitation of *The Pledge of Allegiance.* Following the salute the children are seated and Mr. Latter takes the roll.

"Who wants to take the attendance sheet to the office?" Just about all hands are raised.

"Me, me, me, me," fly at him from all directions. He selects a boy to the groans of all the wannabe's. There are, as yet, no assigned *jobs* posted.

Mr. Harry Latter begins his social studies instruction with a statement about America's past and how we are going to learn all about our country's history; its story. Harry identifies the various eras of our nation's past then pauses to ask questions. Texts are opened and kids are directed to read general introductory paragraphs aloud about *The New World.* Soon Harry notes that a few kids are looking out the window. He calls on one of the daydreamers and asks him to continue to read. The student has lost the place. This triggers Harry's first inconsequential reprimand at Clarksdale.

"I want your eyes on this page and I want you on task," he says in a slightly raised tone.

Principal Myers is in and out of Harry's room for the remaining two days of the first week of school; always noting little obscure items and events that would escape the untrained eye of a Bill Higgins. Dr. Myers observes that her summer suggestion to write a daily schedule on the board for the children remains unheeded perhaps overlooked in the excitement of a new job. She'll speak with Harry before he leaves school today. She has long embraced the title of a song her mother sang to her when she was a toddler. It rates high among her principles of good instruction, *Little Things*

Mean A Lot. The song made an everlasting impression on her.

Harry works after class to align his lesson plan to the curriculum. Aside from the weather unit in science he has much to do. Fractions will be highlighted in math. Critical reading will be the heart of his language arts program while the social studies will feature American History, civics and government. The history curriculum includes the Articles of Confederation, the Constitution and the Declaration of Independence in addition to all the major periods of our nation's past. Though Harry had a similar chronology at Whitewood, he was free to "cover" the material at *his* pace and in *his* fashion.

This year a new obstacle was about to impact his instruction. Jackie Elton, Harry's designated *big sister*, and Jennifer Myers, at their summer meetings with Harry clarified and defined his teaching responsibilities at Clarksdale. He was expected to *lead* the students through the curriculum. He was to be responsible for ensuring that students were actively participating and engaged in their own learning. To assist him Jennifer Myers gave Harry a pamphlet categorizing the intellectual processes by which children learn. Harry listened to the explanation given by Dr. Myers. She is the first educator to acquaint Harry with Dr. Benjamin S. Bloom's work.

Bloom, a University of Chicago psychologist and educational theorist, in the 1950's along with a committee of peers, researched in depth how children learn. At the time of its publication in 1956 it was avant-garde research on higher-order thinking. The work is entitled, *Major Categories in the Taxonomy of Educational Objectives.*[1] Harry had to admit that he had never heard of the study until now. He was reeling under the weight of this added information. Jennifer's pamphlet was designed to facilitate the *Taxonomy* for

---

[1] Bloom, Benjamin, Major Categories in the Taxonomy of Educational Objectives: 1956 (http://faculty.washington.edu/krummr/guides/bloom.html)

classroom application. It simplifies to the extent possible, the terminology of the original study.

Jackie Elton also met with Harry to assist him with the classroom use of Bloom's Taxonomy.

"The six categories in Bloom's work that we use with our students are related to the steps of intellectual development in the classroom, Harry," explained Jackie. He learned that there were also the affective (stressing feeling and emotion) and the psychomotor (motor skills) domains! He was becoming submerged in a whirlpool of facts and knowledge. He was beginning to flounder in the white water rapids of information pouring into and over him.

As he toiled, at the end of his third day of school, attempting to figure how to assimilate the Bloom factor into his lesson plans, Jennifer Myers entered his room.

"Well, Harry, how do you feel about your first days at Clarksdale?"

"Fine, Jennifer, just a little shaky getting out of the gate."

"You know, Harry, I repeat, I'm here to assist you to become the best teacher you can be. Consider me to be a coach and partner and, as such, I'll give you all the support I can. I want to share with you a couple of little things I noticed that, if you take care of, will make your classroom life easier and will be helpful in developing good practices for your students. O.K.?"

"Yes, of course."

"Harry, you must write the kids' daily schedule on the board each morning. They should know what they'll be doing on any particular day. They're accustomed to having that information from previous years here. They'll be better organized, which will make them more productive. Also, Harry, it's important to assign classroom tasks to your children to help them be more conscious and respectful of their environment. Finally, posting a daily list of assignments will keep your youngsters busy until the opening exercises," trust me.

"Sure, Jennifer, I'll have that all done by Monday."

"Good, Have a wonderful weekend and I'll see you Monday. If you need a hand with anything at all, I'll be happy to assist in any way I can."

"Oh, no, thanks anyway, Jennifer."

Harry drives home surprised again at how this principal functions. It was so much easier with Bill but I got no help, he thought. Now he fears that he'll get too much. Harry pulls into his driveway where he is met by Abigail and Jonathan.

"Daddy, Daddy," scream two gleeful little voices.

Chapter 5: Management and Discipline

Harry continues to procrastinate, leaving his schoolwork for Sunday. He takes Dorothy and the kids to Chili's for Friday dinner. He plans to take Abigail and Jonathan to the movies Saturday afternoon to see a re-release of Pinocchio.

Sunday morning, the Latter's go to church and stop for brunch at the Kitchen Kettle, a local eatery. It's the opening week of the National Football League and Harry is anxious to watch the 1 o'clock game, which will be over by 4 P.M. The Giants win and Harry finally gets to work at 5 P.M. He begins by outlining lesson plans for Monday, Tuesday and Wednesday.

"Dinner, Harry," Dorothy interrupts at 5:45. The family finishes the evening meal by 6:30.

Harry returns to his work where he struggles to understand what he's going to do with this "Bloom's Taxonomy" thing to which Jennifer is so committed. He reads the categories over and over again: *knowledge, comprehension, application, analysis, synthesis, and evaluation.* How in hell am I supposed to integrate all of this into my lesson plans, he wonders. He is perplexed and puts the Taxonomy aside. He prepares the three items that Jennifer suggested for the class. He'll post them in the morning.

Monday begins the first full week of school. Harry stops by the faculty room for a cup of coffee and carries it to his classroom. Two teachers were in the lounge this morning, a good sign, but Harry has no time to chat. He has to put his posters up before the children arrive. Jennifer drops in as Harry finishes mounting the day's scheduled assignments, the pupils' designated chores and classroom rules.

"Good Morning, Harry. I thought I'd stop by to see if you need any help from *your partner.*"

"No, but thanks Jennifer. I appreciate the offer. I think I'm all set."

"Good, everything looks fine. The information will help get the class settled. We can talk about the impact in a couple of days."

"O.K."

She leaves as the bell rings.

Students enter somewhat boisterously. This bothers Harry and reminds him of his days in Champlain. He sips his coffee and raises his voice slightly to quiet the youngsters.

"All right, class, I need your attention. Let's all look up here." Harry points to the charts and informs the children that he expects them, when they arrive in the morning, to get busy with the activities posted on the board.

"Now let's all stand and salute the flag." Following the Pledge of Allegiance Harry guides the class through the lists beginning with classroom tasks and explains the day's schedule. "Any questions?"

The week passes and Harry notices more unrest and tedium as he presents his lessons: mostly lectures. A couple of students are ignoring his call for quiet. They keep talking. Harry, exasperated, raises his voice a range or two higher. "Alright Jason, that's enough. Crystal, what did I tell you?" and still louder, "PLEASE QUIET DOWN AND PAY ATTENTION!" Surprised by Mr. Latter's shout, Jack murmurs something under his breath to Crystal who giggles. Irate, Harry scolds the two youngsters who show no remorse. He sends them to the principal.

Few children at Clarksdale are ever sent to Jennifer to be disciplined. Jennifer assumes that because Harry is new he probably decided to send a message to the class. She speaks with Jason and Crystal who admit to having been rude. They are repentant. She has them write notes of apology to Mr. Latter. She reads the notes, approves them and sends the two back to class. Jennifer checks with Harry after school to learn what happened.

"They wouldn't settle down. When I told them to sit down and be quiet they paid no attention. When I raised my voice Crystal and Jason became more disrespectful. They ignored me when I confronted them."

Jennifer listens then suggests, "Harry, have you considered disciplining youngsters separately and privately out of earshot of the rest of the class? You might find that approach to be more effective. That would show your respect for them while setting an example at the same time. It would also let them know that you're able to manage the situation in a deliberate, calm and controlled fashion. You might be more successful reaching them if they don't have an audience. Please try it next time someone is out of line. You may be surprised at the results. Raising your voice to a shout sends a message to kids that you're losing control."

"I hadn't thought about it that way but they don't seem to quiet down until I get their attention."

"Try waiting. Once they're conditioned to not having to settle in until you speak loudly that will continue to be their signal until you change your tactic. Let them know your rule and then stick by it."

On Friday morning, Harry catches up with Jack in the teacher's room. They discuss golf and the pro tour then agree to get a starting time for early Sunday morning at the public links. Jack leaves. Harry dawdles and pours a second cup as the bell rings in the school day.

Three or four of his class are in the room before Harry arrives, cup in hand. He finds the students laughing and running up one of the aisles.

"Whoa there," Harry rebukes the rowdiness with a quieter tone. Fresh in his mind is Jennifer's counsel. "You have work on the board. Let's get with it, pronto." The kids respond but, slowly. Others arrive and note some disorder. They, too, are reminded of the assignment on the board. It takes Harry a few minutes to settle the class. Dr. Myers is two doors away and observes the noisy beginning to Harry's morning. She'll check again a little later.

By the end of the day and week Harry realizes some of his old problems are emerging, in this otherwise orderly school, like dandelions popping up in a lush lawn. He is troubled. Dr. Myers again stops by following dismissal and asks Harry how his week went. He is insincere with his response that it was a pretty good week. Principal Myers asks about the resultant progress from the posted lists and whether he has implemented a "pause and wait" approach. This time Harry is frank and says the lists helped children to get started and kept things more orderly but he noted they were still restless. On Monday he plans to try Jennifer's suggestion, to pause and wait. Two more youngsters were sent to the office on Friday.

"Harry," Jennifer says, "I know you're making an effort to get your room organized and the children to be responsive and respectful. But this has to be done by you and not by me. When you send children to me to be disciplined you are giving away your authority. You're sending an unintentional but clear message to the children that you need someone else's help to control them. This will work against you and erode your authority further until eventually you'll reach a point of no return. The fastest way to lose the respect of your students is to send them elsewhere to be disciplined. There are steps you and I can work on to alleviate this problem. I have two excellent articles that should help. You must be consistent and begin each day in the same fashion. When some of the children finish their opening assignment they could be kept busy in other ways. We have word games and crosswords in the office that are designed to help build vocabulary and other activities that teach American history. Stop by the office on the way out. I'll ask Mrs. Haggerty to have a few things ready and include them with the two articles on classroom management. "

"Thanks, Jennifer. I'm sure that will help. You know, I really never looked at it that way. I mean,....giving my authority away. I see how that can happen."

The second week of September finds Harry and Jack in the faculty lounge where they discuss the pennant race, the weekend golf tournament and their own Sunday golf match.

While playing on Sunday, Harry asked Jack, "What is all this commotion about Bloom's Taxonomy? If I heard correctly the damned thing goes back to the 50's and it's confusing as hell. How in hell can I work it into my lessons?"

"Harry, it's really a logical sequence of steps to ensure that kids are learning. Once you get the hang of it you'll find it to be pretty useful and not all that complex. All I know about Bloom is that he was a psychologist who, with some colleagues, researched how children learn. Their work caught on with a number of educators who were also investigating theories of learning. As you know, Harry, a horde of gurus has come along over the years with their own theories but the Taxonomy remains a logical and useful tool. Jennifer continues to embrace it as her bible for independent learning. Though other psychologists have caught her interest and have expanded her inventory of learning psychologies, Jennifer's commitment to Bloom is unshaken. She insists that all the elements for independent learning are in the Taxonomy and that subsequent researchers have put his work in a box, wrapped it with their own research, tied it with colorful bows of catchy new ideas and pedaled it to interested educators while the Taxonomy inside remains an established and valued tool for guiding children's learning."

"This finely wrapped box, as you describe it, never reached Champlain."

"No, I guess many systems rely on teachers to teach without much instructional support or direction. With good teachers, schools get by but you know, Harry, our public schools are being crapped on by just about everyone because there are not enough outstanding teachers. It's not the teachers' fault. They're simply not being coached by effective principals."

"Wow, I never heard of a teacher in my old school, or anywhere else, complain about not being supervised! Jack, you slay me!"

"I know, I sound brainwashed but I know this works, Harry, honest."

"Yeah, O.K. You keep telling me the Taxonomy is simpler than I'm making it out to be. Would you help?"

"I would, Harry, but isn't Jackie your assigned *big sister* to get you started here? I don't want to mess her up by interfering. Why don't you ask her and then let me know if I can clarify anything for you. Catch you later."

Harry tarries a bit then strolls down to Room 9 again with cup in hand as the bell rings. Some half-dozen youngsters are in the classroom milling around when Harry arrives. The place is bordering on being unruly. Harry, though eager to change his approach, is annoyed and angrily orders the class to get organized, ignoring Jennifer's advice for now and directs them to the day's schedule, which includes their opening activities. He is a U-boat commander lording over his crew of kids who are fast losing faith in their captain and his ability to control the ship.

"Unless you people straighten up, you are going to fail. It starts now, not when you're adults. When you get out in the world you'll remember what I told you." Harry seems to prey on gloom and doom to control the class. His approach is ineffective. He doesn't consider affection and support, two emotions that kids need in elementary school. The world will soon enough teach them about reality and failure. Harry needs something positive to say to his class. In spite of Jennifer's gentle counsel it doesn't occur to him to treat his class courteously. The children are becoming more disenchanted with their new teacher. Harry, during the week, and in spite of Jennifer's warning, sent another youngster to the office; prophetically, his classroom control continues to slip.

Following the Pledge of Allegiance the class begins to work while Harry takes attendance before beginning the history lesson. He drones on like a college professor pouring information into the young heads facing him.

On Tuesday Jennifer notes again what has now become a behavior pattern. Harry never arrives before all the children; he is always toting a cup of coffee. Lately his trousers are wrinkled and his shirts a bit shoddy looking. He continues to lose the respect of his young charges. She must act now. Her coaching philosophy is to build on strength thereby gaining the trust and cooperation of the staff. But she can't wait as Harry's weakness is overshadowing any strength on which she can build and threatening to unravel the school year for Harry Latter's students.

Jennifer informally walks through Harry's classroom at 9:30 and finds children reading from their social studies texts, one after another, paragraph after paragraph. There is no active learning occurring. This worked in her parents' schools but is an unproductive method of teaching today. Some children seem preoccupied; some bored; another pattern that will be shared with Harry along with his problems at the beginning of the day. She notes that Harry is all over the place like a pilot without a navigator. She must take over the navigating until he finds his way. She'll see if Harry, with coaching, can recognize the causes of his troubles and begin to remedy them.

Following dismissal, Jennifer again stops by.

"Harry, let's you and I review your initial days here at Clarksdale. I noted a couple of things I'd like to share with you and elicit your opinion."

"Sure Jennifer." Harry thought, Oh, oh, what's coming now? His thoughts race at a dizzying pace. I made a mistake coming here……I should have quit teaching…….Where do I go from here?

To Harry's surprise, Jennifer is supportive and nonjudgmental. "Harry, beginning a new job is difficult. You don't know your colleagues. You try to understand the expectations of your new assignment and you wonder about your principal."

Jennifer, a longtime football fan, and aware of Harry's love of sports, seizes on a football analogy to explain her supervisory method for evaluating teachers.

"I want you to think of me as your coach, Harry, just like a quarterback coach." She first heard a principal compared to a coach from Dr. Bernard Green when he was hired as the superintendent of schools. It was a comparison that fit perfectly.

"Coach and quarterback are basically partners. The quarterback's success becomes their success; his failures become theirs as well. Likewise, as your coach, I will constantly look to help you modify your performance so we can both succeed. O.K?"

"Uh-huh."

"I want to focus on a comparison between a sports coach and my coaching role. In an elementary school the principal has to be the coach. I trust the similarity will make it easier for you to understand how we'll work together to help with your classroom routines beginning with classroom management and discipline.

"You know that, no matter how a quarterback performs, his performance is continuously analyzed and polished with his and his coach's input. It's the same with teachers. For instance a quarterback whose completion percentage for the season is sixty percent completed only forty-five percent of his passes in his last game. That's a sub-par performance. On Monday, following the game, he and his coach review the game tapes together including the coach's notes, all objective data. They notice the quarterback moved out of the pocket more than usual and noted further that, while out of the pocket, he had dancing feet causing his passes to sail. They agreed that the passes were crisp and accurate when he stepped into the pocket. The facts were before them. There were no judgments about the data in front of them. Their opinions for improvement will be discussed when they work on the problem before the next game. Harry, I try to collect the same kind of objective data regarding classroom performance. Unfortunately we don't have the time to tape the lessons; we rely on my ability to record what I see without prejudice. Does the analogy make sense to you?"

"Yes, it's pretty interesting."

"Will you try a little experiment based on my coaching observations?"

"Sure, I guess so." What else can he say?

"Here are some impartial observations I jotted down for us to review. You can see they are without comment. Harry, tell me what you make of these notes then, together, we'll decide if any of these actions are meaningful one way or another in preparing children to begin their school day. Okay?"

"Okay," Harry replies with a dry throat.

Jennifer hands the notes to Harry. Harry reads, *For the last five days, Harry leaves the staff room just before, or immediately after, the first bell rings; Harry is last to leave the room; Harry carries a cup of coffee to the classroom and drinks while trying to settle the children; many children arrive before their teacher; youngsters are pushing, milling around, hollering to one another as their teacher enters; Harry raises his voice to settle them down; the other classrooms are quiet and busy.*

"Harry, are these notes accurate? If so, what do you infer from them? Do you think any of this has a bearing on the beginning of your day with the children?"

Harry swallows hard, takes Jennifer's notes and reads them again, this time more carefully.

"Am I always the last teacher getting to class?" he asks.

"Harry, I can't say *always* because I've only been in the vicinity on the days I've noted. I will never interject information that I don't observe regarding your work as a teacher. But I can ask, as your coach, if you're satisfied with being last? Are you? Is it a problem that has an effect on your instruction?"

"Well being last, in and of itself, I don't think is a factor but I can see that getting to my class late is."

"Would you like to change that? Obviously it's easily done now that you're aware of the pattern."

"Yeah, I think I should change it in light of the rest of your notes that seem to suggest that I can have a better organized classroom if I do what many of the other teachers do and that's getting to my classroom before the kids. I could direct them to their seats to begin their morning assignment. I do notice other teachers greeting kids."

"There you go. That's an insightful observation and a good way to address the problem. Now, is there some way you can change the kids' perceptions and expectations of their teacher?"

"Jennifer, I think if they see you around the hall it would help to get them turned around. But you made a note about carrying the coffee. What's the problem with that? I've always done that."

"Harry, I'm pleased at the positive step we've just taken in identifying a change that we both sense will help your management of the class. As for the coffee, Harry, I turn back to you. How does it help you as a teacher to bring it to the room? Does it help the kids? Is there a subconscious message to the students? You don't allow them to eat, drink or chew gum in school yet you bring your own pacifier. Yes, you're the authority figure and hold power over them and you can drink coffee without hurting anyone. But is it necessary? Are you sending a subliminal message? Do other teachers do it? Does it fall under our school maxim: RESPECT?"

Harry begins to think of the coffee differently. Jennifer is one sharp lady and she has kind of left this up to him. He suspects if he had come to a different conclusion or didn't see the logic of her input she would have led him to the finding he reached."

"You may be right about the coffee too," he conceded.

"Harry, you're the one who has to decide about the appropriateness of bringing coffee to the classroom. Unless you understand it and it comes from your own logic it will be of no value to you. My job as your coach is to share the objective data I collect. Of course I may see patterns that you have missed. If or when appropriate I will openly but supportively address them with you. I hope that I can motivate you to analyze the information I share with you. We will, together, I trust, find many positive patterns upon which to build and grow."

Continuing with her football comparison Jennifer surprises Harry once again. "I am reminded of what George Halas, the one-time owner of the Chicago Bears once said about Coach Lombardi, *'You might reduce Lombardi's coaching philosophy to a single sentence. In any game, you do the things you do best over and over.'* My job, like coach Lombardi's, is to find those things with you, stimulate your thinking and build your confidence regarding them. Harry, we need to light your fire and to keep it ablaze with the things you do best while encouraging you to do them over and over." Jennifer recalls an old Spanish proverb that asks, *"What good is a candle without a match?"* She chooses not to share it with Harry.

"I'm assuming from what you're telling me, your coach, is that beginning tomorrow morning you will have your coffee and finish it in the faculty room *and* leave the cup there because *you*, Harry, believe that makes sense. Also, if I understand you clearly, you intend to arrive at your classroom door before the bell rings. As your students arrive you plan to greet them and remind each one to get started with the morning task that is posted on the board. Harry, it would be very helpful if you can think of some little tidbit to share with each child as they enter the room. Let's see if all of this will help *us* to eliminate some of the exuberance that is manifesting itself in your room at the beginning of the day." This principal has neatly summarized for Harry what he, himself, decided he must do following this informal chat with Jennifer.

"I'll be nearby in the morning. And, Harry, I don't really have the right to tell you how to dress but I can offer you a suggestion that if your trousers and shirt are pressed the kids will know it. A tie might also help. Please accept my opinion as one based on experience. It's offered in the spirit of caring"

"Well, Jennifer, I'm willing to try. So much of this is new to me and I really want to do well here."

On Tuesday, Harry turns the car radio on to calm his nerves. Sinatra is crooning *Summer Wind.* Momentarily Harry's thoughts shift to memories that ballad evoked of long ago carefree days at Myrtle Beach, a marked contrast to his sentiments this morning. "*The summer wind came blowin' in from across the sea. It lingered there, it touched your hair and walked with me,"*………Briefly, he slips back and forth between the lyrics and the reality of the morning……. *"All summer long we sang a song and then we strolled that golden sand,"*……Harry's emotions sway back and forth between anxiety and nostalgia ……. *"Like painted kites those days and nights, they went flying by,"*……Approaching Clarksdale, *"then softer than a piper man one day it called to you. I lost you, I lost you to the summer wind."*

Harry Latter arrives early in pressed trousers and a clean shirt with tie. He brought coffee from home and drank as he drove. He is so tense he is almost shaking. He feels his breakfast in his throat and is at his classroom five minutes ahead of the bell. He notices through his nervousness that his colleagues are positioned at their classroom doors waiting for the children.

Suddenly Jennifer appears, "Good morning, Harry." She smiles warmly from several feet away. She is a symbol to the children. They like her, respect her and respond to her presence: a help to Harry, for sure.

He feels awkward and clumsy. This is out of character for him. Jennifer backs slightly away and chats with some children in the hall.

"Hi Carter, congrats, you're the first one here,"

Harry welcomes Carter. "Why don't you go to your desk and get a jump on the work I've listed on the board."

This is Harry's first greeting. Harry greets four or five more and Jennifer helps just down the hall.

"Good morning Serita. My, don't you look pretty! Are you ready to get started?"

"Yes, Dr. Myers."

And so it goes. Several days later, Harry's class is a bit more settled and somewhat more focused. Harry was becoming a little more confident and, at the same time, leery of the suggestion Jennifer gave him regarding classroom rules of behavior. But it was beginning to show results.

Jennifer's guidance energized Harry. And the youngsters seemed more motivated because they were better organized to begin the day. Harry was trying to get the kids involved. They were assigned to small groups of four to develop ideas for a class constitution that would, at its core, establish respect for one another by addressing their rights and responsibilities in Mr. Latter's classroom. Because they would be studying the United States Constitution this year the project should take on more significance. Though wary of the *bill of rights* the kids would come up with Harry encouraged the class to create the document they could and would live by in their classroom. What became evident from the onset were the rigid rules and responsibilities they enacted to balance the rights they established. Harry was delighted and pleasantly surprised.

When shared with Jennifer, she responded, "Kids tend to be tougher on themselves if they set up their own parameters than the teacher would be and they will be more likely to honor the work they have proudly created." Harry was once again impressed with Dr. Myers' knowledge of children. The kids elected a president and a Room 9 *supreme court* to deal with *law-breakers.* Classroom discipline and management were slowly improving.

The children remained bored with his class, however, which is causing some disquiet among these active fifth-graders. Jennifer is aware of the ennui.

"Harry, we're doing better with our opening. Don't you agree?"

"Yes, it's better, for sure."

"Of course you know, Harry, the best learning environment is an orderly one. So we're getting through a first step toward that end. Now we need to find the way to *keep* the class organized, interested and active in their learning. That would greatly help to create a positive and stimulating learning atmosphere. While passing through your room yesterday I noted that you were working with the Age of Discovery in your history lesson. Harry, did you feel comfortable with the class involvement?"

"Guess I didn't really notice."

"I know these kids pretty well. I have the advantage of having worked with them for several years. When you and Jackie met in the summer and discussed the kids in your room that meeting was to help you prepare for the opening days of school. Yesterday I noted Ashley and Conner were the two youngsters with their hands raised to answer just about every question you posed as you and the class read from the social studies text. Does that ring a bell?"

"Now that you mention it, yes."

"Harry, you know they are your top students and they'll participate no matter what. I pose the following for your consideration. Were those two motivated to learn or were they simply flaunting their *knowledge*? On the other hand, a couple of your less able kids lost the place while three others were staring out the window. Denham had a Lego T-Rex behind his book. Harry, as I've said, I am a camera while in your room. Those are the pictures I snapped. I'm handing you these photos for your reaction."

"But Jennifer, shouldn't all the kids be following along when I direct their attention to the page? They don't seem to want to learn. Don't they have a responsibility to follow my lesson?"

This was Jennifer's opening. Harry was waving a distress signal. It was her opportunity to finally get started with some serious instructional work with him. She will, of necessity continue to assist him with classroom management until he can stand on his own. Now it's time to address teaching and learning. Jennifer has a portfolio of relevant articles to share with Harry including some exceptional articles from *Education Week* relative to motivating children in the classroom. These will get coach and pupil on the same page. Jennifer will extend her role as teacher of teachers in her partnership with Harry. This is her responsibility as an instructional leader.

It's time to expand her coaching of Harry from classroom management and organization to instruction. It's become necessary to begin formal observations of Harry's teaching. Dr. Myers has ambled through his classroom almost daily since the opening of the school year and noted how he conducts his lessons. Not only is he lacking teaching skills, he is a merchant of doom continually disapproving of what the children *don't do well* rather than praising them for what they do *do well.* Her visits raise no eyebrows because Jennifer drops into a few rooms each day. Though she has a host of other duties and responsibilities to tend, she takes her supervision assignment most seriously; it's her first priority.

Dr. Myers does everything she can to not let her countless other responsibilities keep her from coaching her teachers. She has mentally made note of a few of Harry's teaching patterns during her informal visits. Recording Harry's patterns and sharing them with him will be the first step in helping him to analyze his instruction. She considers Harry to be the most challenging teacher on the staff. Yet she will wait until she completes a formal observation of a lesson before asking Harry to analyze some of his teaching patterns. She has a few more casual chats with him to prepare him for the formal work they will do together.

"Harry, it's time for us to take a good look at our classroom. Let's sit down before school on Monday with a lesson plan to be followed by a classroom observation by your coach."

Harry is somewhat shaken by the suggestion but controls his response. "O.K., Sure, what do I need to bring?"

"We'll need a lesson plan, of course, with *learning objective(s)* written clearly and concisely. Your plan should describe the procedures you will use to teach the lesson and explain how you will assist your students to accomplish the learning objectives you have set for them based on their needs. In other words, what do you want the children to achieve by the end of the class? The emphasis must be on what the children will be able to do that they couldn't do or didn't know prior to the lesson. Also list whatever learning materials you'll use. Finally decide how you will evaluate the lesson. The evaluation should clearly show whether the objective(s) were attained. Stop by the office on your way out and I'll give you a sample lesson plan to guide you.

"Remember, we're partners. We'll meet together to review the plan. I'll transcribe what I see and hear during the lesson. Then we'll each analyze what I record and meet to discuss our findings. My role in the room will continue to be that of a camera. I'll record what I see and hear and only what I see and hear. I will make no judgmental notes. At our meeting following your lesson analysis you and I will identify patterns among the data to determine their effectiveness vis-à-vis your objective(s). Let me once again remind you that a pattern is an action that is repeated enough times to be recognized as a routine adopted by you, or by your pupils. In other words, Harry, a behavior pattern is simply an established habit. We'll build on the habits that we judge to be positive and work to make better those that can be improved. As we scan the data we will, together, decide whether the identified pattern helped or hindered you in reaching your lesson objective or if it really mattered one way or another. Does this explanation help at all?"

"Yes, but patterns, as you describe them, are new to me. Wouldn't patterns of behavior also apply to everyday living as well as to teaching?"

"Absolutely. Harry, before I forget, please bring the Bloom pamphlet that I gave you during the summer to our planning session."

"Just one thought, Jennifer, I'm having a hard time with *Bloom's Taxonomy* and working it into my lessons. I've never been exposed to anything like it before."

"Don't let the Taxonomy intimidate. We'll work it into your teaching as it becomes familiar. Remember taxonomy is just a fancy word for classification or category. For our purposes the Taxonomy classifies several categories of learning. We'll ease into it but it's important that it remain worthy of your attention each time you plan a lesson. The simplest way to explain the Taxonomy, Harry, is to describe it as a guide to steer each of your students through a succession of steps to ensure they are learning. The use of the categories will assist students to become active and independent learners. They will become responsible for demonstrating their scholarship to you. There are some simple steps that are best illustrated in Bloom's triangle pyramid on the cover of the pamphlet you have. Knowledge, you will note, is at the bottom of the pyramid because it is the lowest step on the learning rung.

For example, when you first *learned* to play Monopoly you had to know the rules. That became your knowledge base. What is this game? How many can play? What is the object of the game? What is the money for? When do I acquire property? Where do the pieces go? This was knowledge but it didn't do much for developing your skill at playing or adopting a strategy for winning the game. You can think of checkers or chess or any game in the same fashion. But as you played Monopoly, you *learned* the strategies of collecting money and dispensing it, of going to and getting out of jail, how the bank works, why one purchases property, what is the advantage of mortgaging property, how does one go about mortgaging assets, why are certain properties more desirable than others? You learned about taxes and railroad purchases and how to improve property. You were learning. The more you played, the better you became. You *demonstrated* your expertise. You were analyzing your choices when landing on a property. You were beginning to understand the game when you were able to compete with others. All learning steps were covered as you learned the game of Monopoly.

"Harry, you and I will work to achieve this kind of learning for the children in your classroom. We must remember that each child is different and each child will move at a different pace. Remember, students dream and teachers dream. Their dreams are different. We will allow for that too, Harry. Perhaps this gives you some insight for your lesson plan." Whew, is Harry's silent reaction.

"I have to say, Jennifer, I need to think this all through."

Again extending her sports' analogies, Jennifer says, "Of course you do. Let's say we have a football field of ideas. You will be gaining first downs by rushing and passing. Each positive step of the Taxonomy will constitute a first down. The first downs will lead us, and more importantly, the children to their goal, the end zone. The pamphlet should help simplify Bloom for you.

"I'd like for us to sit and just chat about that last history lesson informally to give you a sense of how we'll use patterns from the classroom during a formal observation. For instance, if I had a class photograph, and placed a check mark over each child's picture as to who was not on task you would count several children. You and I would look for clues as to "why" they were not on task. That's how we'll deal with instruction objectively and candidly. Perhaps we can examine some aspects of Dr. Bloom's work regarding the social studies lesson you'll be teaching and I'll be observing, yes?"

"Well, yes, but I'm still a bit confused about Bloom though you're helping clarify some of the puzzle. But, Jennifer," Harry challenges, "I really think it's up to the students to take on some responsibility."

"I agree they need to do so. You and I will find the ways to make that happen, Harry. Perhaps we can merge the constitution the children wrote and identify the responsibilities that might carry over to their lessons. Will you trust me?"

"Yeah, well, sure."

"We'll examine the Bloom pamphlet at our pre-observation session."

This pre-observation thing is threatening to Harry. Though he is learning to trust Jennifer, he isn't sure that he trusts himself.

All Harry knew is that he had to come up with a lesson design to present to his principal. Harry mused that he was expected to have at least one objective for the kids. Jennifer reminded him that he had to provide a list of materials he plans to use. Geez, what am I supposed to use beside a text, paper and pencil he wondered. And she wants to know how I intend to teach the class and how I will involve the kids. And I have to include how I'll determine whether I met my objective(s). How in hell can I get all this done? And what about this Bloom stuff? Harry tosses in bed, gets up, has a snack, turns on the T.V. and finally falls asleep.

Chapter 6: Jennifer Myers

Jennifer Myers has been a principal for eight years, all of them in Old River where she had been a superior teacher for four years. She rose to the top of a long list of candidates by reputation, composure and eloquence during several intense interviews including a hard-hitting session with the previous superintendent and two principals all of whom she impressed with her knowledge of instruction. Hers was no political appointment. Jennifer Myers is bright, dedicated, confident and strong. She spent her first year as principal at Clarksdale learning how to administer and manage a school. Her second year was devoted to instruction in the classroom.

When Bernard Green became superintendent at the beginning of Jennifer's third year at Clarksdale, she had already been deeply involved with instructional leadership. Bernard Green was steadfast in his belief that it is the principal of the school who is key to improving instruction through a method of coaching teachers based on classroom observations and follow-up interactions between principal/coach and teacher.

It was during an interview with the Old River Board of Education that he compared the labors of ballet coaches who, together with their protégés, study tapes of poses, steps, leaps, turns, plies, arabesques and jetés to improve their skills and techniques, with those of a principal.

"Principals," he told his interviewers, "should be able to analyze learning and instruction with their teachers for the same purpose, to improve performance." He pledged that he would require this manner of coaching from Old River principals. It was this pledge to the board of education that secured the job of superintendent for Dr. Bernard Green.

At the onset of his tenure in Old River, he shared the vow he made to the Board with his principals and expanded the analogy. "Professional dancers, musicians, athletes and a host of other performers in various fields," he told them, "rely on the expertise of their coaches to help them hone their skills and improve their execution. Capable and knowledgeable coaches observe, analyze and often tape their protégés performances searching for precise feedback to extend the talents of their charges. They examine each nuance to determine, with the professional they are coaching, whether it has value for improving one or more skills. Coaches and their performers together scrutinize the data they assemble, look for patterns and suggest modifications to become better at what they do.

"Is it not logical," he asks the principals, "to assume that teachers can profit from the same kind of coaching by an expert in the field of learning? The answer is obvious to me. In the case of classroom teachers, their coach must be *the principal or department supervisor* who has mastered the science of instruction; one who knows how pupils learn and how teachers teach."

Dr. Meyers thought at the time, how simple yet profound. She bought into Dr. Green's analogy, used it often herself and became one of his star pupils. Bernard Green quickly recognized Jennifer Myers' potential to become the kind of supervisor he envisioned for Old River. He encouraged her to focus on teaching and learning methods and psychologies of instruction during her doctoral work.

Jennifer Myers researched and studied several theories of learning and examined emerging techniques of supervision. She completed her doctorate and soon became known for her instructional expertise. Myers also became a resource for Al Antonelli, the district's assistant superintendent for instruction. She continued to explore the works of noted education pioneers from the mid-fifties through the last half of the century.

Benjamin S. Bloom early on became her icon, her guide and her model for understanding instruction and learning. Though Bloom's work was completed in the mid-fifties, Jennifer was convinced that the scholars, whose research concerning the psychology of learning, and who came after him, did not add significantly to his hypothesis regarding how children learn. She was convinced that his most noted work, *The Taxonomy of Educational Objectives,* spanned just about all facets of learning. She worked initially with only the cognitive or learning piece of the Taxonomy keeping the affective and psychomotor domains for future teacher training.

She conceded that other researchers have uncovered new knowledge from their investigations into the psychology of learning. In her mind she saw their scholarly insights as branches sprouting from Bloom's learning tree. They helped to make the tree stronger but did not replace it. Their work, by all means, should be pruned and kept in a healthy state worthy of more exploration. She granted that several branches offered valid insights into instruction helping to strengthen Bloom's research. But she used Bloom's Taxonomy coupled with her coaching skills as her basic tools to improve the act of teaching at Clarksdale. She has stayed with the tried and true just as generations have clung to the traditions of their youth accepting newer ideas but holding onto the values of the past.

Since Green's arrival and her continued fascination with his coaching concept, Jennifer put her research into practice and sharpened her skills to the point that she is confident she can help all her teachers to improve. The tool in this case, Bloom's study, would do the job as long as one knew how to use it. Dr. Myers added several educational psychologies to her supervisory portfolio. Useful common threads were identifiable as she continued her research. The implication of new discoveries was that they could be used to enhance but not replace Bloom's theories. The *Taxonomy* leads children through a process of learning that can be monitored and assessed.

Prior to her work with Bloom, Jennifer used helpful but undeveloped supervision skills with her gift of intuition to determine success in a classroom. She sensed good teaching like she felt the wind. She knew when good winds were blowing but she lacked a main sail for giving them direction.

To complement Bloom's work and to determine its effectiveness in the classroom, Jennifer discovered and studied supervision techniques that would be extremely helpful in analyzing teachers' abilities and children's learning. She recorded patterns of behavior displayed by classroom teachers and their students, which were essentially teaching and learning habits that helped to judge classroom progress. Jennifer turned to some pioneers in the field of pattern collecting. She studied Goldhammer, Cogan, Hunter, Marzano, Pickering, Pollock, Glickman and Gordon among others. The topic of much of their research is patterned teacher behavior. Their work has evolved into a more precise, exacting and effective science and each new finding has contributed to a more efficient way of collecting data on classroom instruction.

As Dr. Myers became more expert regarding Bloom's Taxonomy, she copied a graphic for her staff, for students and for parents. Each year, Dr. Myers, at Open House, explains the graphic to her audience. She sends copies home and has replicated it for the school's website. Subsequently she created a pamphlet to describe the triangular visual of Bloom's categories.

She gave Harry Latter his own copy of the pamphlet at their summer meeting in hopes that he would use it with some degree of proficiency when school opened. Its purpose is to explain and simplify Bloom via a simple triangle.

With her brochure she has included a description of the six steps to learning that each child should experience during the learning process: ***Knowledge*** is at the bottom of the categories and is described by Bloom as the lowest level of understanding. Its focus is on the ability to remember previously learned material: recall *dates, events and places.* When students are working in the knowledge domain, they are listing, defining, telling, describing, identifying, showing, labeling, examining, tabulating and naming. They are mostly responding to who, when, what and where questions. When a teacher is stuck for too long seeking factual feedback the students will not be exposed to meaningful learning. This is a concern of those questioning No Child Left Behind's emphasis on recall.

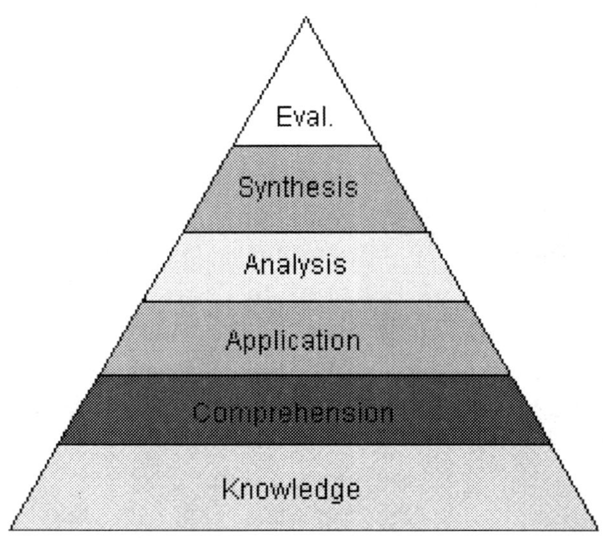

The second step is ***Comprehension***. With this category, children learn concepts, how to solve problems and select methods used to arrive at solutions. They are seeking meaning in their work. The teacher assists students to calculate, illustrate, demonstrate and use information in new situations. ***Application*** follows. It is through application that pupils apply previously learned information to new situations. They articulate, assess, compute, develop and transfer. ***Analysis*** is the breaking down of information into its component parts. Students will pull information apart and study it. Working in the ***Synthesis*** category, they combine information with prior information to produce something new. Finally, learners ***Evaluate*** by judging values, facts from opinions and by determining if answers are right or wrong. They appraise, compare, contrast, conclude, critique, decide and reframe. The steps are not confined to student learning.

Any learner at any age can be guided through these steps to learning.

In the primary grades (K-3), children are led through these steps without knowing the classification of the categories. With a little imagination and the appropriate curriculum, teachers can involve students at the earliest of ages with the entire Taxonomy.

Dr. Myers has long espoused the axiom that one does not remain in one place intellectually, physically or vocationally. One is either moving forward or falling back; treading water is not an option.

Jennifer is not impressed with the common education jargon that is used in professional tomes. The boredom of academic wordiness makes them uninteresting to most professionals and unintelligible to the general public. She is certain such volumes present a dull, irritating and condescending image of education to the public. She scorns them for the most part. She works diligently at presenting the *Taxonomy* as an interesting, palatable and understandable document for students, parents and the community.

For a very long time Dr. Myers has been impressed by very little in the field of learning psychology though she has been encouraged by a few studies. The work of Howard Gardner got her attention.

Ron Comstock, a colleague and principal at Jefferson Elementary in Old River, once asked Jennifer if she had read Howard Gardner's book, *Frames of Mind.* Having admitted that she hadn't, he urged her to do so. Jennifer respected Ron's professional judgment and obtained a copy from the Old River Professional Library. When finished she was intrigued with Gardner's concepts and obtained another Gardner book, *Multiple Intelligences: The Theory in Practice.*

Gardner's work would not need the kind of extensive editing she did with Bloom to explain it to her school community. Yet, how does one march in a parade carrying a *Multiple Intelligences* banner without knowing what the banner is promoting? The titles of Gardner's works, Jennifer was sure, would fail to catch the eye or the interest of the average citizen.

Ah, but his concept makes so much sense. Dr. Howard Gardner proposes that many bright people are unsuccessful in school. Jennifer pondered the thought. She considered tradesmen whom educators call to repair their roofs, fix their plumbing, re-wire their homes, hook them to cable TV, landscape their lawns and repair their cars. A goodly number of these skilled workers admit to having had a difficult time in school. One could run a list of hundreds of skills that imply high intelligence. Many a savvy street person will tell you they struggled in school. Even bookies use a complex system of odds that require sophisticated math skills.

Dr. Gardner's work suggests that educators need more than one way to measure intelligence. Gardner lists seven kinds of intelligences:

- Linguistic: a sense for the meaning and order of words.
- Logical/Mathematical: math ability and a capacity to succeed with other complex logical systems.
- Musical: ability to understand and create music. (musicians, composers, dancers)
- Spatial: ability to think *in pictures* to perceive the visual world accurately and recreate it in the mind, on paper or in a third dimension. (artists, architects, designers, sculptors)
- Bodily/Kinesthetic: ability to use one's body in a skilled way for self-expression or toward a goal. (mimes, dancers, athletes and actors)
- Interpersonal: ability to perceive and understand other individuals, their moods, desires and motivations. (political/religious leaders, teachers, therapists)
- Intrapersonal: understanding of one's own emotions. (novelists, counselors)

- Naturalist: ability to recognize and classify plants, minerals and animals and all variety of flora and fauna. [2]

A significant number of learners may possess one, or a combination of these intelligences.

Before discovering Howard Gardner, Dr. Myers had presided over a curriculum committee to identify the learning styles of kids. She hoped to coach her teachers to use the data effectively. She thought about kids who learned abstractly. They seemed to be the most successful students in school. They can absorb concepts such as addition and subtraction at an early age. She observed others whom she referred to as concrete learners. These youngsters early on, need to count four toothpicks, add them to five toothpicks and count all of them to get the total. They are taught to write the problem as 4 + 5 = 9. Jennifer had made note of these observations and, with the committee, categorized several learning styles.

She eagerly introduced Howard Gardner's work to a subsequent curriculum group and hoped to put his theory to the test during the following school year. She asked if there were any teachers who would be interested in trying a small pilot program in January to test the multiple intelligences approach with their classes. It would become one of her Clarksdale objectives.

She believed that Gardner's research would put meat on the *learning style* bones her committee had created. Dr. Myers' committee mixed the Gardner spice into the Bloom stew and the aroma was becoming the committee's recipe. The two theories were merged and evolved into in-service work with teachers. They were used for P.T.A. presentations, which Jennifer hoped would forge a stronger partnership between school and home in her Clarksdale Community.

---

[2] Gardner, Howard, *Multiple Intelligences: The Theory in Practice,* New York, NY Basic Books, 1993.

Harry Latter, Jennifer knew, would feel overwhelmed by any additional concepts that could lead his students into uncultivated fields of learning. She contemplated his situation as the school year continued its early passage into late September. She chose not to mention Gardner to Harry at this time.

Chapter 7:
Observation of Behavior Patterns

In addition to her research into learning, teaching and supervising Dr. Myers has been a long-time judicious observer of people and is fascinated by human behavior. She is like a botanist observing plant life, looking at constants, at changes and their causes. Over time Jennifer Myers has formed some interesting opinions about people and their behavior. She is gripped by habits that define people: the good and the positive, the bad and the negative, the strong and the weak, the acceptable and the faulty. When observing someone closely she believes she can, in a brief period of time, discern several traits and habits identifiable with that person.

Her first impression generally comes from the physical. Jack is tall; Jill is short. Physical patterns include style of dress, manner of speaking, body shape and body language. Jack has brown hair and freckles, wears muddy overalls and a soiled tee shirt. He complains, grimaces, is cranky and looks tired when carrying pails of water down the hill. Jill has red hair, green eyes, laughs, frolics and is agile. She has fun tumbling after Jack. One's mode of dress or style is often patterned behavior. People may dress fastidiously, fashionably, outlandishly, indifferently or slovenly.

Santa Claus is jolly and is often heard happily "Ho, ho, hoing." Santa smokes a pipe and wears a red suit with a big black belt, a large silver buckle and shiny black boots. He rides in a sleigh. He is plump, has a snow-white beard, is always smiling and loves children. He is generous and benevolent to a fault.

When an action or habit by an individual is repeated often enough to be associated with that person it is recognized as that person's behavior pattern (s). Human behavior is patterned. Describing a person's traits, habits, physical stature, style, characteristics and personalities helps to form a picture of that person.

Dr. Myers has combined her people observations with her research into teaching and learning. She has entwined the essence of learning and instruction with patterned teacher and student behavior, which initially came to light for educators with Robert Goldhammer's[3] work in the 60's. Jennifer Myers' deduction from studying Goldhammer's work is "*that teaching, like all human behavior, is patterned and, therefore capable of being observed, recorded, identified, analyzed and improved.*" Goldhammer's work includes a procedure that he developed and dubbed *Clinical Supervision* designed to provide a structure to validate behavioral teaching patterns. Teaching and learning patterns can be precisely identified and objectively recorded by competent and knowledgeable observers; they shall not be random thoughts that the supervisor recalls.

Clinical Supervision contains several components: 1) The *Pre-observation Conference* where teacher and coach/supervisor/principal meet to refine and mutually understand the lesson plan and the teaching objective to be observed. 2) The *Classroom Observation* where coach transcribes objectively all observable behavior. 3) The *Analysis and Strategy* where teacher and coach, separately analyze the data from the observation and plan for the conference. 4) The Post Observation *Conference* where teacher and coach, together, seek and identify patterns to determine their value in reaching the objective of the instruction. Together, principal and teacher identify patterns

---

[3] Goldhammer, Robert: *Clinical Supervision: Special Methods for the Supervision of Teachers, New York, Holt, Rinehart and Winston, Inc. 1969.*

from recorded classroom data that represent strengths to develop further and elements that can be improved.

A good deal of relevant and effective literature regarding teaching and learning patterns has been evolving for some time. In the case of teaching patterns, the research is providing coaches with tools that are constantly being modified and upgraded.

When observed teaching patterns are positive they need to be extended and enhanced. When teaching patterns are weak an equal effort needs to be made to improve them. The coach will rely on his/her expertise to offer assistance to his/her teacher colleague and accept the teacher's analysis of the data as valuable for improving instruction.

A skilled principal and teacher working together should cull from the transcribed data of the classroom observation: teaching patterns, learning patterns, classroom environment patterns, management patterns, discipline patterns, control patterns, questioning patterns, patterns of respect, motivating patterns, lesson closure patterns, discipline patterns and student behavior patterns. These represent but the tiniest sample of classroom patterns. The list can be extended ad infinitum to include any pattern that affects classroom learning and instruction.

Noting a discipline pattern during an observation when a student creates havoc in a classroom seriously disturbing the learning of others, a teacher or coach may have to stop the observation and immediately address the outburst. In cities discipline issues such as described here can become impossible situations for a planned observation. A youngster's bad behavior is protected by the lunacy of federal and state legislation making supervision difficult, at best. Federal and state laws guarantee all students a public education while disregarding the serious effects disturbed and disrespectful kids can have on the learning of serious students. Can teaching be as effective in such environments even with outstanding supervision? Of course not. Some semblance of this kind of behavior can crop up in any schoolroom where a youngster(s) is out of control.

Jennifer's credo is that, in spite of burgeoning social problems, economic and environmental factors, child abuse, broken homes and one-parent families impacting indirectly on instruction, schools remain responsible for what *they* can control. In the face of mounting odds and negative media schools must deliver the best possible instruction to each and every student within their confines. Dr. Myers asserts that with top teachers, a sound and basic curriculum, a commitment to the parent community and an expert instructional leader, a school can still gain some measure of success within the constraints placed on them over which they have little or no control.

She is also convinced that in the hands of able leaders, there would be no need for magnet or for charter schools. She, of course, works in a suburban district where aggressive discipline problems occur infrequently, are non-threatening and as such, are usually controllable.

Jennifer's dedication to her work with teachers in the classroom takes much of her time. She spends anywhere from 15 to 30 minutes with each teacher at pre and post observation conferences. The conferences, based on classroom observations, link one lesson to the next.

Following the pre-observation conference where coach and teacher discuss and clarify the lesson about to be taught and observed, Dr. Myers goes to the classroom and records the teaching and learning activities taking place in the classroom. She uses a carbon to duplicate what she has transcribed. At lesson's end the carbon copy is left on the teacher's desk showing the data that will be reviewed and talked about at the post-observation conference later that day.

The carbon is confirmation of what the coach observed and wrote; it provides information for the post session. It's a sign of trust; it gives the teacher time to read what was observed, to identify patterns of instruction and/or learning and to prepare for the conference.

At the next pre-observation conference Coach Myers and the teacher will look for connections from the summary of the last observed lesson and the lesson design for the class she is about to monitor.

The normal classroom lesson takes about 45 minutes. Dr. Myers, armed with a lesson plan and a clear understanding of the plan following the pre-observation conference, arrives a few minutes prior to a lesson. As the lesson begins, unfolds and ends, she records all that she sees. At the lesson's closure she brings her copy of the written notes to the office where Eleanor Haggerty will type them onto her word processor and immediately print them making them promptly available to be analyzed by coach and teacher in preparation for the post-conference. A copy is accessible to the teacher as soon as the notes are typed. Though the teacher has the carbon when Jennifer leaves the classroom, words are often scribbled and occasionally illegible. Jennifer, when possible, schedules the post-observation conference with the teacher immediately following dismissal.

The post session can take from 15 to 30 minutes depending on the teacher, her or his competence and the complexity of the data. They will have both analyzed and become familiar with the data by the time they meet. With most of her teachers who have become accustomed to this procedure the post-ob will go fairly quickly as they identify and discuss which patterns helped or hindered the lesson. Once they select the patterns that need to be expanded or improved they begin planning for the next classroom observation. The teacher typically leaves the room knowing what needs tweaking or more emphasis and will incorporate the information in the next lesson plan and observation. The cycles of observations are connected like links in a chain.

The above reflects an extremely time-consuming practice. Jennifer's goal is to schedule three such cycles every week of the school year. In a school with close to 400 children an emergency can change the day's plans in the briefest of moments. Jennifer's supervision translates into more than one-hundred hours of direct coaching with teachers during the school year. She will clinically supervise each teacher for approximately 8 hours each year in addition to walking through classrooms to ensure that identified needs are being addressed. If a teacher is in difficulty, Jennifer will deal with him or her as needed. She does with her teachers what she expects them to do with their students: individualize the coaching program for each one. Dr. Jennifer Myers is a teacher of teachers.

She reads the most current literature regarding magnet and charter schools, the finances and staff necessary for them to succeed and concludes confidently that Clarksdale is delivering quality education. Not a single family opted for the town's magnet program or charter school from Clarksdale.

Supervision of this magnitude is demanding. What Dr. Myers has learned from her arduous work is that she is able to save time for her other responsibilities by spending time in the classrooms of Clarksdale. Because of her time in the various rooms she knows what's happening in her school. She feels its pulse and heartbeat. Not much gets by. She is usually prepared to deal with parent concerns because of her familiarity with current school happenings. She requires that her teachers inform her of any trouble with a parent or student as soon as it occurs. She knows the children by name from her frequent appearances in their rooms. She is often able to nip potential trouble in the bud. Jennifer's time is taken up with parents, both, caring ones and a few unreasonable ones.

When a parent calls the principal with a complaint or concern about a classroom incident or a teacher, school secretary Eleanor Haggerty has been instructed to refer the complainant to the teacher. The teacher is the person closest to the student and should have an opportunity to converse with a parent before the parent contacts the principal. The Clarksdale Handbook directs the parents to follow this practice.

When a complaint is not resolved at its source, Jennifer, because of her propinquity with most of what's going on in the school, is usually aware and able to defuse many a prospective blowup because of that awareness. She is conversant with most problems that come her way. This avoids hours of debate and mending of fences. When a problem festers because it was not resolved quickly enmity spreads. Whenever Jennifer resolves potential time-consuming difficulties through early and knowledgeable intervention, she saves valuable time for other work.

Chapter 8:
Unanticipated Events

Jennifer contemplates the challenge of her upcoming pre-observation conference with Harry. She is hopeful that her coaching will, in time, raise him from the abyss of his past to a level that she considers standard for good teaching. They will meet a week from Monday to prepare for his first formal observation. She has two other observations scheduled before his.

But now there is paperwork to wade through. She is a skillful manager of time. She has learned to efficiently handle papers, mail, notes, junk and messages. She has trained herself to act on each piece as she finishes reading it. She does something with each scrap as she goes through her in-box. Eleanor Haggerty, Dr. Myers' capable secretary, sifts through the incoming piles ahead of Jennifer each day. She pulls the mail that requires punctual responses. Jennifer dictates replies for Eleanor who will prepare them for Jennifer's signature.

Dr. Myers gives short shrift to junk mail assigning it to the round file to be recycled into more junk mail. Some notes require future action. They go into a tickler file with tabs numbered from 1 to 31 representing each day of any month. She will take action as necessary on the appropriate day of the month. Some messages refer to scheduled events that are recorded on her desk calendar. When Jennifer is out of town or attending a meeting, Eleanor sorts incoming papers into 4 piles that are labeled: *High Priority* (read a.s.a.p.); *Medium Priority* (within a day or two); *Low Priority* (can wait) and *Junk* (toss). Eleanor Haggerty opens all Jennifer's mail except that marked *personal* or *confidential*.

What a blessing it is to have a competent secretary. The school secretary is the first contact that parents and the public usually have with the school. The manner in which the secretary answers the phone, how she is able to defuse difficult situations with intelligence, warmth and understanding significantly facilitates the principal's job.

Each morning Jennifer reviews the day's schedule with Eleanor. Committee, parent and central office meetings are marked on both their calendars. Eleanor Haggerty knows Jennifer's daily routine for returning phone calls. She knows that Jennifer walks through several classrooms each day and knows precisely when Dr. Myers' inviolable supervision cycles are scheduled. Together they make every effort to meet the priorities of the day. But schools are such dynamic and bustling institutions that the unexpected is always expected.

It's essential for a principal to be satisfied with his/her secretary. With secretaries' unions, satisfaction too often takes a back seat to seniority and questionable competence holding too many principals victims of the secretaries' union. Jennifer and Eleanor comprise a strong team for Clarksdale. Jennifer fought Superintendent Green as hard as she had ever opposed him on any issue when he once attempted to take Eleanor Haggerty for his own secretary.

Dr. Myers, when in her office alone, takes calls as they come. This saves time and often softens potential problems before anger and emotion eat away at the caller. When Jennifer is not available Eleanor impales phone messages onto a pointed spike that sits on Jennifer's desk. Parents and others hoping to speak with the principal are informed by Eleanor that Dr. Myers begins returning her calls at 1 P.M. and at 5 P.M. Jennifer attempts to reply to each and every phone inquiry on the day they are received. She checks her E-mail in the morning, at noon and, again, before leaving work.

Principal Meyers' job requires her to wear many hats. She is the personification of Clarksdale. Her administrative role requires her to communicate regularly with the staff, the children and their parents. She insists that her teachers do the same.

As Clarksdale's leader she keeps the superintendent apprised of the school's programs, important happenings and needs.

When developing her school budget Dr. Myers seeks input from the classroom and special area as well as special education teachers. She defends the Clarksdale budget requests that she deems reasonable and defensible before the superintendent. When the board or central office make cuts she reorganizes financial priorities according to her best judgment relative to student needs.

Jennifer also supervises the speech therapist, social worker, part-time school psychologist and the music, art, physical education and library/media teachers and all adjunct staff at Clarksdale.

There is the curriculum to assess. She assures the superintendent that her teachers are systematically following the district's curriculum. This includes knowing how youngsters are progressing within the curriculum guidelines. Related to this she manages the school's testing program

Her role in staffing Clarksdale is vitally important. Jennifer is extremely conscientious when recommending the hiring of staff new to teaching or new to her school. She realizes the teachers she recommends for Clarksdale will affect children, their parents and other staff members. When possible she enlists one or two teachers to assist in judging candidates before recommending her selections to the superintendent via the office of human relations. Occasionally, if there are vacancies late in the summer, as in the case of Harry Latter, she will interview alone.

Additionally, Jennifer Myers directs the use of the school facility and equipment ensuring that the school is a safe, sanitary and healthy place for children and the visiting public.

Principal Myers' greatest responsibility is coaching, evaluating and assessing staff on a continual basis. She assists her teachers to develop their personal growth plans while, at the same time, establishing her own program fo improvement, which is monitored by her assessor, Bernard Green.

Jennifer, and all successful principals, as well as good teachers toil long hours and days to achieve an effective learning environment for the children for whom they labor. Though expert coaching is the critical road to improved teaching, there are countless administrative responsibilities that must be successfully executed while running a school. The bottom line is that Dr. Myers is the chief administrator and supervisor of Clarksdale and its personnel as well as its ambassador to the community in her school neighborhood.

At the end of each school day she checks the following day's schedule. If adjustments are needed she makes them before leaving the building. This being Tuesday she scans Wednesday's docket before going home.

On Wednesday when Jennifer arrives she is fully prepared to take on the day. She begins the morning with an 8:15 A.M. before-school meeting in her office with the P.T.A. Planning Committee. Jennifer's office is comfortable and attractive. There is an oriental rug under a rectangular dark oak conference table adding warmth to a cozy office. The conference table accommodates eight people and features a cream-colored Rose Table lamp at one end with a white miniature of Rodin's *The Thinker* under its gentle light. The lampshade is festooned with glass slices of soft pink roses. Two 60-watt bulbs ensure the room's quiet ambience. Jennifer purchased the rug and lamp out-of-pocket. She believes the investment gives the room a friendly and supportive air. She also bought six 18 by 14 inch oak wood frames to exhibit children's artwork on her office walls. The vivid, colorful, pure and innocent images grace three walls. Completing the decor is the principal's dark wood desk with phone, computer, printer and desktop space for paperwork.

Dr. Myers welcomes the three PTA parents and offers juice, coffee, tea, bagels and a lox spread. There are butter knives and dishes placed in front of each chair on placemats. The meeting begins on time. Jennifer looks forward to working with the PTA Executive Committee. This morning's meeting is to determine how the PTA will welcome new families to Clarksdale and how it will encourage new parents' active participation in the association. Ten minutes into the meeting, Samantha Miller, the school nurse, buzzes Jennifer.

"Dr. Myers we need you, Jake Codey fell in the schoolyard and his nose is quite bloodied, it could be broken."

"Not a good call," Jennifer tells the group, "one of the kids hurt his nose badly. I'm terribly sorry but I have to leave. Please have more coffee. I'll be back as soon as I can. Mrs. Haggerty will let you know if I'm going to be detained. Just go on ahead without me. I'll catch up." Such an interruption is rare in the world of business. Corporate America couldn't conceive of regular unexpected disruptions, such as this, to their workdays.

When Jennifer goes into the nurse's room she finds Jake shaking and sobbing uncontrollably. He's a third-grader and is in a state of shock. Third-graders are prone to believe their lives are endangered at the sight of their own blood. Nurse Miller is holding a cold pack on Jake's nose. She tells Jennifer that she will apply the ice for 15 minutes, wait a few minutes and repeat. She has Jake's head propped up on a pillow and is doing her best to let him know that he will live. She doesn't think he has displaced fractures. A doctor might simply prescribe rest and a little pain medicine. Samantha is confident that she can control the situation until Jake's mother is located. Once satisfied, Jennifer returns to her meeting.

Eleanor, who just got to her desk, tries to reach Jake's mother at home: no answer. She tries the emergency number that all parents file with the school, again no answer. Nearly 35 minutes passed before Leona Codey, Jake's mom, is contacted.

Ms., her preferred title, Codey arrives at 9:25 angry and agitated. Eleanor Haggerty escorts the nattily clad Leona Codey to the nurse's office. As soon as Jake, who was by then dozing off, spots his mother he begins to shriek.

Ms. Codey cuddles Jake to her bosom and says, "We're going to see the doctor, honey," setting Jake off again. Mommy is livid. Five minutes pass before she is able to quiet Jake. She tells him to stay with Mrs. Miller for a bit longer and demands to see the principal.

Jennifer Myers returned to her PTA meeting, which was adjourned at 8:45. She is preparing for her observation of Beverly Gillette when she hears the disturbance in the outer office. She opens the door and immediately reads the anger and hostility in Leona Codey's countenance and makes a decision. She will deal with Ms. Codey before she goes away angrier than she is now. Without an explanation there is sure to be trouble over this fall on the playground. Jennifer postpones the observation. The morning is being shaped by an unexpected event, not unusual for an institution full of healthy and active children.

Beverly Gillette had spent a couple of hours carefully planning for her first observation and another thirty minutes meeting with Jennifer at her pre-observation session on Tuesday afternoon only to learn on Wednesday morning that there would be no observation at the scheduled time. This is a major upset for any teacher, particularly one who is brand new to the school and the profession.

Eleanor checks with Samantha who is preparing an accident report for Jennifer to read before forwarding it to the superintendent's office.

Jennifer knows that Ms. Codey can be difficult. She has complained about the cafeteria and is never happy with Jake's teachers. Jennifer has heard that Leona Codey disparages the school to others. She considers what could ensue if she doesn't confront the situation immediately. Postponement now could cost her precious hours from her school responsibilities while possibly having to face litigation.

There are two meetings to attend, a teacher to observe, a newsletter to write, a difficult meeting with one of the custodians who is accused of harassing a kindergarten teacher and a host of other less pressing problems to resolve. She knows, also, other matters requiring her attention may be lurking inside the phone only to be released with its next ring.

Tag-a-long attorneys, a.k.a. ambulance chasers, have become disruptive to the normal operation of schools throughout America. They have happily discovered new arable fields ready for tilling in the face of their ever-increasing numbers and their competitive profession. Our litigious society has created a monster, which impacts severely when unleashed, often for no good reason, on a principal's ability to manage a school effectively.

If Leona Codey takes that approach she could wrap Jennifer in a web of legal frustration and controversy especially if Jake's nose is broken. There might be calls from a persistent and pushy lawyer who would expect her to respond immediately. Any delay and Jennifer Myers could be deemed uncooperative. She may well be hounded to explain why this poor little third-grade boy *was lost in a crowd of children running wild in the schoolyard while teachers chatted with one another unaffected by the plight of little Jake Codey.* The questioning might be followed by a time-consuming account of how this boy fell on the playground with teachers present. Jennifer would lose coaching time. With experience she has become vigilant of the risks that accidents such as this can pose. Jennifer decided to trade her valued coaching time with Beverly to address the Codey accident and to calm Ms. Codey.

Attorneys have found their own playground in the public schools. They represent plaintiffs who hold schools, but never themselves, responsible for student failures, disruptions or accidents.

Scolding a student, or *any* statement a teacher might make during the course of several hours of instructing pupils every day for one-hundred-eighty days can be misinterpreted or misrepresented by a youngster when reporting a day's events to a parent resulting in Mr. Attorney knocking on the schoolhouse door. Teachers are society's targets. They can be accused of incompetence by uncertified and untrained parents and lawyers.

It ordinarily takes a couple of years of post-graduate work beyond a Masters Degree for a university and a state to certify that an educator is ready to pass judgment on a teacher's competence. There are parents like Leona Codey who determine a teacher's ability without ever having met or observed that teacher. When challenged by parents regarding a teacher's competence, Jennifer reminds them that a state certificate for supervision is required to supervise and assess a teacher. Any parent who ignores this fact is skating on thin ice, she tells them, and could be in jeopardy if the teacher opts to pursue anything that could be construed as defamatory by the teacher.

At the moment Dr. Myers is thinking about the irate parent with whom she is about to meet. Ms. Codey stomps into Jennifer's office. "What the hell is goin' on here? Can you tell me? Are teachers supervisin' or just blabbin' with one another out there? Tell me, what's goin' on at this damned place you call a school?"

Dr. Myers has tolerated this kind of aggression in the past and is skilled at handling it. She lets Ms. Codey talk without interruption. When finally she has run her course Jennifer offers her a seat at the table. Dr. Myers seldom sits across her desk or table when meeting with parents. She positions herself next to Leona Codey with her chair slightly aslant.

Calmly Jennifer responds, "Ms. Codey, Jake had an accident. He fell. Has he ever fallen in your yard or in your home, at a neighbor's home or anywhere outside of school?"

She waits in silence as Leona's gaze drops to the desk. Pauses of silence can be effective when attempting to change offense to defense. Jennifer breaks the momentary silence.

"Our teachers can't possibly anticipate an accident when children are running and playing any more than you can at home. They are on the playground to stop roughhousing and play that is dangerous or out of control. They do a fine job keeping kids safe. What happened to Jake was simply an accident. Yes, it was unfortunate. We'd love to say that no child has ever fallen or been hurt at Clarksdale. I wish Jake's mishap had never happened but we have a school full of lively kids who love to run and play. I hope you understand."

"Why wasn't he taken to a doctor? It's apparent that he needed one. Couldn't you people see that?"

"Samantha Miller is not only a nurse but highly qualified as our emergency team leader here at Clarksdale. She's seen many scrapes and bruises. Though she thought there was a possibility that Jake's nose was broken, she applied the first-aid required for such an injury. She could have applied ice packs for several hours without risk to Jake. We wanted to contact you first. We are extremely careful not to arbitrarily haul youngsters off to doctors without parental consent unless we identify a critical situation. I truly hope you understand that we want Jake to be well and wouldn't do anything to jeopardize him or any other child in this school."

Leona Codey seemed somewhat appeased by the time she left with Jake whose nose was no longer bleeding. Jennifer, showing true concern, called Leona at home in the evening to inquire about Jake's injury. He seemed fine: he answered the phone. Dr. Myers never heard anything more from Leona Codey regarding the nosebleed. Jennifer, however, had to reorder her day's priorities and reschedule Beverly's observation. Unfortunately, not all confrontations end as affably.

Fairly often, the anger and dissatisfaction Principal Myers has experienced with aggressive parents have been linked to the parent(s) own failure with their children. Occasionally parents are frustrated and compensate for a home or family problem by using the school as their handy scapegoat for their failings. Parents' refusal to accept the school's testimony regarding their student's misconduct or academic difficulty, choosing instead to blame a reported problem on a teacher or the school is sometime a reflection of culpability. Whether this was the case with Mrs. Codey, Jennifer didn't know.

The media is ceaselessly attacking the public schools and convincing the general population that schools are failing, not the children nor their parents but the schools. The schools continue to be targets for a number of ineffective parents relieving them of guilt associated with their children's problems and taking out their hostility on perceived flawed public education.

Jennifer considers herself to be an advocate for all the Clarksdale children. She also believes that she is fair in making judgments when problems arise while conceding that her teachers and she, herself, make mistakes with the children. When she meets with parents at such times and knows the school is at fault, she listens courteously and always reminds parents that the school and the parents need to be partners and that both have the child's best interest at heart. She is not reluctant to suggest a change in program or course of action when it is clear that the parent(s) challenge is justified. However, she will staunchly but respectfully stand by her decision and her staff when she is convinced the school's action is the correct one for the child.

Chapter 9:
The Litigation Invasion

School principals today are often plagued with nasty and mean-spirited parents whose complaints are seldom resolved to the parents' satisfaction. This relatively new phenomenon has a paralyzing effect on normal school operations. Anxiously waiting in the wings are attorneys looking to expand their offerings.

A nasty litigious issue was about to pop up at Clarksdale at a terribly inconvenient time. The matter would impact Jennifer's coaching of her new teachers, especially with Harry and could not have come at a worse time. Ordinarily Jennifer is philosophical about thorny issues. She believes that she is paid a decent salary to resolve all challenges that come her way. The knotty incidents that, in any school, crop up from time to time can be sorted into three types: some that, with a little time and effort, are worked out to everyone's satisfaction; some that are manageable but only with continual monitoring and communicating and some that are so messy they fail to please the plaintiff. The latter are the heated ones that occasionally end in litigation.

The unpleasant ones become ravenous and consuming and eat away at valuable time. That type has been practically non-existent at Clarksdale. Though unpleasant encounters or disagreements between parents and staff occupy very little of Jennifer's time she manages to resolve most of them with her honesty and by offering sensible solutions.

Long before Jennifer Myers ever considered litigation to be a threat at Clarksdale she learned a tough lesson early in her administrative career. Though the situation was volatile Jennifer and the parents were able to come to an acceptable solution by working to understand each other's point of view. They found a way to solve their problem. Had an attorney been involved, Dr. Myers is certain that many hours of investigating and reporting would have been wrung from her committed time to coach in classrooms. The following incident prepared her for what was looming ahead.

The situation got out of hand because Jennifer was caught off-guard and unprepared. Early one Saturday evening as she was preparing for her dinner date the phone rang. "Good evening, this is Jennifer Myers."

"Dr. Myers, this is Phyllis McGurt, Leslie's mother. I'm sorry to spring this on you on a Saturday evening but my husband just got home from New York and he is furious. He learned from Leslie and me that Ms. Johnson thrust her thumbs under Leslie's armpits and put her up against the girls' room wall because Les left her class early to do her student traffic duty! He is irate and now, so am I. We want to meet with you and Ms. Johnson this evening! Jim has to be back at his job in the city Monday morning and will not be back here until next weekend." Jennifer was quite aware that Jim McGurt was a New York businessman. This kind of Saturday evening pressure was a clear sign of the anger the McGurt's had built up.

A frustrated Jennifer Myers responded, "Mrs. McGurt, yes, it's Saturday evening and I have an appointment. I surely don't expect that Penny Johnson will be available to meet with you on such short notice especially this evening. Can't this wait until Monday when I can meet with you and Ms. Johnson? I'll have all the details for you. Then we can sit together and talk about what really happened and what to do about it."

"What really happened? We know what really happened. If you refuse to meet until Monday we'll press charges against Johnson."

Principal Myers happened to have been leaving the classroom next to Penny Johnson's room when the contended altercation occurred. She knew something about the alleged physical encounter because she, herself, found

Leslie talking back to her teacher in the hall. At the same time she noticed a line of students coming from an art class as Ms. Johnson led Leslie McGurt toward the girls' room. Penny had Leslie by the arm. It appeared that she was trying to move the debate out of the hall away from the oncoming group of children. Before opening the door Ms. Johnson asked Jennifer if she would please watch her class for a couple of minutes.

Jennifer kept an eye on the children until Penny returned. Two of Leslie's girl friends immediately told Jennifer that Mrs. Johnson was really, "…mad at Leslie and was hollering at her." Jennifer knew these three girls were loyal to one another and tended to be naughty from time to time. This togetherness against the world was a typical trait that sometimes emerged in girls as early as the fifth grade; they could be unshakeable in their loyalty.

Jennifer's early mistake was not following up with Penny before the weekend. She had only asked if everything had gone well. This was a lesson that she would not repeat.

"Mrs. McGurt, is Leslie injured? Is she marked?" Jennifer asked.

"She was physically manhandled and you'd better produce Johnson and yourself to explain how and why this happened."

Because this occurred during Jennifer's first year as principal she had let an important incident pass without investigating it thoroughly with the teacher. Yet she had learned that, by being in and out of classrooms, she was often aware of what was happening throughout the school. She had some personal knowledge of the accusation referred to by Mrs. McGurt but she hadn't followed through. She had no basis for argument over the phone. Now she'd have to break her dinner date and try to reach Penny Johnson. This would not happen again she vowed. It's called learning from experience and Jennifer was a quick study.

She told Mrs. McGurt that she'd try to reach Mrs. Johnson. She called Penny. "Hello."

"Penny, this is Jennifer. You don't know how I hate to call you but something rather serious has come up that I don't know enough about because I didn't pursue it with you yesterday. "

"What is it, Jennifer?"

"Well, Mrs. McGurt just called. She's accusing you of taking Leslie into the girls' room and sticking your thumbs under her armpits and propping her against the wall because she left early for traffic duty."

"Oh my God! I did no such thing. You saw me walk her into the girls' room."

"She said that other kids told her that you took Leslie to the girls' room and were hollering at her."

"Well, yes, I first brought her into the hall. With another class walking down the hall I decided to scold her out of range of the other kids as long as you were willing to take my class for a few minutes. What prompted the whole deal was that I had told the class that I didn't want to hear a peep out of anyone until dismissal.

"They had been rowdy during the afternoon and I was going to keep them after school if I heard anyone make a sound. Not a good threat, perhaps, but they all needed to straighten up. Leslie defiantly whispered to Keisha next to her and got up to leave. I told her to sit down. She said she had student crossing-guard duty and got up anyway."

Sophisticated children through their parents' influence have been made aware of their right to express themselves. More and more, children have become emboldened by this knowledge and brazenly and disrespectfully too often sass their teachers. Fortunately, this was unusual at Clarksdale where the concept of RESPECT was regularly stressed.

"I directed her to wait for me in the hall. I took her into the girls' room and scolded her. She can be very snotty, not the little angel everyone thinks she is. She is always testing."

"Unfortunately, the McGurt's want to see you and me at school in an hour."

"No way, Jennifer, we're going to the movies."

"Penny, I just broke a date that I was looking forward to and you will need to do the same unless we want to face charges, justified or not. I do not intend to meet the McGurt's alone. I don't really have a handle on the issue. We'll meet at 7:30."

"Shoot, Jennifer, this is insane. O.K. I'll be there dammit," she responded disgustedly and slammed the phone down.

The four of them met. Penny Johnson denied having abused Leslie and was very adamant about it. Mr. McGurt began to simmer down but it was obvious he didn't believe Penny. It appeared that Mrs. McGurt, though agitated when Leslie got home and told her side of the story, was stirred up all over again when her husband reacted as heatedly as he did when he heard Leslie's story.

The meeting lasted forty-five minutes. Dr. Myers' presence and testimony to the fact that Leslie and Penny were only in the girls' room for a couple of minutes and that Leslie appeared to be angry but hadn't complained about having been hurt was not completely believed by the McGurt's. Though they weren't entirely satisfied with Penny's version of the incident they did admit that Leslie was capable of stretching it. Parents today are more likely to believe their children than their children's teachers: a condition whereby youngsters have learned how to work a system of creating waves while they remain comfortable in the ebb of the tide.

Though the McGurt's weren't convinced, they were satisfied that Jennifer was on top of it and that nothing like what Leslie said happened would happen again, if indeed it ever happened in the first place.

Jennifer never again responded to parent concerns unprepared. Her teachers know to inform her of student or parent issues that might need to be handled by her. Though Dr. Myers' routine of walking through the school and classrooms on a regular basis is time-consuming Jennifer believes the trade-off in time saved when speaking

knowledgeably with parents is worth the effort. She commands the respect of just about all of Clarksdale parents who are confident that Dr. Myers knows and understands the children, the school, the parents and the program. Yet there remain a cynical few at Clarksdale, as at any school, who remain skeptical and wary of teachers and the school.
Enter the Cassidy's and their attorney!

Chapter 10: The Cassidy Attack

Jennifer Myers' interest in patterned human behavior has helped her cope with and understand an occasional intolerant, demanding, rude or inconsiderate parent who can upset a school's routine for a couple of hours or a day at most. But nothing prepared her for George and Louise Cassidy, parents who embodied each and every one of these characteristics. The Cassidy's, whom she would soon learn, could undo the routine of a school for days, weeks, months and longer with relentless interruptions, threats and litigation. From the moment they enrolled their son, Adam, at Clarksdale, fireworks were set off beginning with sparklers, then lady fingers followed by M-80's.

The Cassidy's were cut from the same cloth as some parents Jennifer has observed at her nephew's Little League games: parents who shout verbal affronts at coaches and umpires who volunteer their services at these little people's games. Though few in number some of these boorish parents callously use offensive language in voicing their disagreement for what they believe is unfair or inept coaching of their offspring. Far too often they will even bark at their own youngsters for striking out, committing an error or for lack of hustle. Their own children cause them embarrassment. They have little respect for authority whether in the athletic arena or the schoolhouse. They are the parents who live vicariously through their children. They put undue pressure on their kids and demonstrate slight regard for anyone who questions them.

They are immature and offensive. They believe their child's coach is a bungling imbecile. These parents display bad manners for all to see and hear. Their rudeness makes a mockery of what was intended to be fun for their kids. Their children either become extensions of themselves or are humiliated by them. Their kids are often the children who have little respect for their coaches or their teachers.

They are condescending and nasty and believe whatever their children tell them about their teachers. These young people have learned to be rude, disrespect authority, curse, fight and lie. They know their parents will believe whatever they tell them. These children have cunningly learned to work one side against the other.

The Cassidy's were cast from this same mold. Throughout Adam Cassidy's first year at Clarksdale the Cassidy's had been complaining about his program and teacher. His year at Clarksdale began in early November when the Cassidy's were forced to transfer Adam from St. Elizabeth's Catholic School to Clarksdale.

St. Elizabeth's principal, Father Michael Russell, told the Cassidy's that Adam would no longer be able to attend St. Elizabeth's because of continued disruptive behavior, constant bullying of smaller children, foul language and parental unwillingness to meet with his teacher. Father Russell had several nasty encounters with the Cassidy's regarding young Adam's intolerable classroom antics before expelling this malicious third-grader: *there was no discussion.* Father Russell simply told them to leave this private school. The Cassidy's angrily slammed the priest's office door and left with Adam in tow.

Private schools have every right to expel children who don't meet their rules of conduct or academic standards. Public schools do not. There are strict guidelines for suspending a public school student and state mandated regulations for expulsion. The public schools are required to take in all comers and, to all intents and purposes, keep them.

In the Old River School System it is the school principal who determines whether a student's behavior warrants a suspension. If a student is suspended the principal decides the length of the suspension not to exceed ten days for a single suspension. Parents or guardians are informed before any suspension is enforced. In most states no student may be suspended more than ten times or fifty school days in one school year: an extremely rare circumstance. A monthly suspension report is forwarded to the superintendent's office from each Old River School.

Expulsion is far more serious and gives the student the right to a formal hearing unless there is an emergency such as a threat to the safety of the student being expelled or to others before a hearing can be scheduled. In Old River, following state law, a hearing is conducted by, at minimum, three board members. The local board of education has the option of appointing an impartial hearing officer in its place. The board or its appointed officer may expel a student following presentation of evidence serious enough to oust the youngster. The parents or guardians of the student being expelled must be notified of the time, date and site of the formal hearing according to state statutes and may, of course, attend the hearing with or without legal counsel.

Public schools must enroll all students no matter their label as long as they reside in the appropriate school district. Though Adam Cassidy was expelled from St. Elizabeth's private Catholic school for intolerable and disruptive behavior he has the right to a public education. Parents of students attending private schools agree, usually in writing, to follow school rules to ensure the continued attendance of their children. They need not make such a pledge in the public domain.

America's public schools are responsible for educating the infirmed, the mentally retarded, the emotionally disturbed, the learning disabled, the non-English speakers, the poor, the butcher's, the baker's and the candlestick maker's children. A goodly number of well-to-do families send their children to public schools yet many who can afford private school reject their public school entitlement thus skimming many fine scholars from the rolls of the public institutions!

Adam Cassidy was at Clarksdale's front door in the time it took to drive him the two miles from St. Elizabeth's. Eleanor Haggerty greeted the Cassidy's who came to drop Adam off at his new school. There had been no previous contact with Clarksdale. No one at the school expected a new student on the day the Cassidy's arrived. Eleanor buzzed Dr. Myers who was in a classroom.

Jennifer knows not to ask Eleanor if the interruption is important. Eleanor knows when a problem might be brewing. She told Jennifer that new parents were determined to leave their child at the school without properly registering him. Jennifer left her teacher observation in mid-lesson.

Jennifer, once introduced to the Cassidy's by Eleanor, explained to them that she could not register Adam until she was able to confirm his residence, his withdrawal from St. Elizabeth's and, most important, until she received a copy of Adam's birth certificate and his immunization record. George Cassidy became increasingly irritated. Jennifer noticed that both Cassidy's were showing an unusual degree of impatience while waiting for her to validate Adam's withdrawal from St. Elizabeth's with a phone call to the school. George Cassidy kept checking his watch. He was visibly aggravated by the delay. He soon let Jennifer know that he was a businessman and had important things to do that she probably wouldn't understand.

Jennifer learned later that Mr. Cassidy ran a small florist shop in Old River called *Smell the Roses.* She learned that he employed a clerk and two other workers, one who drove a delivery truck; the other maintained the flora.

Finished with her call to St. Elizabeth's, Jennifer repeated that Adam could not be enrolled until she received the required papers.

"It's the law," she advised. She asked the Cassidy's to please return with Adam on the following day and bring the essential documentation.

George Cassidy sneeringly said, "You have to be kidding. What's the big deal?"

"Mr. And Mrs. Cassidy, it is customary for parents to notify the school at least a day ahead when a student is to be enrolled so we can make the arrival as comfortable as possible and apprise you of what we ………" George Cassidy rudely interrupted her in mid-sentence

"This is a joke and it looks like this school might be a joke. Here's a student, you have a room and a teacher and you can't deal with that immediately? If he was at St. Elizabeth's you surely know he has all the necessary papers."

"I'm sorry. It's incumbent on me to confirm the paperwork. It's my responsibility. And, Mr. Cassidy, there's more to just placing a child in a room. It's also necessary to inform Mrs. McRaney that she will be getting a new student. As soon as I notify her she'll tell the other children to expect another classmate. She'll prepare her children to give Adam a warm and friendly welcome. This is for Adam's benefit. Also, the custodian will have to bring a desk and chair to the class that fit Adam. It's obvious that he's a big boy. We don't store extra furniture in the classrooms. There are textbooks the teacher will have to get from the storage room. It is also important for Mrs. McRaney to speak with *you both* about Adam, his needs and his strengths. There's much to be done to ensure a good beginning for your child. We don't just bring an eight-year-old into an unfamiliar setting not knowing anyone in the class and let him fend for himself."

"Look, I don't have time to play your games. No one is home and I want Adam to begin today."

"I'm sorry, Mr. Cassidy. But you are required by law to follow registration procedures."

"My God, woman. What kind of time do you think I have?"

All the while Adam is listening. When Dr. Myers welcomed him she did so warmly and with genuine affection.

"Adam, I think you'll like it here at Clarksdale. You'll have a nice and capable teacher and some real good kids in your classroom. One of our mottos here is respect for each other and for the school building. You will see evidence of that respect when your new classmates welcome you to their room. Are you pleased to be coming here?"

"I guess so," he mumbles.

"What's your best subject?"

"I don't care. I don't like any subjects."

"Oh, I see." This is going to be interesting Jennifer thought. She glanced at the boy throughout her exchanges with his dad. He twitched and fidgeted, nothing unusual for an eight-year-old-boy. Yet he was coming to a completely new environment and seemed bored by it all. Most kids are edgy or shy or uncomfortable when entering a new school; Adam was none of these.

The Cassidy's stormed out surly and agitated. Louise Cassidy returned the following morning with Adam and the necessary papers. She told Jennifer that she didn't have time to talk with Mrs. McRaney about Adam as suggested.

Her rationale, "As you probably know, I'm a substitute teacher in Albion. I go to different classrooms and schools as part of my job. Often, I have never seen the children before. I have to work with them and don't have the luxury of sitting with their parents to learn their 'strengths and needs' as you put it yesterday. Here's Adam. I'm sure she can teach him."

Dr. Myers brought a somewhat petulant Adam to his new classroom. Mrs. McRaney was ready for him and the students were happy to have a new classmate. Third-graders love to show a new kid the ropes.

A week following Adam's arrival trouble began and the classroom decorum, so patiently crafted, was suddenly being disrupted. Betty saw that Erika, who sat next to Adam, was crying uncontrollably.

She asked what happened, "Adam hit me in the face." When questioning Adam about the incident he looked away without answering. Betty McRaney tended to Erika while Adam hummed under his breath. Mrs. McRaney would call Erika's mom after school and contact Mrs. Cassidy. When she reached Mrs. Cassidy to inform her about Adam hitting little Erika and his belligerent, defiant, uncontrolled behavior since coming to her classroom, Mrs. Cassidy became irritated.

“We never have a problem with Adam at home. You’re supposed to be qualified to handle the children in your class. They’re only third-graders for goodness sakes.” Parents like Louise Cassidy, Betty McRaney knew, invariably refuse to accept teachers’ accounts of the malevolent conduct of their children. They resist discussing their children’s school behavior preferring to remain distant from the school as well as unapproachable. Indeed, as is the case with Louise Cassidy, they rarely admit to a problem choosing rather to hold the school responsible for any and all questionable behaviors of their children. Their position is usually that the child is fine at home and, if there is any trouble at school, it can be attributed to the school’s ineffectiveness. Fortunately for Dr. Jennifer Myers there are no other parents quite like the Cassidy’s at Clarksdale.

Betty McRaney pressed Louise Cassidy and pleaded with her to meet with her as soon as possible regarding Adam’s behavior. Both Cassidy’s decided, though grudgingly, to come to school the following day. When told of Adam’s striking Erika hard across the face and of subsequent outbursts when she assigned him work he didn’t like, George Cassidy asked if the work could possibly be boring, totally ignoring the Erika incident. Mrs. McRaney was attempting to nip emerging signs of a disturbed young man in the bud and all she got was a sarcastic statement from the boy’s father. There were no problems at home George once again assured her so why should there be trouble here. The only sign of a smile that came over Mr. Cassidy’s face was when Betty McRaney showed the Cassidy’s a paper that had, *The techer is ful of shit*, written by Adam who passed it around the classroom. Cassidy’s wry response was, “His spelling needs work.”

The boy had caused lots of trouble at St. Elizabeth’s and was, from the onset of his entrance into Clarksdale, raising havoc there as well. His negative influence was, within his first couple of weeks, recognized throughout the school by staff, students and the bus driver. He became an unsettling influence everywhere.

The Cassidy's blamed Betty McRaney for Adam's troubles. She didn't understand the boy and she was probably an uninspiring teacher. The result of the meeting was the Cassidy's demand for a meeting with Dr. Myers. From the day he entered Clarksdale Jennifer sensed that Adam was in need of psychological testing, which could only be done with the parents' permission. At her meeting with the Cassidy's they steadfastly refused to give it. They stormed out of Jennifer's office with nothing settled.

Dr. Myers recognized that Adam's program did need some adjusting. He was fairly intelligent and, admittedly, bored. She didn't think Betty was doing all she could to meet his education needs perhaps because she was so busy tending to his emotional outbursts, which were detrimental to the rest of the children's learning. Jennifer met with Betty several times and, together, they modified his program but to no avail.

Adam was, in Benjamin Lesser's opinion, a disturbed child. Lesser, the school psychologist at Clarksdale, knew Adam and the Cassidy's from St. Elizabeth's where he also served as the school psychologist. Federal funds are allocated to private schools to provide similar services to those available to public school children. Lesser worked at the Catholic school one day a week under this entitlement.

The Cassidy's had met with him only once at St. Elizabeth's and immediately decided he was a fraud. They rejected the recommendation to have Dr. Lesser work with their son. Because of the Cassidy's refusal to have Adam tested at St. Elizabeth's Father Russell, concerned about the child's uncontrolled behavior, asked Benjamin to observe Adam from a distance hoping he would offer suggestions for coping with Adam. His observations only confirmed Lesser's belief that testing was necessary.

Jennifer and Betty McRaney made several unsuccessful attempts to persuade the Cassidy's of the need to test their son.

Adam swore in class and on the school bus. He sat and pouted when directed to do class work. He often punched smaller kids in the schoolyard. He once said to the male aide who rode on the bus and threatened to carry him onto the bus when Adam announced that he wasn't going to ride, "I'll kick you in your peanut." He was a little imp. He pulled the aide's glasses off when he bent to zip Adam's jacket.

Jennifer met with the Cassidy's several times during the year following their refusals to further meet with Adam's teacher. Jennifer begged them repeatedly to let her schedule a *Planning and Placement Team* (PPT) meeting with them. The PPT would include the Cassidy's, of course, Mrs. McRaney, Anita Crockett, the special education teacher, Dr. Ben Lesser and Jennifer. Its purpose would be to discuss Adam's comportment: his outbursts, his rudeness, his anger, his academic program, his emotional needs and, hopefully, to get permission to have the psychologist test him.

The PPT is a legal procedure that brings school personnel and parents together to share information in an effort to assist a child with any unusual school difficulty he or she may be experiencing. There are names for many learning handicaps. Some are academic in nature such as a learning disability or psychological such as an emotional problem. The intent of the PPT is to establish a set of actions to be carried out by the school with the parents' support to assist a youngster to overcome whatever learning obstacle that child is experiencing. The adopted PPT plan remains in place until a review is conducted to determine its effectiveness. All PPT programs are reviewed and evaluated at the end of each school year, or as needed during the year, with the appropriate school personnel and parent(s) participating. At the time of review the child's program can be modified or continued as originally adopted. If a child has shown enough progress that youngster may be dropped from further PPT assistance.

Each time the Cassidy's met with Jennifer, George became more confrontational and offensive. With Jennifer's continual imploring over a span of several months, the Cassidy's finally, near the end of the school year, grudgingly consented to attend a PPT meeting with Mrs. McRaney present. When Jennifer announced that Dr. Benjamin Lesser would be at the meeting, Mr. Cassidy stated that he would not attend any meeting with someone, "who didn't know his ass from his elbow."

Jennifer decided to go ahead with the meeting in the hope that, once it was convened, she could convince Mr. Cassidy to have the school psychologist join them. When Mr. & Mrs. George Cassidy arrived for the meeting with Jennifer and Betty McRaney, Jennifer could see that George was ready for bear. It was late May. It was time to determine Adam's program for September. The battle had continued for the several horrendous months since Adam's arrival at Clarksdale.

"I am hopeful that we can exchange ideas and digest what is being said as we aim to establish a program for Adam in the fourth grade," Jennifer began. She asked the Cassidy's to please listen to what Mrs. McRaney had to say about Adam's conduct, learning and his lack of interest in class. She knew Mr. Cassidy was one tough cookie but had no idea what lie ahead.

Jennifer followed with, "To make this meeting as productive as possible, I've asked Dr. Ben Lesser to join us shortly. Mr. Cassidy, I'm urging you to simply listen to his assessment of the situation without interruption."

On this particular day she had seated the Cassidy's alongside herself with Betty McRaney across the table. It became immediately apparent that Mister Cassidy had decided to show these so-called educators a thing or two. He struck a rigid pose as he took his place. As soon as he heard Lesser's name he bolted.

Jennifer blurted, “Mr. & Mrs. Cassidy, please don’t leave. We need to be partners. It’s incumbent upon all of us to come together on Adam’s behalf. Surely you know we have a serious problem, actually, a crisis on our hands. Adam is, for all practical purposes, dysfunctional in school. We are doing everything we know to change his attitude. Unless we can work together we’ll function as adversaries. Adam will be the ultimate loser. It will do him no good for us to be confrontational. His success is dependent on the cooperative efforts between you and us. The ‘us’ includes Dr. Lesser.” Cassidy wasn’t buying it.

“When he comes in, I leave.”

Jennifer decided to salvage what she could from what could turn into a debacle. “O.K., because it’s critical that we come to some kind of resolution regarding Adam’s program I’ll reluctantly tell Dr. Lesser we won’t need him. Let’s move on. Betty, please begin.”

“Well, Mr. And Mrs. Cassidy, the fact is that Adam remains unruly in class. He shouts out in the middle of a lesson as I’ve repeatedly communicated to you. I have to stop teaching to quiet him, often without success. He affects the learning of the other children to the extent that I’m receiving complaints about Adam from parents whose children are telling their parents about Adam’s antics. No amount of reasoning calms him. His temper dictates whether he will continue or curtail his outspoken behavior. He is likely to curse if the mood strikes him. He seemingly does not care a whit for his classmates or for me. When last we met, Mr. Cassidy, you made light of his nasty note about me. All you had to say was that he seemed to need a spelling lesson.”

Betty asserted in no uncertain terms, “I believe that Adam is taking his cues from you. If that is a false assertion, then please work with us and show Adam that we are united in our effort to help him to do well here: to succeed at school. He has no respect for any authority in this building. We have used in-house suspensions but they have not been effective. Dr. Myers has asked if I’d advise an out-of-school suspension. I simply hate to do that and admit that we can't help Adam with positive support right here at school but this unruly situation has been going on for months. Surely you are concerned about what I'm sharing with you. We have critical choices to be made for the next academic year."

The Cassidy's and Mrs. McRaney had never reached agreement regarding anything they had discussed while Adam's deportment was worsening. George Cassidy considered Betty to be an incompetent teacher who can't manage young children.

"My God," he once told her, "you can't take care of third-graders? Your solution is to throw an eight-year-old out of school? Adam is just an active little boy." McRaney knew it was ludicrous to threaten expulsion for a third-grader but suspension didn't seem to bother the Cassidy's.

Whenever Betty spoke with Adam's parents she shared her deep concerns about his out-of-control behavior and strongly recommended psychological testing. George Cassidy would invariably boil with rage like an immature despot presiding over a tiny nation of school serfs. She observed in George what was emerging from Adam. An apple was ripening on the branch and was about to fall near the tree. How, she wondered, could this youngster be helped without cooperation from his parents? Can this adult man be brought to recognize that his negative influence is contributing heavily to his son's problems?

"Mr. Cassidy, the school has made some mistakes with Adam, I know I have. We're working to fix them. But, you have built a solid wall between us blocking all attempts to enlist your cooperation. We are pleading for your involvement and support. Adam is already aware of the power he has in the classroom! It's feeding his opinion of himself in a very negative way. He knows you'll fight us on his behalf. This is not the kind of situation that will lead to his success socially or educationally. He is in dire straits at a frighteningly young age."

There was this arrogance about George Cassidy that was repugnant while Louise Cassidy, an unhappy substitute teacher in another school district, was simply rude and crude. She was known for her criticism of the schools where she works. She had been a substitute who was unsuccessful at gaining a permanent teaching position in Old River. She decided to sub in a neighboring town. She tried to create the impression that she was expert on all things educational. She was a faultfinder about everything offered by public schools. She walked with a slight tilt as though she were balancing that proverbial chip on her shoulder. One could only imagine what negative conversations Adam heard at home about school and his teacher.

The Cassidy's were hateful. Yet, their complaint regarding Adam had some education merit. Initially his academic program was falling short of meeting his needs. It was adjusted several times in an attempt to reach him. The purpose of coming together on this day to address his needs was fast losing any positive impetus. The Cassidy's continued to refuse testing for Adam, testing that might reveal clues to his learning and personality problems. Without the Cassidy's willingness to listen to Benjamin Lesser's recommendation for testing not much could be accomplished.

As the meeting concluded again without agreement, an irate George Cassidy took matters into is own hands. It was apparent that the Cassidy's decided before this meeting that George would do the talking. It occurred to Jennifer that she had never seen Mr. Cassidy smile. A receding hairline exposed his permanently upraised, furrowed forehead that, in turn, pulled the curled ends of two bushy eyebrows together near the top of his long nose. His mouth had a waxen and disdainful look. His long index finger was often positioned in front of his right ear seeming to support his pointed chin. He stared condescendingly at Jennifer over reading half-glasses that were part way down his nose. Cassidy had a menacing look carried by an unimpressive reedy frame. Ironically he reminded Betty of Ichabod Crane the clownish country schoolmaster: tall, gangly and seemingly out of shape. Jennifer, on the other hand, assumed that George's body language was intended to project superiority and intimidation but his skeletal physique robbed him of that likelihood.

If nastiness had color it would have made the participants squint to see one another through the dark and angry red hues drifting through the office. The meeting went poorly. There was no give and take. Mr. Cassidy seemed to be interested only in intimidating these *school marms,* a term he used when referring to Betty and Jennifer. George and Louise Cassidy had, up to now, come to Clarksdale together.

This was about to change. George decided to take charge of Adam's schooling and began, what would become, a relentless attack on the teacher, principal and school system. His teacher-substitute wife was herself about to be substituted for by George's attorney.

Jennifer would finally be confronted with the legal action long threatened by these two unhappy parents. These angry individuals had no intention of cooperating or compromising with the school in seeking a solution to their grievances. They refused to accept observations made by teachers who saw their child daily in his school environment. The Cassidy's came riding into Clarksdale with guns blazing and always with the threat of a lawsuit. In some schools there are several of these interruptions during a school year practically bringing a school to a standstill.

Litigation that disrupts public schools has sprung up like Jack's beanstalk and been growing slowly but surely for nearly three decades. Lawyers have begun to thrive on this fertile ground, ground where they have pitched their legal tents. Their goal is often to intimidate teachers and principals with legal hammers. They, like their clients, seldom seek amicable solutions to festering problems.

This hard-line approach forces staff and parents into hostile and opposing positions. Words at meetings are more carefully measured; teachers are guarded as attorneys attempt to dominate the proceedings with legalese and requests for written information. The possibility of a cordial meeting where ideas can be explored and exchanged is unlikely in antagonistic climates such as these. There is little give and take in such unfavorable conditions and the likelihood of resolution between school and home on behalf of the child is remote if not improbable.

Ian James, Esquire, was about to become George Cassidy's major ally in an all out assault on Clarksdale and a significant piece of the problem. Due process would soon rear its head in the school. Growing litigation, in a number of cases, has begun to ravage public education while stripping faculties and principals of power, respect and valuable time.

Jennifer was disheartened. There had been no effective PPT, no cooperation, no willingness to identify a problem and no happy ending. She spent many hours on the Cassidy Case; hours that would affect the entire school. She would discover how legal action can slow a school's timing and have a controlling effect on its progress.

Jennifer learned that two days following the aborted PPT meeting, George Cassidy with Ian James accompanying him, had taken the liberty of walking through the school and peeking into classrooms without invitation or permission! Several teachers called the office to report two unidentified men in the hall. George Cassidy surely had gall she thought. She had reminded him once before that, for the safety and security of the children, all adults visiting the school were required to stop at the office to identify themselves and pin a visitor I.D. on their clothing. He laughed then and here he was again.

With only a few weeks left in the school year Jennifer's time became severely impacted by George Cassidy and Ian James. Mr. Cassidy apprised Jennifer of his intent to have the school system pay for his attorney. Old River's Corporation Counsel, serving the town council as needed, advised Jennifer to write to Mr. Cassidy immediately and inform him that he can bring anyone he wishes to any meeting regarding his son, however, the district would not pay his attorney unless directed by a court to do so; another assignment that Jennifer had little time for.

Principal Myers was often disturbed at inopportune times and forced to immediately gather meeting minutes, teacher notes or to answer some other question about state mandates and guidelines for Attorney James. If Jennifer's responses weren't forthcoming on the day they were requested, she was warned that her delay would be recorded as a sign of failure to cooperate. When she was unavailable, James's secretary would leave a voice message that Dr. Myers was expected to Fax the requested information before leaving work. Finally Attorney James informed Jennifer that legal action was being initiated on behalf of Adam Cassidy. Jennifer was appalled. She called the superintendent's office to notify him of the threat.

Superintendent Bernard Green acknowledged that he had already received notice of the intended litigation. He told Jennifer to summarize all she knew about the suit. Though she had dozens of end-of-school tasks to complete, she was forced to table everything and write her summary, which filled four 8 ½ x 11 pages. Mr. George Cassidy had decided to play hardball. Jennifer left Clarksdale at 7:15 P.M., drove to Dr. Green's office with her recap. She rang for a custodian to let her into Dr. Green's office where she left her work on his desk.

Having read her detailed account, Green directed her to implore the Cassidy's to attend a PPT with Dr. Benjamin Lesser present. The Cassidy Case was really cutting into her effectiveness as her teachers' coach and their end-of-the-year evaluations.

Following Dr. Green's directive she called George Cassidy to schedule the PPT with Mrs. Cassidy and him. She stated that she expected them to attend and that Dr. Lesser would be present.

"Look, Ms. Meyers," he said, "we just finished with one of your PPT's and nothing was settled. And, by the way, my wife will not be attending any more of your so-called meetings. She is too upset with *your* process. And I don't want you bothering me again. Please direct your intrusions and requests to Attorney James."

"Mr. Cassidy you are avoiding the one avenue we have left to help Adam. I am asking, begging, urging you to attend this PPT in good faith. Our aim is to reach an agreement regarding Adam's behavior, his progress and his program at Clarksdale. His situation remains dire. I ask, on his behalf, that we collaborate by attending a PPT together!"

"I see no value to your PPT's. But, you know what, I've just changed my mind. I will come this one time with Attorney James so he can observe, first hand, what a debacle your meetings are. Are you satisfied? Attorney James will call to set the date with you."

"Thank you. I hope I'll hear from Mr. James within 24 hours." George Cassidy hung up without a response or a good-bye. Jennifer followed the conversation with a letter to the Cassidy's and a copy to James offering several dates for the meeting.

Jennifer tackled her many school closing responsibilities. School would soon be out and some of her staff had vacation plans. She didn't wait for James's call. She phoned him. He was unavailable. She left a message with his secretary that it was extremely important that he get back to her for the purpose of scheduling the meeting Mr. Cassidy agreed to attend. Two days passed before he returned her call. His reason, he offered, for not responding sooner was because he was researching special education laws and appearing in court. Jennifer learned that attorneys could delay returning phone calls to principals but principals could not delay responding to attorneys without being admonished for lack of cooperation.

Each date suggested by Dr. Myers was inconvenient for Attorney James or his client. Jennifer was certain James was deliberately being an obstructionist. James said he had an opening on his calendar at the end of the second week in June. Before Myers could respond he said, "Please clear your calendar for the 14th at 2 P.M." The 14th was not one of the options Jennifer had sent him.

"Mr. James, I have a school to close and an important meeting on the 14th. That would be a very difficult day for me."

"Well, that's all we have until the last day of June. Are you telling me you won't meet with us on the 14th?"

Jennifer was speechless. This was yet another member of the public who was oblivious to the heavy responsibilities of a school principal. She would have to re-arrange two entire days to be at a June 14th meeting and would have to insist that her special education team, which had to, by law, conduct end-of-year PPT's with more than twenty sets of parents, make itself available and cancel other PPT's scheduled for that day and time. This would cut into still more precious time. She had no choice, the district was being sued and the superintendent and board of education are expecting her to resolve this sticky situation at her level.

"I hope, Attorney James, that you realize what a critical time of the year mid-June is in *your* public schools. If there is any other open time, I ask you to please re-consider."

"No, *Miss* Myers," a deliberate slight of her title, "the 14th will have to do. I'm a busy man." Another slight.

Jennifer began to put the wheels in motion for the June 14th meeting. She made clear the whys and wherefores and asked that each member of the special education team try to understand the kind of dilemma into which they had been placed.

Try as she might Jennifer could not expunge from her mind the ruddy face of Ian James, a face topped by thinning blonde hair and framed by two pinned-back ears. He had a used-car salesman's disingenuous eyes and a wee know-it–all shady smile. In two encounters with Ian James, Jennifer concluded that his professional competence was limited to chasing after lawsuits. Schools were particularly vulnerable to this low level counselor. There wasn't a full-time attorney employed by the school system to challenge the likes of Ian James but it was Jennifer's opinion that he was very ordinary and very pesky. She learned that he had attached signs to over fifty parking meters along streets leading to City Hospital that read:

Recently Injured or Disabled?
Call Atty. Ian James at 644-7676
Free Consultation for any and all injustices
No fees unless we win.

James was like the attorneys who sued McDonald's on behalf of a woman who spilled hot coffee on herself. They perched like birds of prey waiting to bring suit for anyone who had an accident. Attorney James was of that ilk.

He didn't begin his day with the sports page, no indeed. He went right to local news looking for *possibles,* as he referred to anyone involved in an accident. His firm took out a half-page ad in the Yellow Pages that implied immediate wealth if your case were worthy of its time. His motto could have been: *The Individual is Never Responsible.* She was sure that he would spend as much time as it would take to bring people and small businesses to their knees. He would don his Sherlock cap, pull out his magnifying glass and hunt for any clue of error of omission or commission. His type was causing medical costs, insurance rates and small business expenses to skyrocket in bringing about frivolous lawsuits.

Such attorneys reach far beyond the sense of fairness while chasing everything from hot soup to rotten nuts! Though not in the upper echelons of the very crafty, Ian James sought every opportunity to strike the unsuspecting. If you fell in a parking lot on the one three-inch sliver of ice without sand, his magnifying glass would find it. It made no difference if an entire acre had been completely sanded it was James's contention that anyone getting out of a car or on foot, has no responsibility to be careful. He once brought suit for a person who slipped on the *sand* that covered ice*!* All liability lies with the proprietor. With school litigation in full bloom, Mr. James had a brand new set of victims to avenge.

At 11:00 A.M. on June 14th, Eleanor Haggerty's phone rang.

"Good-morning, Clarksdale School, Mrs. Haggerty speaking."

"Good morning, this is Shelly Prosper, Attorney Ian James's secretary, calling to inform you that Mr. Cassidy has to be out of town this afternoon on an emergency forcing him to postpone the 2 P.M. meeting. We'll call for a new date and time as soon as we can."

"Excuse me! Just a moment, please. Could you hold while I ring for Dr. Myers? I'm sure she will want to speak with Attorney James."

"I'm sorry, he's in court. He just called a couple of minutes ago." Eleanor was able to quickly connect and inform Jennifer.

"Please hold for Dr. Myers." Eleanor handed the phone to Jennifer.

"Ms. Prosper, you tell Attorney James that three of our staff have changed important meetings with other parents to attend this afternoon's session."

For the first time in her memory, Eleanor saw Jennifer become unruffled. In fact she was irate.

"Miss Myers, Attorney James won't be there either. He will not appear without his client. I'm sorry." She hung up.

Again, Jennifer had to inform each of her three staff members of the postponement. She would do this in person because of the trouble each of them went through to alter their schedules. Then she would inform Bernard Green of the change and follow-up her call with still another written summary.

When Shelley Prosper's call came, Jennifer had been attending a meeting with her custodian, Whitney Holder, and his union representative regarding the harassment charge by Su Akami one of the kindergarten teachers at Clarksdale. Jennifer suggested to the two men that they have lunch in the school cafeteria and return in 30 minutes to finish the meeting. They agreed. Another day disrupted and a significant part of it lost.

It was the 16th of June when Ian James's office contacted Eleanor Haggerty to re-schedule the PPT for the 21st, two days before the end of the school year! Jennifer was in the office and when Eleanor motioned that it was James's office she picked up the extension and requested to speak with Ian James. Again, he was not available. Again, Jennifer made note of that. Then she scrambled to pull her team together for a PPT on the 21st.

She assured the PPT team that, if there was another no show, they would hold the PPT in the Cassidy's and James's absence, write Adam's Individual Education Plan (IEP) for his return in September and forward it to the Cassidy's for, hopefully, their acceptance.

Things were becoming hectic at Clarksdale. Most of the other PPT's, though squeezed in during lunch and early evening, went fairly well and were coming to fruitful conclusions. There was generally cooperation and agreement with parents on how to support the children who were in need of special help. There was concurrence regarding actions to be conducted at home and at school. Communication links between parents and school were established. Some of the children were from one-parent families yet, the guardian parent was usually thankful for the direction provided by the school. Occasionally a grandparent was the custodian of the child and particularly grateful for the school connection. All were made comfortable by the openness of the Clarksdale staff. Teachers were willing to speak with parents at mutually convenient times. Though the PPT process took time, it was worth the teamed effort between teacher and parent.

A PPT for a child with educational or emotional difficulties that interfered with the child's education can be initiated at anytime during the school year and might need a follow-up during that span of time. All PPT's were reviewed during the last part of May and the beginning of June.

It became impossible for Jennifer to schedule her team for the 21st. The team was working feverishly to complete the last few PPT's before the school closed on the 23rd. She called Attorney James's office to re-schedule for the 26th. An hour later, Shelly Prosper called Eleanor Haggerty.

"Attorney James," she told Eleanor, "believes your principal is stalling." Eleanor asked Shelly Prosper to hold and again gave the phone to Jennifer.

"Ms. Prosper I have been directed by Superintendent Green to make every effort to schedule a Planning and Placement Team meeting with Mr. & Mrs. Cassidy at a mutually convenient time. We have done everything possible to accommodate everyone's schedule. The 21st is simply not convenient for out team, which had to postpone other parent meetings to the 21st. State law, which Attorney James certainly must respect, requires that these meetings be held at this time. The school will close for the summer on the 23rd. I have no right to hold my staff beyond their contracted time. They have personal plans and travel plans that cannot be changed. Each member, however, is willing and able to come back to school on the 26th to meet with the Cassidy's and Attorney James. As soon as we're finished with this conversation I will call Mr. & Mrs. Cassidy and urge them to come to the meeting. Please share this information with Mr. James. I will confirm our conversation by registered mail. I am scheduling the PPT for the 26th." Jennifer was more concerned that the Cassidy's be present than Ian James.

Jennifer called George Cassidy at his flower shop. Following a brief conversation he told Jennifer that neither he nor his wife would come to her meeting. Jennifer advised him the meeting would be held on the 26th and pleaded with him to come.

Jennifer then wrote a summary of the past few days' events, notified Ian James that State regulations authorize the PPT to gather without parents who continually refuse to attend a PPT as long as every effort has been made to get the parents to come and that sincere attempts have been made to find mutually convenient times to come together. Failing that, the school may hold the meeting without the parents but is required to notify the parents of the date, time and place of the session and to again ask them to attend. Both parties were notified that the PPT would be held with or without them.

The Cassidy's did not show. The team met and designed a plan for Adam. Together, the PPT wrote several behavioral objectives for Adam. The first was to have Adam remain in his seat for fifteen-minute segments and write 10 vocabulary words from a reading lesson. At the end of fifteen minutes, if he complied, Adam would earn points toward a reward. When he accumulated a realistic and achievable number of points, he would be allowed to go to the art room and work on an art project for fifteen minutes. Adam loved to draw. If Adam could extend his on-task time from fifteen to twenty minutes, he would earn more points toward his perk and gain five more minutes to work on his drawings. The team compiled behavioral objectives that would provide incentives for Adam to work toward a goal. The program results would be reviewed at the end of September. The intent was to increase Adam's work time and reduce his outbursts. There was little else the school could do without the parents' consent. Nor could Adam be programmed into a special education class without the parents' permission. Adam's Individualized Education Program (IEP) was sent, registered mail, to the Cassidy's and to Ian James still with the hope of gaining input from them. It would be filed as proof of its having been offered to the Cassidy's.

Several days passed. There was no response from the Cassidy's or James. According to state statutes, there was little left for the Old River Public Schools to do. One of three options left, if Adam continued his disruptive ways, was to continue with in-school suspensions. Jennifer decided that she would limit this option to one week. They had proved to be ineffective during the past year but the team thought Adam might have thought things over during the summer.

A second option would be to suspend him from the school building for a day or two. Jennifer was certain that would get the Cassidy's attention. This was an alternative that Jennifer had never used nor did she ever believe that course of action would be necessary for any child in her school. The board of education would ask serious questions, and rightfully so, regarding a fourth grade boy who had to be removed from school. Jennifer would, again, be required to use valuable time to write, respond and manage all activities related to a suspension. The work necessary to comprehensively document the grounds for suspending a nine-year old to the superintendent and to the Board would again cut into her supervision hours with the Clarksdale teachers at the beginning of the school year; an important time for coaching.

The very last choice the school had was to file for a due process hearing and request that a hearing officer order an evaluation of Adam. Even if the Cassidy's were ordered to have their son tested and the evaluation findings recommended special education placement, the Cassidy's still are not required to place Adam in a special education program. Jennifer did not want to even think about taking that action at this time. It would be time wasted.

Just one little boy who knew he had the power to wreak havoc at his school, one domineering father and one eager minor league attorney were disrupting an outstanding school program. And, because Jennifer kept abreast of education topics, she knew this was part of a national trend. How horrific, she thought, that attorneys could tie-up schools for what are, for the most part, trivial lawsuits.

She believed that, among the large number of litigious actions challenging school programs, only a small percentage had merit. The force of law, she thought, should be used to upgrade those who are responsible for providing quality education to the children of America not for the purpose of disruption.

The Cassidy's obstructions continued into September of the new school year. The situation did not improve. Adam's fifteen-minute work periods did little to change his compulsive behavior. A return to in-school suspension became necessary to protect the right to learn for Adam's classmates. They proved to be no more effective than they were the previous year. Dr. Jennifer Myers had no alternative but to suspend Adam from school for two days. This action, as she suspected, got the Cassidys' attention. The suspensions were followed by phone calls of protest from Ian James. George Cassidy continued to bully, coerce and threaten. He used any tactic that he felt would upset the school.

Cassidy and James marched into Clarksdale unannounced. Again they refused to wear identification badges as they roamed through the halls, checking classrooms until Jennifer saw them and threatened to call the police. She explained to James and Cassidy once again that, "*another silly rule,*" as they called it was for security reasons and for the safety of the children. Though she had, the previous school year, explained the rule to them, Cassidy and James continued to challenge at every opportunity. How could there be hope for Adam with a dad like George for a role model?

Adam's deportment did not improve. Jennifer pleaded once again with George Cassidy to allow testing. He responded by accusing Adam's new teacher of being as incompetent as McRaney and Jennifer of being just as inept.

Jennifer told him that he would do well to speak with his trusty attorney before labeling a teacher incompetent. She repeated what she had told two other parents over the years about judging a teacher's competence without the certification to make such pronouncements.

George wrote letters to the local newspaper and even took out an ad questioning the caliber of the schools in Old River, always being cautious about naming any one school. One day late in September, George Cassidy announced his candidacy for the Board of Education. When next he saw Jennifer he warned her that, "Things are going to really get tough around here if I'm elected." She believed him.

The lateness of his decision to run for the Board and his political campaign took up much of his time and his harassment of Jennifer and Clarksdale abated. He did, however, find enough time to attend a PPT meeting with Ian James, chaired by Benjamin Lesser. At the meeting he agreed to have Adam tested. Jennifer believed that George's decision to attend that meeting was to help him better understand what he loathed about Clarksdale and the special education process.

Candidate Cassidy used his PPT experience in his campaign. Citing his experience he condemned the entire school system. His legal suit at Clarksdale seemed to be losing steam. Yet his refusal to work with school staff left him with a biased opinion of people for whom he had little regard. But at last, he accepted a modified special education program for Adam. Jennifer was certain that George was determined to "get her" from a new vantage point.

His half-truths, during his campaign and in his campaign circulars, became the cornerstone of his run for the board. Jennifer believed that George Cassidy would win a seat on the Board.

She pondered negative campaigning and its path to power at all levels of government. Anti everything candidates lead crusades to tear down all that is in place: the bad and the good. However, their success in our culture has resulted in the emergence of a divisive and confused society, she believed. Our *immediate reward* pop-culture refuses to give the "ins" any time before the next carping season begins. It appears that the losers hope the winners will fail in their attempts to make life better for their constituencies so they will have a better chance of winning at the next election. Confrontation is the tool for settling differences of opinion. The "outs" attack but, often, offer no positive plan of action to improve what they condemn. Frequently an unknowing and overtaxed local public is persuaded to vote for the most strident of these challengers. George Cassidy became tired taxpayers' icon.

George and Louise were blind to the school's commitment to their son. Though accepting Adam's special education placement, they refused to have any contact with the school. All of George Cassidy's unrest, disruption, threats, contempt and litigation led only to Adam's continued unruly behavior. Adam, now 9 years old, was learning from his parents and their attorney rather than from his teachers.

The election gave a seat on the Board of Education to George Cassidy from where he would brandish a critical voice and would challenge every school report brought to the board. He was especially vigilant and confrontational whenever a special education program was brought to the Board's attention.

Between his business and his board responsibilities, George had little time for further harassment at Clarksdale. He chose to cut his ties with Attorney James fearing a conflict of interest charge regarding his son's placement in special education and the related litigation.

Slowly, Cassidy yielded. He learned of the respect the other six board members had for the Clarksdale staff and especially its principal. He began to see the detail through which the Old River special education staff sifted as it sought to bring help to students with social, emotional, physical or learning problems. Though George was on the board and had many opportunities to learn of Dr. Jennifer Myers's outstanding work, he never took to that *school marm* whom he had fought tooth and nail.

Adam's special class placement very slowly began to help. Some improvement was noted but the outlook remained less than bright for this young and unruly fourth-grader.

The Cassidy case had impacted the school operation for much of a school year. Dr. Myers, school principal and coach to her teachers, was distracted from her main responsibility to improve her staff's delivery of instruction.

Mostly, the PPT process at Clarksdale worked well. Parents, though concerned when a child needed special help, were put at ease by Dr. Myers and had confidence in her and her staff's ability to help their children.

Often, the school, in concert with the parent(s), was able to identify a difficulty the home had overlooked that might have contributed to the child's school problem. Occasionally, it was a problem the parent(s) chose not to face; at other times, the home situation, itself, was unsettling for the child. From time to time, a program or teacher problem surfaced in the classroom that required notification of parents. In those cases, Dr. Myers gained credibility for recognizing the school's failing. The case of Gordon Clay was one of these.

Kayla and Jerome Clay worked different hours and at the end of each school day, their son, Gordon, was unsupervised for a couple of hours when neither parent was home. When Beverly Gillette, Gordon's teacher, noted that Gordon was losing interest and beginning to lag behind at school, she apprised the Clay's and Dr. Myers. Both, she and Jennifer initially thought something at home might be affecting Gordon.

Beverly contacted Mrs. Clay to share her observation that Gordon seemed to have lost interest in school. Kayla Clay said that she saw no change at home except that Gordon seemed less interested while doing his homework. She asked if Miss Gillette thought her work hours might be affecting Gordon. That's when Beverly asked the Clay's to meet with her. Kayla said that she would have to meet without her husband who could not get the time off.

"Does Gordon have any new friends in the neighborhood? Is he tired at home? Does he ever complain that both, you and Mr. Clay are not home when he arrives from school? Does he talk about school? Has he had any problems with any of his friends?" Beverly, a first-year teacher, posed these and other probing questions to Mrs. Clay. Both Kayla and Beverly sought answers together. They agreed to watch for patterns or changed habits and try to motivate Gordon to do better in school.

But Beverly did little to change anything in Gordon's program. She remained convinced that the problem lie elsewhere. When Jennifer inquired about the session with Mrs. Clay, Beverly opined that the problem was probably home related. Though the Clay's were cooperative and concerned, they must be overlooking something she suggested.

Jennifer spent fifteen minutes in Beverly's language arts class on Monday, fifteen in her math class on Tuesday and five minutes each on Wednesday and Thursday observing Gordon. She walked through the class for shorter spurts a couple of other times. She took a look at Gordon in the cafeteria and on the playground. She did not let her findings wait for a formal and planned observation cycle with Beverly. She shared her objective observations with her!

"Beverly," she offered, "Gordon is bored and he is bored in the classroom. We need to know why. He's a fairly bright young boy. Let's sit after class today and see what we can work out."

Following dismissal Beverly came straight to Jennifer's office.

"O.K. Bev, what do you think?" Jennifer always deferred to her teachers first. They knew the children better and they often preferred to offer their suggestions before the coach offered hers.

"I've spoken with Gordon every morning since I met with his mom to ask him why he was so unresponsive in class. He had no clue. He didn't even realize he *was* unresponsive! He hasn't changed one bit."

"But now we need to do something."

"Jennifer, I'm kind of puzzled as to what I should do, especially after what you noted yesterday and today while observing him."

"Well, first, I think you have to get to know more about Gordon. What are his interests? What can he do to improve? Why is he bored? Does he like dinosaurs? Is he a baseball fan? Is there someone he admires? What are his hobbies? Once you learn something about this young *person* you can help him to work on a project that will require him to use skills from the curriculum. If it's baseball he likes he could learn how to figure batting averages, winning and losing percentages, even earned run averages. If it's dinosaurs, he can use the research skills you're teaching to find unknown facts about those great creatures. He could create a time line and determine when the dinosaurs roamed the earth and report to his classmates. He could use his math research to write a report and share those findings with the class. Beverly, you know you can design active learning activities around any interest. If those don't work to motivate Gordon, we'll have to find something that does. AND we will have to let him know that he has a responsibility to do some things he may not like to do. Remind him of his mother and father and how they have their own responsibilities to maintain the family. They don't always like to go to work, I'm sure. Both work to provide for him and his siblings with the many comforts they enjoy; they expect him to work at school in return."

Seeing little change at home, Mrs. Clay called Beverly a couple of times subsequent to their meeting and not long after Jennifer had conferred with Beverly. Beverly didn't follow-up with Mrs. Clay to learn anything more about Gordon. Jennifer returned to observe Gordon and was disappointed. She didn't see much in the way of change. There didn't seem to be anything geared to Gordon's needs. Mrs. Clay, still not satisfied, called Jennifer and asked to meet with her.

Jennifer scheduled a meeting with Beverly, the Clay's and herself. Kayla said it was important enough for, "Jerome to attend though he will have to miss a couple of hours of work." Dr. Myers welcomed the Clay's and began the meeting with her usual greeting.

"Mr. and Mrs. Clay, we're so glad you could both come. Please make yourselves comfortable. We know this is an unfamiliar setting for you both and that you are giving up costly time to be here. Rest assured that Ms. Gillette and I are here with you, not against you. We're here for Gordon. Hopefully we will work together as a team to try to solve *our* mutual problem." The Clay's, of course, agreed.

"I trust that our goal is the same as yours. We, at Clarksdale, want Gordon to be successful here. It is clearly in our collective best interest for him to do well in school. If you have unanswered questions when you leave here today, our task would be more difficult. So, please be frank and don't worry about offending us. I am confident we can address the issue that has brought us together and exchange ideas that will aid us to assist Gordon to overcome his math difficulty, his trouble with word problems and his seeming lack of interest in school. Gordon is bright enough to be doing better. It's our hope that, by sharing pertinent information, we can begin to resolve Gordon's problem.

"Please know that we make every effort to live by our district motto: *Children Are Our Most Important Product.* We are committed to succeed with each and every child. On that basis we urge you to openly share your concerns with us. The bottom line should be that, through our joint efforts, Gordon will get back to where he needs to be academically and attitudinally. With that said, let's examine our dilemma. We know Gordon is simply not up to speed and he's bored. We must do something more here at school and we believe that you can help by monitoring Gordon at home and by sharing with us some of the things that interest Gordon."

Jennifer has reason to believe that Ms. Beverly Gillette has been lax in adjusting Gordon's program. Jennifer told the Clay's that she and Beverly realize, that, up to now, the school has failed to find the solution to Gordon's difficulties. Her willingness to share the school's failure made a lasting impression on the Clay's. Together they identified Gordon's academic and outside of school interests. Jennifer suggested learning activities similar to those she had earlier shared with Beverly.

The principal has to balance her support of her staff while maintaining credibility with the public, a very difficult balancing act. Jennifer often thought there should be a course in administrative programs to emphasize this concept. Teachers make continual observations, suggestions and decisions every few minutes of every hour of every school day, and according to some parents, they must *all* be the right ones.

"Johnny, no, you may not sit there, Rachel turn to the page we're on, Jim, it's not time for your music lesson, Billy, where is your pen? We're going to lunch in five minutes why don't you wait? Do you really need to leave the room now? I want you to get organized before we go to recess. Please close your books and sit up straight. Whose turn is it to lead the line?"

All it takes is one Leslie McGurt, at the end of the day to challenge her teacher and speak to her friend as she leaves for crossing guard duty and for Penny Johnson to take her to the girls' room and be accused of shoving her thumbs under Leslie's armpits for the wheels to come off on a Saturday evening.

Jennifer realizes that teachers make mistakes; some that are difficult to defend and amend. She handles these thoughtfully and gathers as much data as she can before meeting with parents. There are youngsters who dislike their teacher and some teachers who may dislike a particular child. Situations can emerge where there is no defense for a teacher's behavior or action toward a particular child. At those times, Jennifer MUST address the teacher face to face. Usually a parent whose child has such a teacher will try to get the child through the year and make it a learning experience. Sometimes that can't be done.

Jennifer's integrity and honesty are recognized and appreciated by parents and teachers alike. They all know that she is dealing as candidly as she can with everyone. Parents are almost always impressed with Dr. Myers and her apparent regard for and her commitment to children. It is her credo; it is no pretense. Her words usually translate into a team effort between home and school to resolve whatever problem arises or is cause for anxiety.

Gordon Clay's parents describe Gordon's frustration with his math and word problems and ask what they can do at home. They don't see any other issues regarding Gordon at their house.

Ms. Gillette, following Jennifer's suggestion for this meeting, brought a book of interesting word exercises to the meeting that begin with simple and lead to more complex word problems. She informs the Clay's that she will design learning activities based on some of his interests. And finally she makes a commitment to the Clay's to learn even more about Gordon. She is grateful for Jennifer's guidance prior to the meeting. She asks if one of the parents could monitor Gordon each evening for a week and see how far he progresses with the word problems.

Jennifer advises the Clay's, who were hoping for help from the Clarksdale professionals, that, "We'll see how this goes. If and when Gordon becomes frustrated, please call Ms. Gillette and tell her on which page and which problem he begins to have difficulty. Direct Gordon to take that page to his teacher. That's where she'll pick it up and see what she can do to help. Let's begin with this first small step. And, let's all encourage Gordon when he succeeds." The four adults around the table proceed to examine the proposed action plan. Gordon's program at school and at home is clearly defined before adjournment. Beverly Gillette got the message without losing face.

"We ask that you and Ms. Gillette touch base daily for the next week. Let Gordon know that *we are working together* on his behalf.

"And, please," Jennifer continues, "call Ms. Gillette to clear up any problem Gordon has that troubles you. She is our front line."

Dr. Myers's words are persuasive with reasonable people. Mr. Clay sat passively throughout but was interested in every word that was exchanged about his son. The participants left the meeting with a clear plan for Gordon. Though a couple of uneasy months passed, the communication between home and school kept everyone on their toes. Gordon's program was adjusted, modified and tweaked many times. All parties remained steadfast and united. Gordon did better and seemed to be back to where he should be. Though not overly enthusiastic, he was productive.

Dr. Myers frequently reminds herself of what she considers to be her failure with the Cassidy's when she compares so many successful PPT's and parent meetings to the breakdown that happened with them. Jennifer keenly recalls how her approach simply didn't work with Mr. George Cassidy who came to school with, not a chip, but a block of ice on his shoulder and wasn't about to leave without causing chaos for his son's teacher, the principal, the superintendent and the school board.

There are times when appeal to reason fails. The Cassidy assault was Jennifer's first, and up to now, only encounter with the lawyer brigade.

She, her teachers and the students paid a terrible price throughout that school year for that lawyer assault. Immediate demands from the attorney, the superintendent and the board of education for information related to the Cassidy attack on Clarksdale tied up too many hours for several months; all because of one obnoxious, know-it-all father whose student brought home stories that misrepresented his teacher and the school. Sadly, Adam lied because it paid dividends.

Perhaps she could have handled it differently, she wonders. She recalls one incident with George Cassidy that typifies most of her encounters with him, which usually ended with Cassidy arrogantly and rudely stomping out of the school.

"Children can misread comments or actions," she had proffered to Mr. Cassidy. "Please understand our situation," she went on, "when an eight year-old child goes home with a tale about school, we have no idea how it's presented. Mr. Cassidy. I'm certain you would not remain successful for very long if your establishment hired an eight-year-old to sell your product. Yet eight year-olds are selling ours every day.

You would not gamble your company's reputation on the interpretation of an eight-year-old. But that's on whom we rely to establish our reputation daily."

Cassidy's half-glasses slipped slightly. He sneered and scoffed at the analogy and left for his little flower shop.

Chapter 11: Principal vs. CEO

The school principal is a *platoon leader* whose motto should be *Follow Me* on the schoolhouse battlefield; *the* CEO is a *general,* directing operations safely inside a corporate war room. It's front line versus shelter harbor. When the school day begins, the principal has no idea what might change his/her agenda.

The CEO, on the other hand, is, "*Yes sirred or Yes, ma'amed,*" all the way to a luxurious office or suite where "coffee….*and*" are waiting with, perhaps, phone messages needing a response. Prepared and carefully placed on the CEO's desk is the day's sacrosanct schedule to be maintained as precisely as possible.

On this particular Friday, our CEO arrives at 9:00 AM and inspects his day's agenda. He is pleased to see it has not changed since he left work late yesterday afternoon. Subsequent to a meeting with the Chairman of the Board at 9:30 to review his Board's recently updated goals, followed by a second meeting at 10:30 to examine the status of an important advertising project with his financial officer, he is scheduled for a 12:30 business luncheon with the local Rotary at the *Inside Passage Country Club.* After lunch he and three members of the Chamber of Commerce will discuss the Chamber's current business promotion. The foursome plans to tee-off at 2:30.

It's 8:00 AM at Clarksdale School on this same Friday morning. A panicked deer bolts across the school lawn from a wooded area near the school and smashes through the large plate glass window of the cafeteria terrifying several screaming children who are having their before-school breakfast. The frightened deer bounds through the cafeteria, jumps across a corridor into the auditorium tripping over bolted-down chairs and spilling blood everywhere until, finally, exhausted it collapses near the stage. Jennifer, beginning her day like our CEO, is scanning her Friday agenda when she is jolted by the sound of breaking glass and the shrieks of shocked children.

She drops her day's plans, runs to the scene, immediately rings for the school's two custodians and has Eleanor call the police and Superintendent Green. Two custodians and two male teachers manage to lift the exhausted and flailing animal onto a tarp and drag it out a side door where they drape the tarpaulin over a tree branch to hide the trembling beast from several wide-eyed youngsters who have gathered around before being shepherded into school. Some are crying; some are frightened.

Newly arriving children beg the police not to kill the animal. Jennifer calls the local humane society for guidance. The society's agent arrives within twenty minutes and advises that the animal be destroyed. Jennifer and several teachers have assured the children that the school would do what is right for the animal. Shortly thereafter, a policeman's gunshot rings out. There is dead silence in the classrooms. No certification program prepared Jennifer for this.

The cafeteria and auditorium have to be cleaned of drying blood. Superintendent Green assigns three custodians from three other schools to help scrub the bloody stains from the two locations, which are placed off-limits. Once the dead animal is removed from the premises, the large tarp, used to hide the deer from the children, is moved to cover the open space where the animal had smashed through the plate glass window.

Jennifer monitors the situation before returning to her computer to draft a letter for the children to bring home to their parents explaining the bizarre accident. While working on the letter, she's interrupted by a reporter from the *Old River Observer*.

Another school day is underway for Principal Myers while our CEO, following some phone calls and dictation between meetings, assigns several important tasks to underlings. He tidies his desk and leaves for lunch before his 2:30 tee-off time.

Jennifer has experienced countless unexpected incidents before, during and after school throughout the course of her principalship, all of which took significant time from her day's priorities. The deer incident, a once-in-a-lifetime occurrence, represents the many disruptions that all too often reorder the operation of a school day. Earlier in her career a first-grade teacher fell dead entering her classroom as innocent eyes witnessed the dreadfulness of sudden death.

Though the deer episode was a one-time astonishing occurrence, there are scores of unanticipated incidents that require a principal's swift and rational response almost daily throughout the school year. Such events, usually handled alone, force Jennifer and all school principals to chuck their day's plans and take appropriate and immediate action. Dealing with disturbances, whatever they may be, that interrupt the most carefully planned day is, of course, the responsibility of the leader of a school.

Johnson City provides a safe haven for CEO's who toil in their alabaster metropolitan bastions. By contrast, that same city often claims a chunk of Jennifer's day. There are kids who, with free passes, ride commercial buses out of the city to suburban schools passing executives' automobiles going in the opposite direction.

The executives' city is quite different from the children's who come to school with inner city baggage that often, when opened, reveal background conditions that severely obstruct their education. A limited number of city children are bussed to the suburbs as part of government-funded programs that supposedly offer a better education outside of Johnson City.

CEO's days are different. It's true that CEO's constantly function in pressure cookers that allow little, or no, margin for error. Daily decisions affect their job security but the CEO is ordinarily sheltered from unexpected adversity unless it comes when the Wall Street bell is rung. Their pressure cooker, unlike the principal's, is most intense when the financial health of the company is presented to the Board and to the company's stockholders. No question that pressure is gargantuan and often requires a shot of Pepto-Bismol. The CEO's, however, usually have the luxury of thinking through and planning what their actions will be relative to problems needing resolution. Their plans of action are typically deliberate, managed and controlled.

The school principal, making a salary of one-twentieth or less than the average CEO, walks on eggs and his/her pressure cooker includes dealing with unexpected emergencies always with threat of litigation should a procedure or decision made under fire be challenged. Public school principals are accountable for maintaining a safe, orderly and organized learning environment for their student body and the public, something a CEO never need consider.

There are the required observations of classroom teachers to conduct. The notable instructional leader, such as Jennifer Myers, regards coaching teachers as his/her top priority. Dr. Myers runs an effective system for supervising and evaluating the teaching and non-teaching staffs at Clarksdale, a time-consuming but necessary task.

The *Coach/Principal* must also manage the school. There are before and after school bus altercations, playground accidents, ailing children and a host of other interruptions happening on a daily basis. There is no lunch at the *Inside Passage* or golf on Friday afternoon for the school principal.

There are vouchers and pay slips to be signed, communications to prepare, administrative council and evening meetings to attend, school concerts and P.T.A. meetings to go to. There are monthly awards ceremonies to organize, P.T.A. fund-raisers to plan and town-wide committees on which to serve at the superintendent's discretion. Principals of secondary schools have athletic events to attend and department head meetings, graduations to plan and guidance departments to oversee.

There are monthly fire and evacuation drills required by law. Rules must be established and enforced to ensure that no strangers gain access to the school building. Principals have to make judgments regarding visitation rights and court orders concerning divorced parents' guardianship.

Principals welcome substitute teachers, some of whom they've never met, at school the first thing in the morning. It is incumbent upon the principal to bring substitute teachers to the classroom, orient them to school procedures, apprise them of children who have medical conditions and what to do should an emergency occur. The principal has to scan the lesson plan and review the day's schedule with the substitute who needs to know when the class goes to lunch, recess or to music, gym or art class.

Additionally, principals are required to understand the numerous statutes that apply to education and fully comply with complex special education laws. They interpret and administer Federal laws such as *No Child Left Behind.* CEO's have a corresponding responsibility regarding business related statutes of which there are many but ordinarily they have access to a corporate lawyer.

The school chiefs are obliged to remain current à propos of magnet and charter schools and participate in professional growth programs.

The public school principal is required to: oversee test administration (No Child Left Behind [NCLB] and state testing programs); analyze school-wide test results; attend countless Planning and Placement Team (PPT) meetings throughout the year; oversee and guarantee the implementation of the school district curriculum; assess program effectiveness; be alert for possible child abuse; assure the well-being of handicapped children.

The principal must develop a budget; monitor all special area programs; promote a positive learning climate for students and staff; check the daily attendance report; inform parents of school events and happenings; respond to parent concerns and questions; complete accident reports; check on the cafeteria operation and its personnel; know all students by name; schedule art, music and physical education classes; assign playground, school bus and cafeteria duties; record and report suspensions, produce an annual parent handbook; generate daily staff bulletins; be cognizant of education issues and trends; all challenging and demanding undertakings. BUT: never mid-day golf.

Not a day begins with the assurance that it will unfold according to plan. From the moment the buses arrive and the school day begins until the last bus safely drops its last student can the principal rest. That's when the principal's school portion of the day is finished. The principal's responsibilities for all facets of running an educational institution must be attended to every day. The job is stressful and exacting.

As any veteran principal can attest, there will be several days during the year when a youngster decides to skip the bus ride and walk to a friend's house or that a new bus driver will let some tiny first-grader off at the wrong stop. Those are the times the phone jumps as a panicked parent screams from the other end that her child is missing! The bus driver is contacted, the police are alerted and neighbors are called. Usually the panic subsides when the child calls home for a parent to pick him up at Rob's house. And half the time, the parent, being relieved and breathing again, forgets to notify the school while the principal remains in limbo or is it hell?

John Doe, CEO, just missed a three-foot putt on the eighteenth hole. Time for a couple of beers. Ahhhh, TGIF!

NOTE: The deer account as herein described actually happened at the Henry A. Wolcott Elementary School in West Hartford, Connecticut. Each description of a school happening used in this book reflects an event witnessed or experienced during the author's time of service in the West Hartford Public Schools.

Chapter 12:
Harry's Lesson Plan Ordeal

Harry grapples with the lesson plan he is struggling to complete for his introduction to clinical supervision, which will be the pre-observation meeting with Jennifer that will take place prior to her observation of him teaching. He is unsettled as he mulls over his lesson plan objective.

Jennifer sat with him Friday, when he said he was unsure of how to write a suitable objective. She clarified still again that an objective is what is aimed for. It's an intended outcome. Harry's supposed to be writing plans daily that begin with learning objectives.

"For example," she tried to simplify, "Jack's objective is to carry his pail of water down the hill without dropping any. When he reaches the bottom of the hill he can immediately determine by checking the result whether he achieved his objective.

Your lesson objective is what you, Harry, want your students to accomplish by the end of the class. The outcome of your intent for the class can be measured by testing, observing, or describing what the students could do following your instruction." She added that specificity is a quality of a good objective. Harry sought Jennifer's approval to design a lesson that introduces the children to the study of The New World. She agreed.

With Columbus's birthday just around the corner Harry decided to begin with an introduction to Columbus. To motivate the class he planned to read from a Columbus biography, *Meet Christopher Columbus*. The one concept Jennifer continually referred to regarding the science of teaching is that students must be stirred to learn. Harry knew he would have to focus on motivating his class hence the rationale for the biography. He hoped it would appeal to the kids and encourage them to learn about Columbus, especially the boys.

Harry had no trouble coming up with ideas for lessons. He was bright and often thought of good classroom activities. His problem was, and remains, an inability to transfer his ideas into sound teaching practices, which are critical for student success. This lack contributes greatly to his discipline problems.

His inability to succeed evolved from his helplessness with classroom management at the beginning of his teaching career. His inability to organize a classroom environment gave rise to an atmosphere that degenerated into persistent classroom control problems. Like Captain Queeg in *The Caine Mutiny*, he had, early on in his career, lost control of his ship and subsequently his crew and, finally, his confidence. Principal Bill Higgins had been oblivious to Harry's loss of control.

Principal Jennifer Myers was making every effort to pump water from the bilge of his listing classroom ship. But it was incumbent upon Harry to pump with her. In a relatively brief time Harry, with Jennifer's concerned coaching, began to right his Clarksdale classroom; at least at the beginning of the school day with the improved management procedures Jennifer helped him to put into place. Early morning discipline was better and lately there was some minor progress during the day when Harry reminded the class of the *Room Nine Constitution* they had written and agreed to abide by. Yet, there continued to be a humdrum feeling in the room when Harry presented his lessons.

The daily and dreary instruction took place with little connection to learning. Harry talked at the children. He attempted to pour his knowledge into their young heads. He followed his recitations with quizzes to find out what facts they retained and could regurgitate back to him, still oblivious that knowledge, as defined by Bloom, is the lowest level of understanding. It was as though Harry were thinking

I am giving all this information to these kids and, if they paid attention, they would *learn* from what I'm *telling* them. All they have to do is give the information I'm presenting back to me accurately and correctly when I quiz them.

Harry was a font, full of knowledge, trying to fill the empty glasses sitting behind the desks in front of him. As he poured his facts, he was able to fill a few glasses, half-fill several more and squeeze a few drops into others while the remaining droplets evaporated into the deadness of the room.

This is the reality that Jennifer faced in her attempt to coach someone who lacked the teaching skills of a beginning teacher. She was not coaching a diva or a concert pianist; she was coaching a novice.

Harry was grappling with an objective. He wrote and rewrote his objective several times. He was lost. What is it the children will learn from his teaching? According to Jennifer's explanation, the students should gain something from the instruction that they didn't have before the class began. Part of Old River's format for lesson plans included a section for listing materials that would be used to teach the lesson.

Harry labored trying to think of what materials he could use for his lesson beyond the paragraphs he would read from the e-biography of Columbus that he acquired from the Internet. There were the encyclopedia and the children's textbooks that he could list. Jennifer reminded Harry that the curriculum standards of performance must be considered in his planning.

Finally, after more than an hour of wrestling with it, he wrote an objective. Next, he wrote his plan for carrying out the objective. He pored over the Taxonomy but failed to see how he could use it for this lesson. Harry completed his lesson plan. He was as ready as he was going to be.

Uncertain of his work and exceptionally on edge Monday morning, he ate very little for breakfast. He didn't bring his customary thermos of coffee for the ride to school. His stomach quivered as he pulled into the school parking lot. His pre-observation meeting was scheduled for 7:30.

Chapter 13:
Lesson Plan Review

"Good morning Harry, you're right on time. How was your weekend?"

"Pretty good."

"Did you play golf?"

"No golf. We took the kids hiking."

"Great weather for it."

Jennifer was trying to put a very tense looking teacher at ease; it didn't seem to be working.

"Let's go to the conference room where we can be comfortable."

"Comfortable? Jennifer, I'm too nervous to be comfortable. I really had trouble trying to work any of the Taxonomy into my objective." Harry thought his opening ploy might gain some empathy from Jennifer and lower her expectation for his lesson plan. Harry had some traits of a con artist.

Jennifer, without comment, asked Harry to sit. She sat next to him. He placed the lesson plan between them on the conference table.

"Okay, let's see what we have."

Harry, concerned that Jennifer had ignored his statement, lay the following on the table:

Lesson Plan for Observation: October 6

***(<u>Note to the reader</u>: The lesson plan re-write is shown in bold print. It illustrates the changes he made following his pre-observation conference with Coach Jennifer. His original objective is underlined.)

Objective: *To have the children learn why Christopher Columbus sailed for the Indies.*

***Modified Objective following conference with Jennifer: **To introduce the students to Christopher Columbus and for the students to know the reasons Columbus set out for the Indies.**

Action Plan:

1. Tell class they are going to find out about Christopher Columbus.
2. Ask who knows anything about Columbus. Wait for answers.
3. Ask if they know why we are learning about him this week (October 6th).
4. Read from the e-book, *True Story of Christopher Columbus, Admiral.*
5. What is an admiral?
6. Following my reading, have children list what they know about Columbus from the reading or from their own knowledge.
7. Have class open their texts to chapter entitled, *The New World.*
8. Encourage individual children to read aloud from the text.
9. Have each child read a paragraph.
10. When finished ask children to write any detail that was repeated from my earlier reading, from their individual knowledge or from the class readings.
11. Have children name the ships that sailed with Columbus.
12. Ask how long it took Columbus to reach the Americas.
13. Have a volunteer look up Columbus in the encyclopedia and find three facts we didn't learn from our readings.
14. Recommend the purchase of *Meet Christopher Columbus* by James T. DeKay.
15. Recommend the E-book from the Internet.

Materials:

1. Library book: *Meet Christopher Columbus*
2. E-book referred to in action plan.
3. Textbooks, encyclopedia, paper and pens.

Evaluation:

1. Short quiz
2. List and recall five facts presented by the teacher.
3. Exchange papers for corrections.

Jennifer perused the lesson plan with Harry then offered, "Harry, let's look at the Taxonomy together." She wasn't about to be duped by Harry's feigned opening helplessness. On the other hand she dropped her idea of introducing anything new into the lesson. She realized it would be foolish to overwhelm Harry while she was attempting to gain his confidence for the coaching approach to supervision. Piling anything on right now wouldn't serve any good purpose.

Harry retrieved the Taxonomy pamphlet from his attaché case.

Jennifer began with Harry's objective. She was going to make him work at analyzing what he was about to present to his class.

"Let's examine "our" objective," she said.

To have the children learn why Christopher Columbus sailed for the Indies.

"Tell me about the verb *learn*. We need to agree with definitions if I'm going to observe productively. Yes?"

"Well, yeah, sure."

"Harry, share with me your definition of *learn* as you present it in your objective."

Harry felt the pressure of uncertainty. He became flustered as he grasped at straws seeking a logical response. He paused for what seemed to be a very long time. Jennifer waited. This was her time to make Harry face the reality of the task for which he was responsible. She was cautious, gentle and yet, forceful. He'll remember this in the future she thought. She didn't want to take over or he would become defensive and dependent as well as lose confidence in her commitment to their partnership. This would be the first test of their alliance and she meant to honor it.

"I guess it's to know something," he muttered.

"About what?" She coaxed.

"About something that's important."

Jennifer flipped through the dictionary.

"Here is this dictionary's definition of learning: *'….learning pertains to a body of ideas acquired and retained with great effort by a learner who can subsequently explain that learning to another'.*

"Is the verb *learn* accurately describing what the children will accomplish during this lesson?"

"No, I guess not," is Harry's weak response.

"We need to be precise with terms used to explain our objective. The purpose is for us to agree about what we're doing with the children. It might appear to be nit-picking but it's really important for us to be accurate.

"This might be a tad unfair, Harry," she continued. She wanted Harry to be at ease. This was another delicate moment for his professional growth and she didn't want to step on his lines. She proceeded cautiously.

"As you know, I've been at this for a long time. I've studied and deliberated a lot about learning throughout my career and I've analyzed the Taxonomy to death. So I have a great big jump on your contact with it. Let me give a try and see if I can influence you to follow my thinking as we look at Benjamin Bloom. Note, Harry, that you used the word learn in your objective. Reflecting on the dictionary definition you concluded that to be inaccurate."

"Right."

"Let's scan our action plan and compare it to the first category listed by Bloom.

Harry reads, "*Knowledge* is the lowest of the learning categories. Its focus is on the ability to recall *dates, events and places.* When students are working in the knowledge domain, they are listing, defining, telling, describing, identifying, showing, labeling, examining, tabulating and naming."

"Looking at your plan and your evaluation of the children following the lesson, which category of the Taxonomy are we working with?"

"Knowledge, I guess," Harry timidly responds.

"And what word does Bloom use to introduce the lowest level of understanding?"

"Knowledge," Harry repeats.

"Didn't we agree when you first decided to introduce Columbus that your introductory lesson would lend itself to a *knowledge* approach?"

"Yes."

"So we're on the right track as long as we change to a word that better describes what you are seeking with the kids."

Jennifer couldn't help but notice the smallest sigh of relief escape from Harry's throat and a slight nod.

"Okay, so if Bloom's research is valid, *knowledge*, as you just noted, is but a first step to learning. I submit to you that *understanding* is what learning should lead to and learning is what we're seeking for our students. Yet this first step in your new lesson is best taken by providing the children with knowledge they can use to eventually pursue independent learning."

"Yes, I guess I follow your logic."

"Good, you see Bloom is not so difficult if you take some time with his work.

"Would you consider for future planning that when a teacher is mired in the knowledge domain, so are the students? One concludes from the verbs listed under the *knowledge* category that children, if their so-called learning ends with knowledge, may become good at *Jeopardy* and *Wheel of Fortune* but their education would be vacant of any real and meaningful learning. Of course that's not our consideration for today's informative lesson.

"So, do we want to use *learn* in this objective?

"No. You're right. I need to change *learn* to *know*. For this lesson, then, the kids will be in the *knowledge* category."

"Exactly. Now you know why this is a *knowledge* lesson. As a teacher, you need to recognize when such a lesson can and should be taught and understand why you have to move the children to the next step as soon as they are ready.

"Do you see how we can use the Taxonomy as our guide to learning? We need to substitute *know* in place of *learn* in our objective but we must be consistent in explaining what we are hoping to accomplish with the class."

"Yep."

"So, by making this tiny change our objective becomes more accurate and precise, does it not?"

"Yep, again."

Harry muses for a bit and re-writes the objective to read,

To introduce the students to Christopher Columbus and for the students to know the reasons Columbus set out for the Indies.

The modification is simple and uncomplicated. It is a very basic first step toward which Jennifer has steered Harry. It is this kind of clear-cut conclusion that a coach must be able to coax from a teacher as inexpert as Harry. Though the revision Harry made seemed pretty uncomplicated to him, much skill was needed by Jennifer to extract this change from him without being directive. Working with Harry, she knew, was going to be a lengthy process. She hoped they had taken a positive step in lesson design. It was a very deliberate step like taking a child by the hand who is just learning to walk.

To make the leap from *learn,* to *introduce* and *know* is a substantial one for this teacher. Harry becomes attentive to the difference and begins to recognize an application of Bloom to his lesson.

"Harry, are you satisfied that *our* plan reflects what you believe the class needs to begin a study about Christopher Columbus?"

Harry is hesitant as he looks at his Action Plan before responding. Quietly he answers. "I think so. But I do need to use *knowledge* to introduce them to Columbus," he half states and half asks needing still more assurance.

"Yes, of course, you're presenting a new lesson; a new piece of information which they will use as a starting point for their study of Columbus. Some initial knowledge is key before moving to more independent work.

"You have listed, in your objective, what you expect them to demonstrate during the lesson and at lesson's end to prove they know what you want them to know as preparatory information," Jennifer waits.

"I guess that would include recall of information; knowledge of dates, events and places; recognition of major ideas that I or they read during the lesson."

Harry scans the Bloom pamphlet. "I'll look for them to list, define, tell, describe, identify and name," he proudly asserts.

"Excellent. That is precisely what is needed for our lesson. Now let's examine our *Action Plan* to be sure I know what I'm going to observe, what your role will be and what the class will do."

They scan the action plan and Jennifer raises a question to clarify item 4. "I'm not familiar with the book to which you refer."

Harry informs her it's an e-book, *The True story of Christopher Columbus Called the Great Admiral* by Elbridge Streeter Brooks (1846-1902). He hands her the first chapter, *Boy With an Idea,* which he had downloaded. It's the chapter he plans to read to the children.

"It looks interesting and appears to be something the kids can enjoy. How much do you plan to read?"

"A couple of pages then ask questions. My purpose will be to motivate them."

"That's the key to learning isn't it, Harry? We, as adults, are learners and whenever we seek to learn something it's because we're motivated one way or another. Motivation of students is critical to their learning yet it is the most demanding teaching skill for which we're responsible," she said. "Long ago," she continued, "Jerry Lewis, who appeared weekly on his own variety television show, paid tribute to teachers when he declared that he had a talented and well-paid staff that worked all week to find ways for Jerry to motivate a nationwide audience for one hour. Lewis said, in effect, that he was humbled by the fact that teachers were expected, without much help or pay, to motivate students for several hours each school day for 180 days!

"Yet, Harry, it's the key to teaching. Motivated students will seek to learn. There is a variety of ways to motivate. Kids are often motivated once they begin working on a project. Unfortunately too many teachers use threats to motivate. We must be aware of all opportunities to motivate positively.

Harry sheepishly believes that Jennifer is rebuking him. Hollering and threatening are the kind of negative motivations to which she is referring, he is sure. Those behaviors have been at the core of his teaching at Whitewood and also since coming to Clarksdale. Still, Jennifer makes no direct mention of this.

"I'm clear on items 5, 6 and 7," she states, "but I need to better understand you reasoning for number 8. What is the purpose to have each child read from the text?"

"I want to keep their attention while they gain some knowledge about Columbus at the same time."

"And what if you aren't able to keep their attention? Do we have a strategy if their attention wanes? Some of your pupils struggle when reading aloud while a few read in a monotone. Neither is conducive to exciting reading. Might that strategy cause many to lose focus and interest?"

"I don't know. But, Jennifer I ask again what I asked you when you were suggesting ideas for me to manage my classroom. Shouldn't I expect them to be disciplined enough to remain engaged during the class?"

"Do you believe that more information would be retained if they are engaged throughout the lesson?"

"Well, of course."

"Suppose it's going well with the reading. Would it make sense to continue?"

"Yes, but that doesn't answer the question."

"Well, Harry, you know my response. Of course you should expect them to follow directions and pay attention, it's part of growing and maturing but when students become restless because of a questionable teaching technique, the responsible teacher will have other cards to play. Yes?"

"I guess so."

"For example, could you prepare a few provoking questions to ask during your reading with the intent of stretching the kids a bit. I note an engaging thought in the fifth paragraph. *'Every boy who lived near the sea and saw the ships and the sailors, felt as though he would like to sail away to far-off lands and see all the strange sights and do all the brave things that the sailors told about.'* Couldn't we do something with that sentence? Couldn't this be an opportunity to have the class imagine what was going through Columbus' mind as he pondered the vastness of the sea in front of him? We could ask what thoughts those in your class have had as they watched the ocean and how they felt about its enormity. Could they possibly imagine that, during Columbus' youth, no one knew what was out there. Most believed the earth to be flat and at some point a ship would fall off the edge! There are several ideas that could be used to motivate your class. There could even be a writing assignment suggesting they imagine being Columbus looking out over that great expanse of water.

"Understand, Harry, these are questions and suggestions I'm posing for us to mull over. I'm in this with you. If the lesson is successful, we'll be successful together; if not, then we'll fall short together. If you think your way is better, try it and we'll determine its effectiveness as a team. Fair enough?"

"Yes."

"Harry, it's always important to be conscious of the type of lesson you present to the children and whether it is the appropriate mode to meet your objective. Does your action plan determine that your lesson will be teacher-directed, student-centered, interactive, student dependent or student active?" She waits.

"I guess it's pretty much teacher directed; not what you want is it?"

"Remember, we're a team. It's what *we* want that's important. You should be comfortable with a teacher-directed lesson if you believe that's what this introduction to Columbus calls for." She was pressing Harry to see if he would stand his ground.

"Well, yes, it is a directed lesson."

"Okay, but you must be aware of why it is and how long you want to extend this style of teaching for the Columbus study."

The above is the kind of give and take an instructional leader must be prepared to engage in while discussing a lesson to be observed. This is how coaches prompt and guide their protégés in many professional fields. Each step must be understood by both coach and student and candidly discussed.

The remainder of the lesson plan is clear and the two are prepared to take the next step, the classroom observation. Harry's plan of action will guide their mutual analysis in preparation for the post-observation conference. Jennifer's observation and collection of data will help to determine the lesson's and Harry's effectiveness. The pre-observation analysis of a lesson plan requires mutual understanding and trust. Such a session, as described above, may take twenty minutes or more depending on the quality of the objective and the clarity of the action plan. When observing, Jennifer will be a camera. She will transcribe everything she observes and is able to transcribe.

Writing and collecting data while in a classroom, is hard work and takes intensive concentration. Principals who are skilled classroom supervisors often create their own shorthand systems. For example, a transcriber might use "u" for "you" or skip vowels e.g. *vwls.* The goal is to gather as much of the classroom activity as objectively as possible. Jennifer has established her own shorthand. With any new teacher at Clarksdale, like Harry, Jennifer writes everything she can throughout the initial observation(s). Usually, enough patterns emerge for her to eventually collect data based on selected patterns for extension or improvement such as questioning patterns, motivation patterns, closure of a lesson patterns. There are hundreds of patterns that teachers exhibit during a teaching year. Jennifer has discussed all of this with Harry in an effort to have him think of how he can improve his classroom delivery.

Jennifer concludes the conference by asking Harry if he is clear about her role. He nods twice. Coach and protégé wrap up the session. The pre-observation phase of the cycle is complete. The two are ready to take the next step.

Verbatim data, teacher talk, student talk, student activity, body language of both teacher and student(s) will comprise the data that Jennifer will compile. She'll leave a copy on Harry's desk of everything she has written when she leaves the classroom. He will have in his possession, though he may not be able to read every word, the data that he and Jennifer will examine at the post-observation conference.

As quickly as she can, Eleanor Haggerty will type an easy-to-read double-spaced version of the lesson, place it in Harry's mailbox and notify him that it's ready.

Jennifer will also get a copy and analyze what she has recorded prior to the post conference.

During their discussion of the data they will mutually possess, she will encourage Harry to identify patterns that support his objective. She'll ask if he's satisfied with what he's found. Which patterns show that he reached his objective? Which worked for the benefit of the children and which patterns would he like to improve? Harry will be encouraged to build on positive patterns and to attend to weaker ones. These two factors will be reflected in his planning and teaching of subsequent lessons. He will use his findings to show progress during Jennifer's next classroom observation: informal or formal. It is important for the *teacher* rather than the supervisor to have the opportunity to identify satisfactory or patterns for improvement. The discovery of patterns by a teacher more effectively brings change than do those identified by a supervisor. One usually feels pride in having rid one's self of a bad habit without another calling attention to the habit. Then the change is more likely to be permanent.

(Subsequent lessons, Jennifer hoped, would be designed to guide the students through a learning exercise eventually leading to their understanding of Columbus and his impact on the discovery of The New World.)

Chapter 14:
Don't Just Drop In

It's Tuesday morning. The time for Harry's formal classroom observation is upon him. Jennifer will observe his 9:00 AM lesson. One may question the strategy of scheduling and planning so carefully for an observation. Wouldn't supervision be more authentic and effective if the principal dropped in on the classroom unannounced? Wouldn't the supervisor find a more legitimate situation? What if the teacher had no lesson plan ready? Wouldn't the children more likely be in a normal routine? Why give a teacher like Harry the opportunity to prepare for an observation?

Any principal who is a skilled instructional leader knows what is going on in the classrooms. Jennifer Myers appears in several classrooms each day at different times when other job requirements are not keeping her in the office. This principal, like any competent principal, is aware of the learning environment in their classrooms. She recognized during that first week of school that Harry had few classroom management skills, was a poor disciplinarian and had poorer teaching skills. This she learned from informal observations and visits. Jennifer didn't wait for a formal teaching cycle to deal with his management problems. She dealt with Harry at once. The situation called for immediate intervention. Should any circumstance become urgent, anywhere in Clarksdale, Jennifer would intercede without delay.

Harry's pattern for beginning the school day was a condition that required attention. Dr. Myers spoke to him without rancor. She made positive suggestions as she attempted to help him plug his management dike; some he followed, some he didn't. She recognized many needs while passing through Harry's class and made mental notes, which she used constructively and supportively during Harry's first few weeks at his new school. She and Harry made some small inroads with classroom management and some with discipline techniques during the month of September but so much more needs to be done, especially with his teaching skills.

The formal cycle of supervision, as compared to drop-in supervision, is an effective tool for improving the teaching act. There is no way for teachers to hide their basic teaching patterns for a 45-minute period anymore than they could hide their personalities. Preparing for an observation does not give the teacher any particular advantage except to, perhaps, pre-plan more carefully for the lesson about to be observed, which is, in and of itself, improving one's instruction.

Harry's pattern is non-stop lecturing, a boring approach with students of any age. Harry is a talker, he lectures and reads to his class, has kids read, directs lessons and tests often only to find that his young charges are doing poorly. They lose interest; they are bored. He seldom checks for understanding but poses questions that the brighter kids can and do answer. That is his measure to conclude that the rest of the class should be *learning*. He is oblivious to the fact that many are confused. When kids do poorly, Mr. Latter places the blame on the children and their parents. He is offended by their lack of interest in what he is telling them. After all, he believes, he has so much to share with these lazy and thankless kids.

If Harry's classroom management, discipline and instruction don't improve with the assistance she provides, Jennifer will be forced to execute a more direct approach. However, it is assumed by effective leaders that progress is quicker and more successful when coach and protégé are able to work cooperatively and in harmony with one another.

The formal planning that is required for an observation focuses on what will be taught and/or learned, what has been successful and what is weak or has failed in the past. By planning together with a coach to accomplish a common objective, the teacher is conscious that the coach will be observing teaching patterns for the purpose of helping to improve his/her skills. This approach is organized and logical and designed to assist the teacher to grow. Shooting from the hip seldom works to permanently improve teaching.

To storm into a classroom unannounced, find problems, call the teacher to task and confront him/her with an opinion without data is a haphazard tactic. It is based on judgment and opinion but not necessarily on fact. It offers little chance for the teacher to defend his/her position. There is not much opportunity for the teacher to explain what might have been a rational action for a particular situation. If a teacher is jumping from a desk to the floor it may have been to teach something important about gravity. The supervisor must always weigh the data with the teacher before making judgments.

Also, if a principal were to apply a *drop-in* supervision strategy for a teacher whose competence was in question that principal would be hard-pressed to prove a case of ineptitude. To begin a formal action against a teacher with no proof of having coached and assisted the teacher, a union representative's first questions would be, "Where are your data? What have you done to assist the teacher? What are you basing your decision on?"

The objective data that are shared at the post-conference following a planned-for observation are summarized in writing and filed with data compiled from numerous formal observations. Without such accumulated summaries, it's the principal who is vulnerable and helpless when dealing with an incompetent teacher. Case closed.

With extensive coaching, discussion and closure such as occurs in formal supervision cycles, if it's determined that the teacher is incompetent, there are substantial data to support a case for dismissal. It should be stressed however, that the pre-observation conference, the observation, the post-observation conference and the written summary, which comprise the clinical supervision cycles are first, and foremost, used for teacher growth with a trained supervisor serving as a teacher's coaching partner for their two-person team. To employ supervisory cycles to dismiss a teacher would be counter-productive and would only be used as a last resort. Then, and only then would written data be used to fire a teacher. The collection of data is critical to all phases of teacher growth or lack thereof.

But, one may suggest, the teacher has plenty of time, in a pre-observation conference, to *set up* the coach. The rejoinder is that no matter the length and depth of the planning, patterns will emerge during the classroom instruction. Planning for an observation forces the teacher to focus on instruction. By coaching with a disciplined formula such as required for a supervision cycle, growth can more easily and quickly come about. Unless the situation is calamitous and/or dangerous, there is no need, nor purpose for barging into a classroom and playing the autocrat.

It is time for Harry's observation. The phone rings. It's for Jennifer. It's a call that can wait 45 minutes. She tells Eleanor to hold calls, leaves her office, and enters Room 9.

Chapter 15:
Jennifer Enters Room 9

When Jennifer Myers observes her proficient teachers, the focus is on active teaching and learning unlike what she witnesses in Harry's room: lethargic presentations and passive learning. Clarksdale teachers are expected to lead and assist children to become independent, creative and probing learners. It is the teacher's job to motivate students to become self-reliant under their instructor's guidance. To attain such an environment, teacher direction, classroom discipline, management and organization are fundamental prerequisites; essentials still lacking in Harry's class. While walking to Harry's room Jennifer has no clue how Harry will carry out the lesson design they just discussed.

For this first formal observation Jennifer is comfortable with Harry's planned teacher-directed lesson as long as she observes good management techniques, an orderly classroom and a reasonably accurate delivery of the lesson plan. She anticipates that, if he can stay on track for this initial formal observation, she might be able to coach Harry and bring him to a level of competence that will ultimately benefit his fifth-graders. Jennifer is hopeful that she and Harry will take, at least, one positive step in the right direction this morning.

Because the children will be introduced to Christopher Columbus for the first time, Harry is pleased that Jennifer validated for him that his lesson lends itself to teacher-directed instruction. He has more than enough to consider with class management always a question mark in and of itself. Harry is simply not ready to handle anything more complicated for his initial experience with the kind of supervision Jennifer employs.

If Jennifer can ease him through a successful lesson and build trust at the same time, she believes it will raise Harry's confidence and encourage him to attempt more challenging and productive teaching strategies. Harry, on the other hand, is still not convinced that supervision is a positive tool. There remain remnants of a threat in the word and the deed. As he prepares for the lesson he is about to teach, he perceives Jennifer as the personification of power and wisdom: a lightning bolt, coming dangerously close to his often-stormy classroom.

Jennifer's scrutiny of Harry's lesson, from planning, to presentation, to analysis, is the nucleus of the coaching process that she uses as her basic tool to help her teachers. Whatever the process is called in Old River or elsewhere the components for teacher supervision should be similar. The process is the essence. A rose by any other name is still a rose.

Rather than chronicle for the reader the entire written collection of data accumulated by Jennifer during her 45-minutes of observing Harry's lesson, a 15-minute segment of the lesson is presented in the following chapter. The purpose of the segment is for clarification of the principal's recording function and to introduce the concept of teaching patterns. Dr. Myers will script as much of the entire classroom activities as she can.

One might question why a video camera is not used to record the instruction. Simply, there is not enough time. Recording would require teacher and supervisor to review the entire lesson together, frequently stopping the tape to discuss patterns. The 45-minute classroom observation would be doubled in time alone and extended for pattern searches and discussion that can be otherwise accomplished by a skilled supervisor. The time needed to review taped segments with the entire faculty is just not available. Also, additional time would be required to technically set up for taping a class. There would be need for someone to operate the equipment who is proficient enough to capture the teacher's *and* the students' actions. If the necessary human resources and technical hardware were available in public schools, a tape could be useful for further study at one's leisure. A competent principal, armed with a pad and a writing instrument can collect the data for any lesson and use them effectively in collaboration with the teacher during the post-observation meeting.

Principal Myers enters Room 9 a couple of minutes ahead of schedule to ensure that when Harry begins there'll be no interruptions. She will write verbatim everything she observes using her personal shorthand. When she places the carbon copy on Harry's desk, she'll thank him and the children and leave.

Chapter 16:
Observation and Analysis

Jennifer, back in her office, gives Eleanor her shorthand copy of Harry's lesson to decode, type into MS Word and print two copies double-spaced: one for her and one for Mr. Latter. Eleanor will put Harry's sealed copy in his mail slot.

"I'll take mine a.s.a.p."

Harry, still sweating and feeling clammy following Jennifer's observation, wonders what's on the papers she left on his desk but doesn't have the nerve to read them in the presence of his students. He was so nervous while Jennifer was in the room that he isn't sure how the lesson went. He wants to quickly scan the data but feels restricted. He's like a cowering puppy restrained by an invisible electronic fence. He is too tense to remind himself that everything on those papers represents what actually occurred in the classroom. Yet, he is unable to convince himself that the written record is without bias. He takes his class to gym and returns to Room 9.

Summoning his courage, Harry picks up Jennifer's transcription. He is able to read and easily decipher the notations included in Jennifer's shorthand, review the lesson and recall it almost completely. Much to his surprise her notes are without comment or judgment.

Later, when notified by Eleanor that the finished copy was typed, printed and in his mailbox, he rushed to get it before his class returned from their physical education class. He read the content, compared it to the scribbled notes Jennifer left with him and found that it contained precisely the same information as the original. Subconsciously he was trusting Jennifer more with each succeeding contact with her.

Mutual trust is critical for a positive and successful supervisory program.

Eleanor reminded Jennifer, "You have three calls; the one I told you could wait 45-minutes sounded fairly important, the other two are for appointments to see you. I took care of those. Also, Brian Hoffler punched Greg Porter in the eye in the hall. It's swollen and red. His father is on his way to pick him up. I didn't interrupt you because Samantha assured me it wasn't an emergency."

Jennifer isn't certain that Mr. Porter will agree. She goes immediately to the nurse's room, speaks with Greg, assures herself that he's O.K. and hurries to Greg's classroom to get the details from his teacher, Bill McFadden, before Greg's father arrives. Bill seldom has problems of this nature in his room. Jennifer needs to know exactly what happened and how Bill handled it. Bill is one of three male teachers on the Clarksdale staff. He told Jennifer that the teacher on duty reported that Brian and Greg were yelling at each other on the playground. They were still bantering when they came into the building before they settled down. Once the children were back in class and seated, McFadden turned to write on the board and heard Greg holler, "Owww!" When he turned around Greg was whimpering and holding his hand on his eye.

"Alright, Greg, come here. Calm down and tell me what happened."

Bill McFadden told Jennifer that when he took Greg into the hall, Greg told him that Brian punched him when he wasn't looking. Brian admitted to having struck Greg. McFadden told the boys that he would deal with them at the end of school and sent Greg to the nurse. Bill didn't know what brought the quarrel about.

Jefferson Porter is calm and accepts Jennifer's account of the confrontation. He shrugs and says, "Kids fight. All I want is to be sure that it's finished and done with."

As soon as Mr. Porter leaves, Jennifer calls Brian's mother. When Jennifer shares the teacher's report of the scuffle with her, Mrs. Hoffler tells Dr. Meyers that she is terribly upset and embarrassed by her son's actions.

"If Brian was out of line, I'll take care of him personally. Dr. Myers, do what you feel is appropriate." Jennifer heard from McFadden that Brian and Greg weren't getting along.

With the parental notifications completed and Greg back in class Jennifer asked Bill to send the two boys to the office. Her major disappointment, she told them, was their obvious disregard for Clarksdale's tenet: *Respect*.

"You've ignored the daily reminders of caring about one another and for the school itself. You've paid no attention to all the notices throughout the school or to the daily reminders about *respect.*" She does not pursue the reason for their feud leaving that to their parents and Mr. McFadden. She tells the boys to face one another stare into each other's eyes until she tells them they can stop. Of course, the boys are soon giggling.

At that moment Jennifer says, "You can't possibly be angry with those grins on your faces. Now shake hands and go back to class. I expect that you will resume the friendship that has been so meaningful to you both." Once again, Principal Myers has to re-order her day's plans. One of Dr. Myers' many strengths is her ability to solve problems quickly and efficiently.

She begins to analyze her observation notes in preparation for her meeting with Harry.

Just as she settles in, Mandy, a slight little third grade girl, comes to the office accompanied by her teacher. She's crying uncontrollably. Her sobbing is gut wrenching. Jennifer drops her notes. Mandy's desperately trying to catch her breath between sobs. Jennifer embraces her. Her mom and dad are going to be divorced she splutters. Her mother tried to make her understand before Mandy left for school that these things happen and told Mandy that both her mommy and daddy love her. She tried to lessen Mandy's hurt and insecurity by assuring her that she will always be with her dad and her mom, only not at the same time.

"You need to be brave," her mom had told her. But it had taken two days before Mandy was able to come to school. She made it part through this day before she fell to pieces.

Jennifer loved her Clarksdale kids. She wondered how two parents could choose their personal happiness, if that is the case here, in the face of their child's devastation. She realizes that her thinking is not politically correct for the age in which we live. She witnesses so much of this in her role. Parents, like Mandy's, rationalize that it's unhealthy and foolish to ruin their lives by staying together. They hang onto the modern psychiatrists' exculpation of sacrificing their children's happiness for their own. Counselors assure them that children rebound quickly. After all, nearly half of marriages end up this way. The kids get through it. Ah, but do they, Jennifer wonders. She sees too many broken children who go into shells or act out their aggressions negatively following separations and divorces. They often mistrust adults and many have little respect for their elders. Yes, some behave well, are good students and succeed: perhaps working through their hurt positively. How can I help this poor child? She recalled Barry Manilow's *Mandy* and felt a desperate ache for *this* poor little Mandy as she thought of her parents' decision.

> *"Oh Mandy, well, you came and you gave*
> *without taking, but 'we' sent you away,*
> *Oh Mandy."*

"Come on, sweetie, let's take a walk outside and talk." Trying to catch her breath, Mandy felt the warmth of her principal, which made her cry even harder.

"My mom and my dad are not going to be together anymore and I want them to stay so bad." Mandy shook and wept. "They don't care about me."

"Of course they do sweetie. They both love you very much. You're not the reason they are getting a divorce.

"Then how come they don't care how I feel?"

Jennifer calls Mandy's mom and informs her about Mandy's hurt and urges her to come to school to pick her up if she possibly can. Mrs. Thornton expresses her discomfit with the conversation, thanks Dr. Myers and promises to come to school immediately to get Mandy.

Jennifer invites Mandy to sit with her in her office until her mom comes for her. She has a shelf of children's books of varying interests on her back wall and selects *Swamp Angel* for Mandy to read while she examines Harry's lesson, underlines patterns and seeks clues to the attainment of the objective.

Oh, for the life of a CEO Jennifer thinks but would never trade her job for that of a corporate executive's.

She tries to concentrate so she can be prepared to go over the data with Harry. She peeks from her reading to check Mandy.

Which patterns show whether the objective was met? Do the data show that the teacher stuck with his action plan in his lesson design? Will Harry be able to show supportive evidence to answer these questions and will he find some patterns of his own? As Jennifer continues to underline obvious patterns she contemplates how she will begin the post observation conference. She plans to be positive with the intent of moving Harry ahead even if it's only a step or two. For Jennifer to succeed with Harry, she must help him to trust in the process designed to help him. It's difficult to remain focused with the image of Mandy's sadness clouding her thoughts. Struggling to deliberate on the task at hand Jennifer, following her analysis of Harry's lesson, is ready for the conference.

She has a sliver of time to read several messages before their meeting. She was unable to conduct her planned and required monthly fire drill due to the unexpected events with the two boys and Mandy, both of which required her attention. She postponed the fire drill until tomorrow.

When Harry's class goes to lunch, he reads the typed copy of Jennifer's transcription more carefully. Once he re-

read her notes he was again amazed at how much of the lesson she was able to accurately accumulate. Boy, she's really skilled at using her own kind of shorthand for both speed and accuracy, he thought. Basically, he noted on the original copy, that she leaves out vowels, uses the first and last letters of words, and uses homonyms. For non-verbal actions, she uses numbers and symbols.

For example Harry read: T: OK gys wnt u 2 trn 2 p 42."

Interpretation: Teacher says, "Okay guys I want you to turn to page 42."

Rptd: Interpretation: a repeated pattern.

Tchr rds Chp 1, 4 mn

Interpretation: Teacher reads Chapter 1 in 4 minutes.

Jennifer's symbol for a child raising a hand is ^. Three children with hands raised: ^^^. The symbol 0 is used for no response to a teacher question. When a student asks a question, Jennifer jots *q* in her transcription.

She uses a seating chart to identify the children who respond or raise questions. She begins with blank squares that display the class seating arrangement with each student's name above a corresponding square on which to make notes. The squares identify the location of each pupil's desk. The squares are also numbered. Eleanor, during the summer, designed the charts with a variety of seating arrangements for Jennifer. Before each observation the office clerk sets up the chart for the classroom where the observation will take place. Some classrooms are organized in rows, others with desks clustered in groups of four while still others are setup in two opposite rows facing each other.

Alicia, who sits in the first seat of the first row in Harry's room, is student a1/1. The letter a, is the initial of the pupil in seat 1, row 1. Interpretation: a1/1q translates: Alicia asks a question. a1/1^ means Alicia raised her hand. Jennifer jots the time of day in the margin at 3-minute intervals.

Harry, now quite impressed with his ability to accurately translate Jennifer's original notations will have thirty minutes following dismissal to analyze Jennifer's work and prepare for the conference. That should be enough time for Harry to review the data, circle some patterns and be ready to discuss the lesson with his coach.

Mandy's mother arrived fairly soon following the call from school.

"Hi, Dr. Myers, it's me, Mrs. Thornton!" Jennifer stopped what she was doing, returned the greeting and watched the child bolt to her mother.

"May I speak with you?"

Jennifer replied to the soon-to-be Ex Mrs. Thornton. "Of course."

Jennifer made no move. Cindy Thornton asked if they could meet now.

"I don't think we should wait," she said.

"I agree, but I believe that Mandy should be alone with you for the rest of the afternoon, if that's at all possible. I'll meet with you anytime after that; the sooner, the better."

"I have time this evening, Dr. Myers. I could be here by 5:30. My sister loves to stay with Mandy."

"Fine. If you and Mr. Thornton could be comfortable together, it would be better if both of you could be here. I would feel more secure having the two of you interpreting the same information at the same time. You know how much can be lost in translation"

"I have no idea whether or not he would or could come but I'm pretty sure I can reach him."

"Please try to impress upon Mr. Thornton that it would be to Mandy's advantage if you're both here but, in any case, I feel it terribly important to share what happened a while ago with at least one of you as soon as possible."

Mandy, with puffed, red eyes was sitting a few feet behind her mother just out of earshot looking very sad.

"I'm so embarrassed about all this."

"You needn't be. I believe it's a good thing if we can talk frankly about how this is affecting Mandy. I assure you, Mrs. Thornton, I don't intend to butt into your personal affairs. I do, however, feel a responsibility to help Mandy cope here at school. Any input that can assist us at

Clarksdale and you at home would be to her benefit. I simply, as you do, want to help Mandy get through her distress and be able to function successfully here at school."

"Thanks, Dr. Myers. I'll be here this evening with or without Paul."

The dismissal bell signals the end of the children's school day. Harry finishes his examination of Jennifer's text. Her direction to Harry was for him to find patterns, scan his objectives and be ready to discuss his findings at their post-observation session.

Jennifer, returning from checking the buses, greets Harry without referring to the lesson. It's important to maintain an objective and collegial atmosphere throughout a teaching cycle. By not commenting on the lesson, she avoids a trap that could undermine the concept of objectivity by offering a subjective opinion.

"How about a cup of coffee before we get started?" Harry accepts her offer. Jennifer pours two cups and sits with Harry. They'll work from the lesson plan, which includes the objective, action plan, materials and student evaluation. They'll use the classroom data to determine the congruence of the plan and the delivered lesson. It should be noted here that a lesson plan or design is used as a guide for teaching a class. It's not meant to stifle spontaneous and/or positive teaching opportunities that had not been anticipated in the plan. However, Harry must learn to recognize unplanned adjustments and be able to rationalize the purpose for mid-stream changes.

The lesson plan is replicated here for the convenience of the reader.

Lesson Plan for Observation: October 6

Objective: *To introduce the children to Christopher Columbus and to know his reasons for wanting to sail to India.*

Action Plan:

1. Tell class they are going to learn about Christopher Columbus.
2. Ask what they know about Columbus. Wait for answers.
3. Ask if they know why they are learning about him this week (October 6th).
4. Read from the e-book, *True Story of Christopher Columbus, Admiral.*
5. What is an admiral?
6. Following my reading, have children list what they know about Columbus from the reading and from their own knowledge.
7. Have class open their texts to chapter entitled, *The New World.*
8. Encourage individual children to read aloud from the text.
9. Have each child read a paragraph.
10. When finished ask children to write any detail that was repeated from teacher's reading, from their individual knowledge or from the class readings.
11. Have a volunteer look up Columbus in the encyclopedia and find three facts we didn't learn from our readings.
12. Ask how long it took Columbus to reach the Americas.
13. Recommend the purchase of *Meet Christopher Columbus* by James T. DeKay.
14. Recommend the E-book from the Internet.

Materials:

1. Library book: *Meet Christopher Columbus*
2. E-book named in action plan.
3. Texts, encyclopedia, transparency of world map, paper and pens.

Student Check:

1. Short quiz
2. Exchange papers for corrections.
3. List 5 facts presented by the teacher.

Evaluation of the Lesson:

1. Analyze collected data from principal's notes.
2. Discuss with principal positive feedback and strengths of the lesson
3. Discuss areas for improvement

NOTE: Eleanor Haggerty retyped the following classroom observation from Coach Myers' raw shorthand notes. For purposes of succinctness and clarity, the typed version is presented below. The underlined words, phrases and sentences are Jennifer's patterns found in the data. The writings in bold are notes in Jennifer's analysis for her to share with Harry as necessary. The data presented here are but a brief segment of Jennifer's 45-minute observation. The intent is to use enough of the lesson to demonstrate for the reader how clinical supervision is employed in the hands of an instructional specialist while not boring the reader with extensive data:

Coach Myers entered the classroom before the start of the lesson to let everyone settle down and get ready for the class to start. She will write only what she sees and hears: no opinion, just facts.

Classroom Observation: Mr. Harry Latter: 10/06

DR. MYERS' NOTE AT BEGINNING OF CLASS: children restless: settle down quickly when principal enters.

Teacher begins lesson: "Okay guys, what are we studying in social studies?" Several hands shoot up "Yes, Serita?"

NOTE: In a shorthand version the notes for the opening interaction between teacher and student would look like this: T. ok gys, q. ?studying in ss ^^^^^ (j1/2, f6/5, r5/4, ja3/2, s4/1.) *Yes, s4/1?"* (Five students raised their hands to answer the question posed by the teacher.)

"The Discovery of America."

"Good."

Teacher: "Okay guys, can anyone tell me the name of a famous explorer from the Age of Discovery?" Several hands are raised (here Jennifer again lists the initial and number of the volunteers). "Carter?"

"Christopher Columbus." **(Jennifer, in her analysis, found a pattern of one or two-word responses for each question and underlined the pattern for the post-observation conference.)**

Teacher: "Good." **(Jennifer identified a pattern of teacher using *"Good"* for rewarding a correct answer but not using children's names when using the reward signal, "*Good"*)**

With these student responses Harry begins to breathe a little easier. He continues with several more *what, who* and *where* questions, which he will see as patterns in Jennifer's transcription. Soon he notices a few kids becoming antsy. I'd better begin reading, Harry reasons. So far, so good, he thinks

Teacher: "Okay guys, **(Clearly a pattern) Have Harry speak to it if he doesn't recognize it.)** Sit back. We're going to learn a little bit about Columbus and his plan to reach the Indies by sailing west. I'm going to treat you to a little story to begin our study of Columbus."

This announcement gets the class's attention and is noted by Jennifer; the children seem to enjoy being read to. **(Jennifer notes this as a positive change of pace.)**

Teacher has difficulty getting the children settled. She notes: **(some limited progress since teacher has been using classroom charts for organizing the class at the beginning of the day.)**

Teacher reads:

CHAPTER I. BOY WITH AN IDEA

Men who do great things are men we all like to read about. This is the story of Christopher Columbus, the man who discovered America. He lived four hundred years ago. When he was a little boy he lived in Genoa. It was a beautiful city in the northwestern part of the country called Italy. The mountains were behind it; the sea was in front of it, and it was so beautiful a place that the people who lived there called it "Genoa the Superb." Christopher Columbus was born in this beautiful city o Genoa in the year 1446, at number 27 Ponticello Street. He was a bright little fellow with a fresh-looking face, a clear eye and golden hair. His father's name was Domenico Columbus; his mother's name was Susanna. His father was a wool-comber. He cleaned and straightened out the snarled-up wool that was cut from the sheep…

A good place to stop and discuss how this process works.

…so as to make it ready to be woven into cloth. Christopher helped his father do this when he grew strong enough, but he went to school, too, and learned to read and write and to draw maps and charts.

How did this shape his thinking…….? stop to discuss; another opportunity

These charts were maps of the sea, to show the sailors where they could steer without running on the rocks and sand, and how to sail safely from one country to another. This world was not as big then as it is now -- or, should say, people did not know it was as big.

What does this mean......? <u>No pauses following questions.</u> Pattern: reading without opportunity to check if children understand what he is reading to them.

Most of the lands that Columbus had studied about in school, and most of the people he had heard about, were in Europe and parts of Asia and Africa. The city of Genoa where Columbus lived was a very busy and a very rich city. It was on the Mediterranean Sea, and many of the people who lived there were sailors who went in their ships on voyages to distant lands. They sailed to other places on the Mediterranean Sea, which is a very large body of water, you know, and to England, to France, to Norway, and even as far away as the cold northern island of Iceland. This was thought to be a great journey.

The time in which Columbus lived was not as nice a time as is this in which you live. People were always quarreling and fighting about one thing or another, and the sailors who belonged to one country would try to catch and steal the ships or the things that belonged to the sailors or the storekeepers of another country. This is what we call piracy, and a pirate, you know, is thought to be a very wicked man.

But when Columbus lived, men did not think it was so very wicked to be a sort of half-way pirate, although they did know that they would be killed if they were caught. So almost every sailor was about half pirate. Every boy who lived near the seashore and saw the ships and the sailors, felt as though he would like to sail away to far-off lands and see all the strange sights and do all the brave things that the sailors told about. Many of them even said they would like to be pirates and fight with other sailors, and show how strong and brave and plucky they could be.

Columbus was one of these. He was what is called an adventurous boy. He did not like to stay quietly at home with his father and comb out the tangled wool. He thought it would be much nicer to sail away to sea and be a brave captain or a rich merchant.

Following two pages, teacher stops and poses questions.

Teacher: "What **(Questions begin with what, where, who throughout the lesson inducing one-word answers.)** did Columbus want to do, Willie?"

"Be a sailor."

Teacher: "Good. What didn't he want to do, Virginia?"

"Be a weaver like his father"

Teacher: "Good." **(Jennifer confirms pattern of teacher not using children's names while using the same reward system, *Good*)**

Teacher: "Where did he live, Kanye?"

"Genoa"

Teacher: "Good."

Teacher: "Where **(note the "what" and "where" questions: appropriate for this kind of directed lesson?)** is Genoa, Oscar?"

"In Italy."

Teacher: "Good. **(Jennifer re-confirms pattern of teacher not using children's names while using the same reward system, *Good*)**

Where did sailors from Genoa go?"

Alicia's and Anita's hands are raised; some fidgeting and looking around.

Teacher says "Well?" **T. calls on his best students (pattern): Ask teacher to give reason for calling on his best: to bail out the class.** Carter, Serita?"

And so the lesson began and continued along similar lines. The above is a sampling of the beginning of the class. Below is the last segment of the instruction.

Part of Jennifer's data is a notation of time along the margin of her pad. She jots the time at regular intervals enabling her to give Harry input as to the length of portions of the lesson and when they occurred. For example, when Harry finished reading to the class she was able to record that his reading ended after 4 minutes. His introduction took 7 minutes of teacher talk. Questions related to the reading took 8 minutes. **(Does this information help to determine when kids began to fidget?)**

When Harry exhausted his questions, he projected a transparent map of Europe onto the white board. He had scanned it with a couple more from a library book. Harry was competent with technology. (something Jennifer will try to build on. **positive**

He next projected a map of Italy onto the board. Harry asks for a volunteer, many children raised their hands to locate Italy on the map of Europe followed by a volunteer who found Genoa and another who pointed to the Mediterranean Sea. **(actively engaging children: positive)**

Teacher: "Open your texts to page 42 and Christopher Columbus. Jack, please begin reading." Jack reads tentatively, stumbling on words. **(teacher skips vocabulary opportunity)**

Teacher calls several students to read. "Ashley, continue, please. Conner, you're next. Oscar, go on." Oscar reads slowly and softly. Many don't hear because of his monotone. Several children fidget. Teacher reads the next two pages then has the class close their books.

"Maria, go to the encyclopedia, please and look up Christopher Columbus." By the time Maria finds the entry, more kids are squirming and looking elsewhere. **(a strong clue that it's time to change the pace of the instruction again)**

Teacher: "Please read, Maria." Maria reads haltingly. **(skips vocabulary opportunity again: pattern?)** and struggles through several paragraphs as children look bored.

Teacher: "Okay you guys, **(pattern)** listen up. Time for a quiz. Take out your pencils." *Groan.* The announcement of the quiz jolted most back to reality, but not all.

Teacher: "Did you hear me, Willie? Warren, what are you up to?" (teacher appears to be frustrated by the way things are beginning to deteriorate) Harry feels beads of sweat on his forehead.

Teacher: "Okay guys." **(pattern)** Teacher hands the multiple-choice quiz to the pupils in the front row who pass them back. **Jennifer notes the two minutes this takes.**

Teacher: "Any questions?" A couple of hands are raised. **(Unable to hear the two questions)** "You've got 10 minutes to finish."

Teacher walks among the desks as the children write their answers. At the end of the ten minutes he directs the class to exchange papers.

When all papers are traded Mr. Latter calls on students for answers to each question. Following each response, he asks the class to raise their hands if they agree with the reply. Students mark the incorrect answers with an "X" then write the number correct over the total of 20. **(opportunity for math lesson: 5th grade division)**

Teacher: "These scores will go into my marking book," he tells the children. **(How will he provide for individual needs without scanning the tests himself?)**

Harry's fearful 45-minute bumpy ride through his day of judgment is coming to its painful end.

Teacher: "Okay guys, **(pattern)** let's wrap it up. Let's get to our math lesson." *Groan!* **(lesson closure?)**

Post-Observation Conference

Once Harry and Jennifer were settled, she laid her work on the table between them. Harry saw Jennifer's underlined patterns and a few notes in the margins of the transcript. Uh-oh he thought, here comes the hammer. He had been leery of how the conference would be conducted. Jennifer had no particular agenda to follow. She was hoping for Harry to take the lead. He had not jotted notes for himself during *his* analysis.

With the lesson plan and the classroom transcript side-by-side Jennifer starts, "Harry, why don't you take the lead. Using our data, can you verify whether our *objective* was accomplished? We need to confirm that first."

Jennifer paused to show the effect a brief halt could have on a learner. But Harry misinterpreted the pause, this was a slider; he was expecting a fastball. Jennifer had turned the tables by having Harry address the lesson's objective. Not quite prepared for this initial parry though forewarned at the pre-observation conference that Jennifer hoped he would take charge of the conference, he is silent for several moments as he tries to deflect, what he perceives to be Jennifer's opening gambit. Now, again not fully prepared, he has to shift gears before moving to his Action Plan.

Harry still views supervision as a skirmish, a chess game, and Jennifer had begun with an unanticipated opening. A sound opening is often the key to a strong ending. He must react with a solid defense. Harry's suspicious mentality is already creating resistance to Jennifer's attempt to guide him.

He collected his thoughts and finally said, "The introduction to Christopher Columbus went well. The reading that I did helped to meet the objective. So, yes, I think the objective was basically met."

Jennifer stopped him. "Harry, let's use a little time to examine *your* data to prove that your reading helped to meet the lesson objective. We need to avoid opinion."

Harry felt trapped again. Jennifer, sensing his fluster, gently reminded him that she was merely helping him to learn to use data. In *her* transcript she had noted that children were attentive during the reading. She checked the class and didn't find anyone not paying attention. All eyes were riveted on Harry as he read, which confirmed their interest in the teacher's reading. She also noted that they came to attention when Harry connected Columbus with Columbus Day. When she pointed to that observation he was pleasantly surprised.

"So," Jennifer said, "this is proof that your reading held their interest. Can you see that what happens in the room can be objectively recorded and conclusions can be drawn from the data? "

"Well, yes, I guess so. I just didn't think to look at the data that way when I first read it." They moved to the Action Plan.

Jennifer proceeded to ask Harry to find any pattern that showed he waited for responses as he had indicated he would in #2 of his Action Plan: **Ask what they know about Columbus. Wait for answers.** Jennifer's notes did not show any pause to allow students to respond. She had planned to time the pauses. Harry could find nothing.

"I was pretty nervous and just forgot," he sheepishly replied.

Jennifer offered no judgment other than, "Do you feel a need to pause when you ask challenging questions? Should we include pausing as part of our instruction?" Harry said that pausing was a good strategy and he'd remember the next time.

Jennifer reassured Harry that she was aware of his nervousness. She hoped this would put him at ease with this supervisory approach.

"I know you were tense, Harry, but I'm pleased that you recognize the advantage of pausing and letting kids have time to react when you pose questions and that you intend to use the pause to stretch the kids. It's a positive technique that encourages children to think."

Jennifer encouraged Harry to lead them through the rest of the conference.

Coach and teacher identified patterns in the Action Plan corroborating that entries 1, 4, 7, 8, 9 and 13 were completed satisfactorily. Harry is quick to state, before Jennifer asks, that items 3, 5, and 10 were overlooked; he forgot but vows to cover them *tomorrow*. He again blamed the omissions on nerves. May as well use it, he thought seeing that Jennifer recognizes my anxiety. The two recognized Harry's use of the designated materials. The data also confirmed that the student evaluation was completed.

Jennifer gently urged Harry to review his analysis of the instruction to ensure that he hadn't overlooked anything in his notes. He scans his copy. He feels compelled to offer some kind of insight. Jennifer, he knew, was waiting for some comment from him.

"You wrote on your notes that, "children are restless and they settled down when they saw you."

"Is that an accurate account?"

"I guess it's accurate."

"Harry, if you think it's inaccurate, please say so; we need to be honest with one another. We're looking to grow as colleagues."

"No, I can't argue. It's accurate. I guess I'm disappointed that the kids were restless so early in the morning and that your presence is what calmed them. Actually, I'm glad you caught it." This is an opportunity for Jennifer. Harry has made an interesting observation and shared it with her! The children's demeaner is a problem, which has plagued Harry from day one.

Jennifer probes, "Are you still using the charts, plans and discipline reminders that we agreed you'd use?"

"Mostly, I do."

"Is *mostly* working?" she pressed.

"Not as well as it should."

"Harry, you know that consistency is essential for good classroom management."

"I know, I know, I'll be sure to greet the kids at the door and get them settled and working right away."

Because classroom management remains a serious problem in Harry's room, Jennifer takes the opportunity Harry afforded her and changes the focus of the conference to this more crucial topic. She urges the daily implementation of the rules generated by the kids in *their* established classroom constitution and reminds Harry that his students worked hard to draft that constitution and had agreed to abide by it.

"Harry, you're the administrator of their Room Nine Constitution and responsible for helping them to carry it out. When a disciplinary situation occurs in the classroom, it's your job to address it by reminding the students of their responsibilities to the rules they drafted and accepted."

She presses on, "I have an article for you that I would like you to read. It's a description of a good teacher. The title is *Best Teacher Description* by Dr. Glen W. Probst. In his article, Dr. Probst identifies time-tested attributes, characteristics and practices that contribute to teacher success. It's an easy read: comprehensive and filled with valuable, uncomplicated information. I am convinced that, if you read it carefully and conscientiously, it will be of great use to you."

An expert instructional coach, such as Jennifer, is able to refer to pertinent articles and books related to a variety of instructional issues designed to help teachers.

"Harry, I want to help. If you don't see what I see, it's my job to lend a hand. Classroom management has to remain our priority. "Now let's get back to our lesson. What patterns have you underlined or circled?"

"Well, I noted that I told the students that they were going to learn about Columbus."

"Yes, that's obvious and the feature was that you informed the children what you were going to do with this lesson. It's a plus when the children know what you're looking for in any lesson. Do the data suggest that you asked who knows anything about Columbus?"

"Yep, here is the question." Harry points to the record.

Jennifer moves to the lesson and asks if Harry found other patterns.

"Well, I see that I used 'Okay guys,' each time I addressed the class and said, 'Good' each time a correct response was given."

"What do you make of those patterns?" She kept the ball in his court.

"Well, they seem kind of trite."

"Do you think they impact the lesson?"

"Not really." How easy it is to sway this man, she thought. He has few convictions when it comes to teaching.

"Will you continue using them?"

" I guess not."

"Why not, if they don't affect the lesson?" Another pause. Anxiety grips him once again.

"I guess maybe they're pretty bland."

"Could that affect the lesson?"

"I don't know."

Jennifer offers a thought for Harry's consideration. "Is bland likely to motivate students?"

"No, it wouldn't inspire."

"Harry, please always remember, *we*'re in this together. Should we be satisfied, with *trite* or *bland* words?"

"No."

"Then we are of the same mind. In and of themselves, they may not have a great effect on the lesson but we agree they make no positive impact."

"Jennifer, trite is certainly a negative. I'll change the "*okays*" and the "*goods.*"

"Marvelous! Might we consider better words then? Remember, Harry, when we tell children they are correct with a response, *we're* rewarding them. Kids love to have their teacher's approval however, if the reward is trite or bland or has little meaning, do you think it will motivate?

" I guess not."

"Then, what words could we substitute?" She again pauses.

Harry is quick to come up with several. "Terrific, is one," he offers. "How did you ever get that? could be another; you're right on target; now we're cooking; what a thoughtful answer. I'm sure I can come up with lots more."

"Those verbal rewards you just cited should be more effective and meaningful. Another thought while we're looking at these two patterns, the use of children's names might contribute to the effectiveness of *your* rewards. Do you agree?" Jennifer wondered if Harry would see this as useful practice.

"Sure."

"Can you find among the data where you used any-one's name following a child's response?"

Harry scans the sheets. "Geez, I didn't use any names except to call on someone."

"Kids," Jennifer adds, "as we all do, like to hear their names used positively."

" Yep, you're right."

"Should we build these changes into our next obser-vation?"

"I can change those two patterns tomorrow. I don't have to wait."

Though Jennifer realizes she is working with the most primitive of teaching techniques, she also knows that if she has any chance of helping Harry to become a competent teacher she must be patient for now.

"Harry, let me know if you detect any change in the youngsters' reaction to your expanded reward comments and the use of their names over a period of a few days. Let me know if they respond positively.

" Let's move along. How do you evaluate your use of the maps?"

"That went well, many kids participated."

"Exactly, it's right here. Your timing of changing from reading to the map lesson was perfect. You changed the pace and maintained their interest, a very positive piece of the lesson. Obviously you see how visual aids and changing the pace of the instruction can enhance your lesson."

"Yeah, I really do."

At this point in the post-observation conference, Jennifer stops and encourages Harry to adopt these minor adjustments, not only for the next day but also for the next formal observation. She believes the changes will affect his children and their learning even if only slightly. These will be, as noted earlier, the smallest of steps but fairly significant ones in establishing the clinical process with Harry.

This is a point of decision in the conference for Jennifer. She chooses not to overwhelm Harry with her notes and will hold off regarding the many "discussion" opportunities from his reading until the next time.

In every conference there is a moment when a teacher finds a pattern that he/she feels good about or one that he/she identifies as needing attention. Those are usually effective times to stop. They can offer good breaks from which to begin planning for the next observation. They can be used to reinforce. If a teacher misses something momentous during the analysis, the coach has the responsibility to lead the teacher to the pattern.

Though Harry has completed his initial experience in fair fashion he lacks countless teaching skills and is still extremely deficient with classroom management. Jennifer's intent is to gain Harry's confidence with the process by the beginning of November. She is willing to take tiny steps forward for a couple of weeks and observe the results. If she were to overwhelm Harry at this first post-conference, she is sure he would become dysfunctional; she would have lost him and would have to begin to decide whether he can meet the expectations she has for all her teachers. Jennifer tells Harry that she's satisfied that they've made progress.

"We can stop here," she says. He is baffled but inwardly he is delighted. This principal has made another unexpected move. Checkmate!

"To be certain we're in agreement, I infer from what we've discussed that if I step into your classroom tomorrow, you'll be using your expanded reward statements, you'll be addressing your students by name and using pauses when posing questions. And I'll find some improvement in your classroom management, correct?"

"Yep, you'd see all that."

"Also, you will have read the Probst article. For the next observation, I'll recognize the changes we've discussed to be a permanent part of your instruction," she continues while pouring more coffee.

"Harry, would you be comfortable taking this a little further and plan to work Bloom into your instruction? You have some notion now, how that can be done fairly easily. I'm sure we can continue to move within the *knowledge* category and extend it a bit now that you've seen that it's not difficult to work with it. You can look at the list of verbs in the Taxonomy. I know you can weave a few into observable tasks for the children. Just scan them. Perhaps you can already recall some of them. If you consciously take two or three new ones from his *knowledge* list you will improve your instruction. Consider each one as you decide, which would broaden your instruction. Harry, are you game?"

One notes that Jennifer is employing good instruction techniques during her exchanges with Harry. She refers to him by name, she encourages him to make the changes he, himself, has decided to make, she pauses, she challenges him to adopt something new and, lastly, shows confidence in him.

The conference ends on a positive note. Harry agrees to try. Jennifer hopes for the best. She leaves Harry with the simple follow-up he has chosen to work on, which could possibly reap some initial success and, at the same time, boost his confidence in the clinical cycle as a means of becoming a better teacher.

Though choosing not to overpower Harry, a coach with Jennifer's instructional expertise gleans immeasurably more from the data than has been addressed with Harry.

Jennifer will keep her notes from this post-observation discussion until their next pre-observation conference. Her written summary will include all that was noted during the post-conference. She'll prepare a copy for Harry and file the original and use it at their next pre-observation planning conference.

Chapter 17: Preparation of Summary

As stated in the previous chapter, there are several additional patterns Coach Myers could have called to Harry's attention during their meeting. Also noted, she chose to accept the three rudimentary patterns uncovered by Harry to get him moving toward more serious work as soon as possible. In addition to establishing Harry's trust in the clinical process she hoped to quickly expand Harry's ability to identify patterns of teaching *and* learning, gain his confidence in her as a coach and improve his instructional skills. At the conference she decided also to suggest a rather simple Taxonomy assignment for him. She hoped the Taxonomy might shed some light, faint as it was, on Harry's teaching. Lastly, she wanted to keep pressure on Harry to manage his students in a favorable learning environment.

Once Harry circled his two patterns: "*Okay, you guys*" and the overuse of the word "*Good*", Jennifer opted to let Harry work with that pair of uncomplicated patterns. Overwhelming him at this time with the poor teaching patterns she identified could jeopardize all of what she was trying to achieve with this below average teacher. The irony is that she had to work quickly AND also slowly with her approach.

Jennifer's work with Harry is an illustration of how data are compiled and used for improvement even with a poor teacher. She had been hoping that Harry would find some patterns, any at all. To her pleasant surprise at the post-conference, he had identified those two obvious ones.

She and Harry worked from his findings. She believes the literature to be accurate when it suggests that one is likely to change one's pattern of behavior if he/she is the one who recognizes the pattern(s) without the help of another. A good example of this premise is when one first hears his/her recorded voice.

Usually the reaction is, "Do I really sound like that? How awful." Soon, re-taping begins and is not completed until the voice has been improved to an acceptable tone and quality. We are our own best critics.

As witnessed in Harry's lesson, when Harry had identified, "Okay guys" and "Good" (without using students' names), he pledged to change those two patterns. Chances are good that he will. A hopeful beginning will have been achieved.

When Harry questioned Jennifer's notation about the children being restless, Jennifer took the opportunity to get right to the management problem that persists in Harry's classroom.

Harry had opened the door; she felt obliged to enter. She put the observation sheet aside for the time being and addressed the most critical problem facing Harry. She moved the subject directly to the classroom management issue. By putting the observation data aside she was keeping it separate from his management troubles.

When she was satisfied that Harry understood his corresponding problem, she returned to the classroom data where Harry found the two simple patterns *he* had *discovered!*

During the conference, it is customary to work only with the classroom data from the lesson observed. This keeps the focus on the teacher's most recent instruction. However, if something demands immediate attention, as did Harry's continuing classroom management problem, it becomes incumbent on the coach to address it.

Harry's opening was a bonus for Jennifer. It was an unanticipated opportunity for her to address the problem that was a constant in Harry's room. With Jennifer pressing him, Harry was quick to declare his re-commitment to the classroom charts and the constitution.

Another significant pattern from this lesson that Jennifer will file for future observations is the tendency of the children to respond to Harry's questions with one-word or one-phrase answers limiting classroom interaction and lots of thinking opportunities. Jennifer noted that Harry used who, what, where and when questions almost exclusively with his introduction to Christopher Columbus.

She'll also note at the next pre-observation conference whether he is able to work any of Bloom into his planning. To generate interaction and to stimulate thinking there should be *why* and *how* questions. She didn't press this with Harry because she agreed that the lesson was designed to be informative: not investigative or exploratory. She will, at their next planning session, show Harry how teacher questions influence learning.

As important as finding what needs to be improved is the recognition of positives. Jennifer cited Harry's *change of pace,* when he stopped reading and moved to the map instruction, as an effective tactic. Thus she planted the concept of changing pace with him. She believed he would include this pattern into his teaching.

Chapter I: Boy With an Idea offered countless openings for classroom feedback. Coach Myers will address these as Harry becomes more learned. She underlined only a few examples to remind her to address overlooked teaching opportunities. The wool-combing procedure might have been interesting for the children. They could have been asked how one gets wool from sheep. Another *how* question could have been how Columbus learned from charts and maps and what they might have shown of the world in the late 1400's. She had underlined sentence fragments where Harry could have stopped to ensure that children understood the meaning of those fragments. These patterns were patterns of omission.

Jennifer made note that Harry continues to ask his better students to *bail* him out when the class is losing interest. She could have called Harry's attention to a missed opportunity to slide into a math lesson by using the test score correct responses to compute their personal averages. Fractions are a major piece of the fifth-grade math curriculum. She wouldn't have expected him to try that during this initial observation but could, in the future, show him how to transition from one subject to another when a learning opportunity arises.

Closing a lesson properly is extremely important. It is fundamental to good instruction. Harry's closing of the social studies lesson was weak. The data showed that he abruptly moved from Columbus, a social studies lesson, to a math lesson without warning.

A good teacher takes a few minutes at the end of any lesson to wrap up what has been the essence of the lesson. The competent teacher reviews the lesson with the class, tells the students what will come next and how everything is tied together.

Children are reminded to tell their parents about the lesson when their parents ask, "What did you learn in school today?" If the lesson has homework implications, the students should know why. This approach to closing a lesson, unlike a stop and go finish, is an important teaching skill. It keeps students aware of the sequence of lessons. Jennifer reminds herself to work with Harry on lesson closure. There is so much more to do with this teacher. Will she succeed or will she have to go sheepishly to Bernard Green and admit she made a mistake recommending Harry for Clarksdale and Old River.

Jennifer's written summary of the conference will go to Harry for his reaction and comment regarding accuracy and clarity. She will provide a final copy for Harry to sign and to use in planning for her next observation. Jennifer will file the signed copy for future reference when planning the next formal observation. Her notes will serve as reminders of Harry's instruction needs. Her summary will encompass only what was covered during the conference. Her notes and underlined patterns, though not referred to, will be used, hopefully, to improve Harry's skills.

Summary of Mr. Harry Latter's Instruction: 10/7

To: Harry Latter
Re: Clinical Observation 10/6

This summary of your lesson of October 6th and its analysis will be filed for review and future planning. Should you disagree with its content in any way, please see me and I will be happy to discuss any concerns you have.

You and I began this clinical cycle with a pre-observation conference. We reviewed your social studies lesson design, its objective, its action plan, the materials to be used and your student evaluation proposal. Following our mutual understanding of, and agreement with the contents of the lesson plan, some revisions were made regarding the definitions of, learn and know.

I observed your presentation and scripted a complete objective description of all that was said and done by you and the students during the lesson.

The observation was followed by your and my separate analysis of the collected data prior to our post-observation conference. The purpose of the conference was *to improve your instruction.*

At the conference you noted that you omitted three items from your action plan due to nervousness. You said you would teach the missing items the following day. You expressed concern that I had observed restlessness in the class when I arrived. At that point in the conference we talked about the importance of classroom management and discipline. You agreed to immediately re-employ the class constitution, the posted student responsibilities and rules in a consistent fashion to ameliorate this continuing concern.

Next, you identified two patterns that you chose to improve immediately. We also discussed the importance of pausing when children are asked a question. You decided on a series of new reward responses that you would employ and assured me that I would see that change should I come to your class as early as the following day. Along with that change we agreed that children like to hear their names from their teacher and so, again you agreed to begin the practice of calling your students by name. You stated that you understood the importance of a pause when used as a teaching technique.

We spent time discussing Benjamin Bloom's Taxonomy. You accepted the challenge to work three or four of his knowledge skills into the next clinically observed lesson.

Prior to our next pre-observation, please refer to this summary as you prepare your objective.

Your coach and partner,
Jennifer

Harry read the summary and decided that it was comprehensive and accurate. He told Jennifer he had no problem with it. They exchanged signed copies.

Harry was relieved that his first experience with clinical supervision was over. He was not sure how he felt about continuing under this kind of scrutiny. He recognized a few shortcomings that he wished Jennifer had not recorded in the summary. But, all in all he felt better about the process though his kids did not respond the way he wished they would have while he was being observed.

Jennifer, meanwhile, believed she had made some small headway with Harry and that she accomplished her objectives for their first clinical together.

She'll work at home and carefully scan the patterns she collected. Further, she'll create a plan for Harry's growth. She'll schedule another clinical within two weeks and will continue to stroll through Harry's room looking at the patterns that need work. She has much to teach her inept partner about what is expected of a competent Clarksdale teacher. She'll coach him daily as she continues to work as his partner. She may decide to teach his class for a couple of hours, have Harry observe and record patterns.

Chapter 18: Teaching AND Learning

Because of Harry's limited skills, the patterns he found in Jennifer's data as previously described are simple and obvious. Harry looked only for teaching patterns. As important as teacher patterns are, learning patterns are equally important. All teaching should promote learning and intellectual growth. Jennifer is cognizant that Harry is not yet mindful of student patterns. She is determined to drum that into Harry's consciousness. It's vital for teachers to recognize patterns that reflect students' progress toward independent learning. The teacher's first obligation is to teach students; not just subject matter. For children's learning to occur optimally, a superior teacher must guide them, teach them and challenge them. To do that a teacher has to be astute and observant of student learning behavior. Harry remains fixed on what *he* is doing.

Therein lies still another dilemma facing Jennifer. Her responsibility for coaching Harry to become competent is a considerable challenge. She had hoped for a quick miracle via intensive coaching procedures. A miraculous cure isn't about to occur.

As she ponders what to do with Harry she realizes that she isn't going to change him with the tiny steps she believed would jump-start him.

Following a couple of restless nights Jennifer decides to change tactics. It's time to perform major instructional surgery on her patient followed by a miraculous prescription to turn him into a capable teacher as quickly as possible. She must do everything she can to make a competent teacher of this intelligent but oblivious man. Because he's bright, she continues to believe he can do it. Attitude toward the children, improved teaching skills and growth of his students must be kneaded, shaped and molded into a refined learning organism. Jennifer's task is monumental. She must not only build up Harry's feeble teaching methods but assist him to recognize the children's learning needs as well.

Teaching is not an easy job. It never was and in today's culture with society pulling and tugging in so many directions a teacher's job is especially demanding.

A teacher like Harry is a burden on the children. He remains mired in rudimentary management methods with crude discipline techniques, which make it next to impossible for him to create a positive learning environment. His current teaching focus is two-fold and woefully weak: to implement a simple reward system and to call children by their names; it's already early October.

Harry's approach to teaching is like too many others in the profession: stand in front of the class and talk while expecting students to sit still, be quiet and regurgitate incessant spiels. This method, with some recent modification, has been the traditional mode for a long line of teachers since the establishment of public schools. Fortunately many have shed this milk wagon approach. Students today are bombarded with so many stimulating activities outside of school that sitting and listening to a Harry Latter all day is simply counterproductive. Children must be motivated and active in the pursuit of learning; Harry seems unable or unwilling to make the effort necessary to upgrade his skills and provide a productive learning climate for his class.

Dr. Myers observes negative student patterns in Harry's classes: restlessness, boredom and lack of enthusiasm. The minuscule changes Harry is working on may help a bit but will do little to get the children excited and involved in active learning.

Jennifer hoped that the first small steps of a reward system and the use of children's names would begin the long journey to competence. But Harry is still wearing the shoes of a neophyte and she is becoming more concerned. It is Jennifer's daunting challenge to bring him from his talking-teacher role to that of an instructional leader of children. In an effort to have him see the light Jennifer shared an old Chinese proverb with Harry: "*tell me and I will forget, show me and I may remember, involve me and I will understand.*"

Jennifer, at home, finishes dinner and begins to work on a plan for Harry that she hopes will be logical and meaningful. She compiles a list of teaching patterns with brief examples of each for Harry to emulate. She'll meet with Harry and go over each item on the list. He must understand what he has to do to facilitate learning for his students. She tempers her thinking with caution; do not paralyze him. Make him as comfortable as possible when working with patterns. It will be up to Harry, with her help, to begin to demonstrate his grasp of the teaching act. There is little time to waste.

Dr. Myers functions at a sophisticated level of instruction with her competent teachers. They work on subtleties, a pinch here and a tweak there. They know what is expected and they are committed to the philosophy of helping youngsters become active learners. They trust and rely on Jennifer to assist them to improve. She doesn't have this same luxury with Harry.

The more she thinks of Harry's ineptness, the more she realizes she's kidding herself. She has to act now. She decides to stop the clinical process with Harry and begin intensive daily work with him. She doesn't want to taint the clinical supervision model. To contaminate the clinical formula would be to undermine a method that she is committed to keeping pure. She will rely on defining patterns for Harry. Her line of attack will be direct and demanding. It's her only chance to bring him up to speed.

Jennifer will intervene immediately. Like any good leader she must bite the bullet and take the high road on behalf of the children. She designs a blueprint for Harry. Basically, she is preparing an abbreviated teaching manual for him containing information that he should have acquired in college. She gives her completed work a title, saves it on her hard drive and prints two copies.

Teaching Strategies
Teacher and Student Patterns
Statements, Definitions and Suggestions

Classroom Management & Discipline: Effective instruction can only be achieved in an organized classroom. Actions to be taken by teacher: greet children as they enter the classroom; arrange seating conducive to learning; have children begin work when they reach their desks; ensure that comportment guidelines are visible to remind children of their duties; provide a daily schedule of assignments and responsibilities; require respect; be consistent regarding the implementation of class rules; establish routines. The classroom must be organized and neat.

Teaching to Planned Objectives: The teacher writes effective objectives. The teacher teaches to the objectives. The teacher uses the four following actions to help ensure that objective(s) are met: tells pupils what the objective is; asks questions of pupils to ensure their understanding of the objective; designs effective instructional activities for meeting the objective; takes specific actions to support student efforts and responds to questions.

Motivation: The skillful teacher motivates students. The teacher employs a variety of motivation techniques. The teacher is able to evaluate the motivation procedures according to student response. The teacher's oral and body language that signal good work are good motivators. A little known fact is that children are motivated by their own work, actions and successes when afforded the opportunity.

Lesson Content: The lesson content must be appropriate for the students. The content is consistent with the curriculum requirements and standards.

Communicating: The teacher communicates clearly, using precise language with the children and their parents. The teacher is an effective writer and conveys classroom happenings periodically to parents. The teacher is sensitive to, and respectful of student needs and parent concerns.

Questioning: The teacher poses stimulating questions to the class. The questioning pattern employed by the teacher varies; questions beginning with what, who, when or where will lead to teacher dominated and directed lessons and one-word responses from children. Those four question words tend to elicit factual rather than imaginative responses and mostly lead to ennui. Such questions are to be used judiciously and with foresight. *Why* and *how* questions encourage and challenge student thinking. The intent of questioning is to probe student understanding and to stimulate learning. When planning questions to ask children, Bloom's Taxonomy is an excellent resource to consult.

Checking for Understanding: Teachers need to promote student understanding. Bloom's Taxonomy assists teachers in recognizing clues to student understanding. While instructing or guiding children to understand, teachers modify or adjust the lesson as necessary to suit the learning needs of the students and to take advantage of *teachable* moments that lead to understanding. The teacher has a variety of ways to check for understanding.

Ending a Lesson: The teacher demonstrates an ability to effectively end the lesson. The teacher is able to bring the lesson segments together. The teacher and the class have time at the end of a lesson to review what has been learned. Good lesson closure is important.

Teacher is Sensitive to Students' Affective Domain Students are human and vulnerable. They come to school from a variety of situations and backgrounds; good and bad. Their emotions are fragile. Each must be valued accordingly.

Jennifer includes in her plan the observation skills that she commonly employs in the classroom. In effect Harry will be aware of what she's seeking. Her skills are sharply honed and imbedded in her repertoire. They correlate with the teaching patterns she will present to Harry:

Observing the Teacher

The coach collects verbatim and visible data regarding specific patterns during her observations of:

classroom management & discipline
teaching to planned objectives
lesson content
motivation skills
communication skills
questioning patterns (to be selected and determined by lesson objectives)
checking for understanding
lesson closure
lesson connections (showing correlation between one lesson and the next)
guided practice
preparing students or the lesson
dispensing information
student expectations
teacher modeling
teacher sensitivity

Jennifer knows that Harry needs more than the out-line she employs with her competent teachers at Clarksdale. She plans to coach Harry for several days following dismissal. She intends to rely exclusively on the information she has assembled for him. She's satisfied with her evening's production. Her considerations include a list of student learning patterns. She puts her work aside, takes a break then assembles student patterns of learning that teachers must recognize if learning is to occur.

Students' Learning Patterns

Patterns That Suggest Student Learning: students are alert; students ask questions; students understand (see Bloom); students behave; students are organized; students participate; students demonstrate skill development; student time on task shows their level of involvement; students show progress within the guidelines of Bloom's Taxonomy from knowledge through evaluation; student understanding is demonstrated in a variety of ways: speaking, writing, modeling, creating. Students know what to do to begin the day; students participate in closure of lessons.

Dr. Myers decides on her strategy. She will begin her coaching sessions with Harry immediately in an effort to help him as quickly as possible while assuring him that the sessions are for his instructional improvement. She will inform Harry that she is dropping the formal supervision cycle temporarily to coach him without delay. She will show Harry what he needs to work on to become a competent Clarksdale teacher.

On the following day Jennifer appears at Harry's room as the class is dismissed.

"Harry, do you have plans this afternoon?"

"Well, yes, I do as a matter of fact. I have a dental appointment. Is there a problem?"

"Harry, I've designed a set of guidelines that I'd like to go over with you and it will take three afternoons after school."

"Oh," is Harry's surprised response. "Did I do something wrong?"

"Well, it's really about doing something right. Can we use the next three afternoons to examine what I think will be useful information to help you recognize the skills necessary to motivate the kids and move them forward."

"Jennifer, I used the reward system and the names as I promised and the kids seemed to like it. We reviewed the rules and responsibilities that they put into the constitution. I'm doing what we agreed I should do. I'm even pausing."

"Yes, I know, and I am committed to continuing with that beginning. What I want to do is give you a blueprint of what is necessary to light a fire under these kids. I believe it'll be valuable to you if it helps you to understand what is expected in all classrooms of Clarksdale. Obviously you are aware of the importance we place on Bloom's Taxonomy. We need you to begin using the Taxonomy. You'll need to adopt new teaching patterns."

"I guess I'm surprised and a little disappointed."

"Perhaps you are but I know that unless we move more quickly we are going to lose these youngsters. My intent is for us to avoid that by working together and helping to put a chronological plan together as soon as possible."

Harry realized that he had no choice and hesitantly agreed to meet with Jennifer after school the following day. On Wednesday they began by clarifying the various patterns that Jennifer had compiled for him. Jennifer felt the time spent was productive. She concluded that Harry understood the examples she shared with him. The next afternoon was dedicated to studying how to change Harry's teaching habits from thoughtless patterns to meaningful ones.

Because classroom management and discipline had been addressed a number of times related to specific lapses, Harry's commitment to these needs was always in question. Harry needed no further clarification but required constant reminders of their importance. The bulk of the time on the second afternoon was dedicated to helping Harry with "how to's" with an emphasis on teaching to planned objectives, motivation and questioning patterns. Jennifer's paper provided examples of each; she coaxed, prodded and urged Harry to come up with some on his own.

The third afternoon was used as an information session. Jennifer shared with Harry a list of the various patterns she looks for following the verbatim and descriptive compilation of classroom events. This, she believes, will underscore and support the pattern list she gave him by helping him to understand the interface of the two. Also at the third meeting she focused on the importance of children's learning patterns. How do kids, through their behavior, signal to the teacher that they are learning? "This," she told Harry, "must be a result of how you teach and guide your youngsters."

Jennifer ended the meeting by reviewing their three days of work together. She re-enforced the importance of the tasks that lay ahead for Harry. She assured him of her assistance, availability and support. She made certain that she conveyed her confidence in his ability to implement new patterns. She emphasized her awareness that Harry needs some time to become comfortable with these responsibilities. He can take small steps but they must lead to improved skills.

She hoped the three sessions would help Harry to meet the standards expected of all her teachers. We'll take leave of Harry for now and review his progress in mid-December.

Chapter 19: Harry's Counterpart

Dr. Jennifer Myers' first and undeviating priority is to ensure that classroom instruction is of the quality the children deserve and the community expects. Her responsibilities for all facets of running a superior educational institution must be managed and tended to daily. Her job is difficult and endless.

Principals must work determinedly and tirelessly to maintain a successful school. Jennifer's preference would be to spend a half-day everyday supervising instruction, assisting teachers to improve and observing student progress. With her many other responsibilities she has to settle for as much time as she is able to protect for coaching her staff. Unless there is an emergency, which is common in a schoolhouse full of active kids, she guards, at all costs, her scheduled time for clinical cycles.

Today Jennifer has a supervision cycle scheduled with Grace Linn, a polished, talented, enthusiastic and outstanding fifth-grade teacher, in other words, the exact opposite of Harry. Grace is an expert who is currently in her fifth year of teaching, the same number of years in the classroom as Harry. Subsequent to Jennifer's work with Harry a couple of days ago, coaching Grace is like boarding a luxury liner following several days in rough waters on a barge. Grace, she knows, will be completely and comprehensively prepared. Both Harry's and Grace's lessons were planned to introduce a new topic to their respective classes.

As the two colleagues meet to review the lesson plan, Grace lays out her objective for Jennifer, an opening lesson about electricity.

Introduction to Electricity 10/20

Objective for Lesson # 1 on Electricity

The students will become acquainted with the mystery of electricity, its power and its value in our lives. They will discover that electricity moves through a circuit. They will demonstrate how electricity moves through a simple circuit. The children will begin to develop an *electricity* vocabulary.

Action Plan:

1. Entice students with an invisible mystery guest presently in the classroom
2. Ask if there are any magicians in the class?
3. Write children's guesses about mystery magician on the board
4. Expand to electric circuitry with provocative questions (discussion)
5. Record students' "electricity" vocabulary on the board
6. Life today without electricity. Can children imagine life without electricity?
7. Living in the past without electricity (discussion)
8. Assist with this part of the discussion
9. Involve children in a demonstration of electric current using students and fifteen tennis balls
10. How do we get electricity into our homes? (homework research)
11. Dispense materials for children to produce a simple circuit
12. Seek 100% participation.
13. Closure: wrap-up time and review

Materials:

Thin insulated wire with stripped ends, 10 D alkaline batteries, 10 tiny flashlight bulbs, fifteen tennis balls from gym teacher

Evaluation:

1. Count number of children actively participating
2. Check success of experiments and children's ability to verbalize what happened
3. Record results

Grace reminds Jennifer this lesson is an introductory lesson hence it will be directed to some extent. It's the beginning of a unit of study about electricity; several lessons will be required to complete this science curriculum requirement and achieve this science standard for 5th graders.

Projecting ahead Grace tells Jennifer that the children, at some point during this unit of study, will learn something about Luigi Galvani, Alessandro Volta, Michael Farraday, George Westinghouse, Andre Ampere, George Ohm, Thomas Edison and Benjamin Franklin. She will lead the children to discover that many electric terms come from these scientists' names. She will link Franklin with America's early electricity experiments with lightning and later have the class research Franklin's scientific, literary and patriotic contributions to our nation and the world. Jennifer listens as Grace explains her action plan and its extension over the course of the unit on electricity.

"The materials listed here will be used by the children," she informs Jennifer. She completes her presentation by describing her evaluation plan. She will judge the groups by recording their attempt to create a simple circuit.

Grace tells Jennifer that she'll begin the lesson by asking the class if anyone knows any magic tricks they can show their classmates. Then she'll motivate the children with her invisible mystery magician, *Mr. Electricity*. She'll use their answers to engage them in a free-association exercise to begin the lesson. Before the children are grouped for their attempt to make their own electric circuits, they will act out a circuit with tennis balls. She will organize the class into a large circle. She'll ask them what they are demonstrating in addition to forming a circle, (a circuit). The tennis balls will be handed from one student to another, a tangible display of how electricity flows through a circuit

Grace asks if Jennifer has any suggestions for making the lesson more helpful for the kids. "Does the planned pacing seem to be about right? Do you think the lesson has enough variety, enough oomph?"

Jennifer is supportive of Grace's objectives, action plan and planned closure.

"We'll see won't we?" Jennifer replies. "I like the idea of the invisible mystery guest. I'm sure that'll motivate them; it would tantalize me if I were in the 5th grade. I notice that you don't have anything about *atoms, protons of neutrons* anywhere in this plan. Should they be somewhere at the beginning of your unit?"

"I thought about where they would best fit. After some deliberation, I decided to build from the simple to the more complex. I believe that once the children have grasped the idea of how a circuit works, I can introduce several more invisible mystery magicians whose names are proton, neutron and electron."

Jennifer replies, "Good, they are important little guys."

Grace continues to explain her lesson. "Once the children's free- association activity shows signs of slowing, I intend to pique their interest by introducing them to the mystery of electricity, itself. This will be the essence of my motivation strategy. I plan to instigate a discussion about the effects of this magic power.

"Finally, I'll assign children to groups of three. Each group will elect one of their team to be its recorder. I'll choose someone to distribute an alkaline battery, some insulated wire and a flashlight bulb to each group. I'll mosey among the groups. I'll use a little Socratic critical reasoning and questioning to guide the kids who are fumbling. Their results will constitute my evaluation. To finish up, I'll have them review what happened during the lesson."

Grace and Jennifer take just a couple of minutes to review the plan. They exchange a few ideas and wrap up the meeting.

It's mid-morning and Ms. Linn's class has completed their reading lesson. Her fifth-graders, knowing what is expected of them, are ready for their science class. Jennifer enters to find the class prepared and listening.

<u>NOTE</u>: Significant portions of Grace's lesson will be presented to the reader as it unfolds. Jennifer's shorthand is omitted. The purpose of offering this second lesson is to contrast Grace's lesson, filled with information, questions, activities and enthusiasm, with Harry's dull and shallow work. Grace is the conductor of an orchestrated lesson: a talented leader of her student ensemble, the antithesis of Harry, who is ineffectual, boring and plodding: a soloist playing a kazoo.

Following is Jennifer's transcription of what she observes. I have omitted the specific identification of each student. It's not necessary to repeat here.

Co=Coach's notes; T=Teacher; S=Student; Ss=several students; underlined words/phrases signify coach's observed patterns.

T. "Are any of you magicians?"

Co. <u>Three hands raised</u>.

T. "And what magic can you perform, Kathy?"

K. "Well it's a trick that purifies water. It's an old Indian way to make water pure. I can drop a pushpin into a glass of water and make it dance. When it dances then it's purified!"

T. "Kathy, that's fascinating! Why don't you fill a glass with water and show us. Here, I have a pushpin and you can demonstrate your magic for all of us." (encouragement)

K. "Can I whisper something to you first, Mrs. Linn?"

T. "Of course you *can*, but would you like permission to do so?"

Co. English grammar lesson (teachable moment) between the correct usage of *may* and *can.*

K. "May I?"

T. "Come on up."

Co. Kathy whispers to her teacher, "I really need a bottle of soda water."

T. "Oooh my gosh, that's something I don't have. Why don't you see if your parents will allow you to bring one tomorrow. You can do your trick then."

K. "O.K."

T. To the class, "Kathy needs another prop so she'll do her magic tomorrow. Brad, what do you have?"

B. "I think I need something from home too."

T. "Well, class, our magicians need more time. You can tell me at the end of the day what you need to perform your magic, O.K. Brad?"

B. "Yup."

T. "Now I'm going to tell you about a magician who can do astounding things and who is always near to help us all with his incredible power. Can anyone guess who this mystery magician is? I can tell you only that the magician is invisible and is here with us as I speak!"

Co. motivating

Co. No hands are raised; the children seem captivated; look askance at one another; eating out of her hands. They haven't a clue.

Co. Mrs. Linn waits; her timing is like a stand up comic's punch line, perfect. (pauses to wait for children)

T. "Do you want a hint?"

Ss. "Yessss," they cry out in shrill unison.

T. "This magician can bring a lion into your home, sing songs and make darkness disappear!"

C. Still no hands; they look suspiciously at one another.

T. "Our invisible guest can make your toast…….."

C. Several hands are waving.

T. "Nykeisha?"

N. "A television."

Co. writes T.V. on board

T. "You got us started, Nykeisha. Is a television invisible? Samantha?"

S. "A light switch?"

Co. writes light switch on board.

T. "A pretty good guess, Samantha. Remember when you played this little game when you were small? You're getting warmer. Are you thinking about my clues? Here's an extra hint, this magician can make you warm in winter and cool in summer."

Co. Hands flying up so high they're pulling their little bottoms out of their seats like puppets on strings. They're exuberant, involved AND MOTIVATED!

T. "This magician can also make ice while remaining invisible."

Co. They can't sit still. There are a couple of answers before Kelly blurts out, "Electricity!"

T. "Yessss, Kelly!"

Co. A Eureka moment for Kelly and the class as they all cheer! (highly motivated)

T. "Here's a very simple *how* question. How do we rid ourselves of darkness? Tammy?"

Ta. "Turn the switch."

T. "Of course, now Tammy, can you repeat your answer with a complete sentence?"

Co. Teacher again takes advantage of a teachable moment.

Ta. "We can make the dark disappear by turning on the light switch."

T. "That's correct and, Tammy, that's a much better response. Class, Is the switch necessary to make electricity work for us?"

Ss. "Yes!"

T. "Now I wonder (extending motivation) what role the switch plays with all these things we named? We know that when we flip a switch we can make lights go on. What other things can you activate (note the teacher's vocabulary) with a switch?"

C. Student responses come at Mrs. Linn like a spray of machine gun fire:

Ss. "T.V, vacuum cleaner, radio, CD player, computer, stove, electric heat, refrigerator, washing machine, dryer, dishwasher, some clocks, fans, humidifier, crock pot, air-conditioner, hair dryer, electric razor, power tools, cars."

Co. Mrs. Linn stops them. "What terrific thinkers," she says. Cars? Wow, we'll take that one separately tomorrow. It's worth a whole lesson by itself.

T. "So, how does this happen, this incredible magic power we have when we turn a switch on or off? Is it simply magic? How in the world does this happen?" motivation

Co. Silence for several seconds; then Rico, whose father is an electrician, raises his hand.

T. "What do you think, Rico?"

R. "There's an electric circuit that the switch turns on and off."

T. "Super, Rico. We're going to come back to your response in a couple of minutes."

Co. Grace is writing all the answers on the white board. The class remains motivated and involved. The teacher has them thinking and she leads them further as she stretches their thinking. She changes the pace.

T. "But first, what would happen if, tomorrow, electricity were no longer available?" (motivation)

Co. Students are suddenly quiet; slowly becoming conscious of such a horrific occurrence. They name disaster after disaster. Could this happen they wondered? They identified several horrific consequences: no lights, no T.V., no radio, no air-conditioners, no refrigerators, Mrs. Linn interrupts and asks if they are aware that it was in 1752 that Benjamin Franklin discovered electricity in lightning. Until then the world had no electricity. "How," she asks, "did humankind survive the cold and, even, the heat?" (rhetorical for now)

Co. **Seeding a history lesson:** earliest man, from cave dwellers to modern times; connections with early American History, Thomas Edison and Benjamin Franklin, all included in the 5th grade social studies curriculum.

Co. Students are rapt as they ponder the dreadfulness of life without electricity and have an awakened appreciation for how people endured life without it. Teacher keeps their minds working.

T. "From where and how do we get electricity into our homes? (pause but no responses) This evening, see if you can find an answer to that question. Use whatever resource you want to find the answer. What would some of those resources be, Steve?"

S. "The encyclopedia, the library, our science book, uhhhh."

T. "Good thinking, Steve."

T. "Now Rico, you mentioned an electric circuit. How do you know that? Do you want to expand the list of resources that Steve mentioned?"

R. "My father. He's an electrician!"

T. "Wow, Rico, you have a unique resource. Does anyone know what unique means?" (teachable moment)

Co. Jill raises hand and says, "Unique means, like, one of a kind."

T. "You got it, Jill. Wow! I'll be anxious to hear what you can share with us tomorrow, Rico."

Co. Rico beams proudly.

Co. Teacher writes each named resource on the white board.

T. "With this list of ideas, class, see what you can find that you can share with us tomorrow. Make your research basic and uncomplicated. I'll pick some of you to teach the class what you learned. I'm going to rely on you to find some answers. In the meantime, would you like to make some electricity?" (motivation)

Co. Ss. "YESSSSS," again comes enthusiastic replies. Teacher holds their interest, continues to motivate, changes pace, involves them in a related activity.

Co. (following is an observation to be shared with Grace) Teacher has enough material from this lesson, including a car's ignition system to work with electricity for a few days. Excitement spawned by thoughtful preparation to pique the class's interest. Children filled with anticipation, she has the class stand and stretch. (change of pace)

Grace has class form a circle.

T. "Now," she says, "we're going to simulate an electric current. What does simulate mean, Mike?" (always challenging)

Co. Teacher gets tennis balls.

M. "It means to imitate something."

T. "Very good, Michael and I like your complete sentence. I'm going to hand Carol the balls one at a time and she's going to hand each one, as I give them to her, to the next person in the circle who, in turn, will hand it to the next and so on until they come back to Carol. We're going to simulate the flow of electrons though a circuit. What constitutes the circuit, Carol?"

Co. <u>precise directions</u>

Ca. "All of us in the circle are the circuit."

T. "<u>Exactly, Carol</u>, so what do the balls represent, Barbara?"

B "They represent the electrons."

T. "<u>Super, Barbara</u>. <u>What a bright bunch you are</u>. When I say stop passing the balls that'll signify the switch being turned off."

Co. Teacher is re-enforcing the circuit concept. The balls begin to move from student to student around the classroom and the pupils keep them going until told to stop.

T. "Essentially, you have demonstrated the concept of electrons flowing through a circuit."

<u>NOTE:</u> The use of tangible objects and/or people to learn an abstract concept can be a powerful teaching tool.

Co. Teacher separates her students into groups of three and has Josh distribute the following items to each group: thin, insulated electric wire with bared ends, 1 alkaline battery, a flat piece of cardboard and a flashlight bulb.

T. "Before we begin, does anyone recall what a switch can do to an electric circuit? Beth?"

B. "A switch can turn the circuit off, oops or on."

T. <u>"Excellent, Beth</u>. Who can tell me how electricity travels, Carol?"

Ca. "Electricity travels through a circuit."

T. "<u>Bravo, Carol</u>! And what stops it from traveling, Rico?"

R. "Turning the switch off."

T. "You're right, of course, Rico. Now let's try it with a complete sentence."

Co. Rico complies.

T. "Part of your classroom research will be to learn all you can about the flow of electrons. Please take out your assignment pads."

Co. Teacher waits for them to open their pads and write: e-l-e-c-t-r-o-n.

T. "Did you all get that? What are we're going to do next?"

Co. Class in unison: "Make electricity!"

T. "From what we've learned during this lesson, can anyone tell me how we're going to make electricity from the simple materials we have? Again, what are we making?"

Co. Re-enforcement.

Ss. "Electricity."

T. "And what does electricity need to do its work?"

Ss. "A switch."

T."What else?"

Co. Following a long pause, Rico says, "A circuit."

T. "That's it, Rico! Now let's see how you can make a circuit with what you have in front of you. The first team to succeed will lead the line all week (reward and motivation) at dismissal and to the cafeteria, art, and physical education."

T. "Rico, you'll be the secretary for the whole class. You'll be the judge as to which group has the most accurate description of what happened to make the lights flash on and off. If I assign you to a group, it'll look like a fix." Again Rico beams.

Co. Teacher is taking into account Rico's individual need. He already knows how to do this so teacher assigns him a responsibility.

Co. The students begin to fumble with their materials. Soon a light bulb goes on then another. Within three minutes all the bulbs are blinking. The kids have a basic concept of an electric circuit. Grace asks the first group to have their recorder read what happened.

Co. Teacher reminds the children that a switch does two things and asks what are they?

Bob “A switch turns the current on and off.”

Co. Chenera reads her notes: “Amanda held the battery sideways on the cardboard and Emma touched her wire to one end of the battery and Amanda did the same with one end of her wire. Then Emma and Amanda touched the base of the bulb in two places and the other ends of their wires to the tip and the screw part. The light went on.”

T. “That’s a very precise report” Chenera, “but I didn’t hear about any switches!”

Co. Silence follows the pause. “Well?” Still no response.

T. “Think hard. What two things does a switch do?”

Co. Maria raises her hand and says, “A switch turns the light on and off when we flip it up and down or left and right.”

T. “Of course, Maria but did you have a switch?”

M. “The switch breaks the circuit or puts it together so when we touched the wire to the bulb from the battery we turned it on and when we took it away we turned the circuit off.”

T. “Bravo! Bravo, Maria!”

Co. Mrs. Linn applauds.

T. “Now please repeat what you said so we can all concentrate on this important and basic concept. And, Rico, what’s a more appropriate electrical term than *put it together*?

Co. Rico thinks and says, “Putting the end of the wire to the bulb connects the circuit and taking it away disconnects the circuit. Amanda and Emma were the switches.”

T. ”You solved the mystery, kids!”

Co. Teacher brought lesson to a close by having the children review what they discovered about the invisible mystery magician. Hands raised and kids participate eagerly ending with a description of a simple circuit; one they built with their own hands.

T. "Now don't forget people, when you are asked this evening what you learned in school today you can describe this lesson from beginning to end."

Co. Teacher employs clever technique to inform parents about what their children are doing and learning in school and avoids the classic, "I dunno," or, "Nothin'."

T. "What is your homework tonight?"

Co. Student hands go up again and Grace calls on Tiffany Allen.

Ti "We have to try to find out how electricity gets into our house."

Co. The class ended with the children having demonstrated through responses and experiment a basic understanding of an electric circuit. Objective met!

At her post-observation conference with Jennifer, Grace brought Jennifer's script with patterns Grace underlined; patterns that confirmed the attainment of the objectives. "Have you circled any patterns I overlooked?"

As they scanned the underlined and circled patterns Coach Jennifer said, "The evaluation section of your lesson plan stated that you would use data from the lesson to determine what percentage of the kids participated. I used your seating chart numbers to record the number of each child who responded. We can use the data to determine, not only the percentage participating, but also the number of times each student asked, answered or offered an opinion. I went so far as to try to also note those who had their hands raised. I used "a" for all."

Jennifer laid out the numbers. They concluded that participation was 100% when the kids, who were waving their hands but not called, were included. More precise info was about the youngsters who were more involved than others, again the more able students. Grace was mildly surprised and would analyze those data when the conference ended.

"That's interesting. I missed that."

Jennifer responded, "We can take a look at it before the next observation and work a flatter, broader and more involved student participation objective."

"I need to do that."

"Well, I underlined this pattern. Did you want to do all the directing?"

"Let's see. Hmm, I did most of it. It looks like all the kids' responses went through me. I need to encourage more interaction among the children tomorrow. Of course we agree that an introduction is usually pretty much controlled by the teacher."

"Indeed," Jennifer responded. "We didn't talk about the strategy at the pre-ob so I wasn't aware either until I scanned my notes."

"I didn't plan for it to be so skewed that way but, for the intro lesson, I'm not too concerned."

At conference's end, each felt that the scripted lesson was, as it often is, extremely valuable for evaluating the instruction and learning and providing the teacher with information about her work and her kids that will make her a better instructor.

Jennifer's job, as Grace's coach, was to identify with Grace ways to spit-shine a pair of already highly polished shoes.

Back in her office, Jennifer is deeply troubled as she thinks about Harry Latter receiving, but clearly not earning, the same salary as Grace. Jennifer's always been troubled by the automatic increases that teachers get for just being on the job. As long as they're considered competent, that's enough to keep them at the level of all others on the same salary step. The old canard the teacher union has used forever is that it isn't possible to determine that one teacher is more skillful than another. Bull, she thinks.

Note the use of children's names; the reward system; the motivation techniques; the involvement and participation of children; the changing the pace of the lesson; the subliminal grammar lesson, the effective use of pauses: all positive patterns that Jennifer and Grace use to build future lessons.

Chapter 20: Signs of Failure

Human beings are endowed with boundless traits and behaviors that spill into their work, their social life and their daily routine. Teachers bring their assorted personalities, including assets and failings to their workplace. Their coach, the principal, needs to identify and assess each teacher's instructional stage of development just as teachers are expected to evaluate their students' individual progress. The teacher's coach must be a teacher of teachers.

Teachers, like the general public, come in all sizes and shapes. Their strengths and weaknesses affect their work. It falls on the shoulders of their classroom supervisor to judge their job-related attributes and evaluate them consistent with curriculum standards and district expectations. Some teachers are warm; some are not. Some feel affection for their students; some do not. Some are intuitive; some are not. Some are intellectual; some are not. Some are dynamic; some are not. Some are followers; some are not. Some are open; some are not. Some are confident; some are not; most are qualified; some are not BUT *all* are certified!

The instructional expert's onus is less a burden than Atlas's but the conscientious and expert instructional leader in our public schools carries a weighty load nevertheless. Unfortunately far too many lack the ability to shoulder their most important obligation, teaching teachers to teach!

Dr. Jennifer Myers juggles her daily agenda in an all-out effort to assist her teachers individually and collectively. Each teacher's observation summaries are neatly filed in a drawer labeled *Coaching Files*. She can, at a moment's notice, verify any teacher's progress. At her own evaluation conferences with the superintendent, always held at the school, she proudly offers the file for his perusal. Jennifer is confident that her staff is exceptional with one exception.

At Jennifer's early December mid-year evaluation conference at Clarksdale with Dr. Green, he had in front of him, as he always does, Jennifer's staff directory. He scanned it before posing his standard question, "Jennifer, who are your best teachers, those you'd place in the top quarter?" That was always the easier response to his two-part question. The second, "Tell me who are in the bottom quartile," was ever difficult because Jennifer judged all her teachers to be above average barring Harry Latter. To rank any teachers in the lowest quarter, she felt, was doing them an injustice. She always voiced her strong objection and told Superintendent Green that his question was unfair. But the corpulent Bernard Green was intimidating when he chose to be: dogged, tenacious and relentless. He delighted in placing his principals under pressure believing that some tension keeps them on their toes. His was a shrewd question and it always added a bit of stress to the principals' conferences. After all, there had to be a bottom quarter even on outstanding staffs. The greater difficulty for a couple of Old River principals was that of having to describe in detail what they were doing about their lowest ranked teachers.

Jennifer placed Grace at the top of her list of best teachers with Harry at the bottom of a bell curved rating of her staff. It was gratifying to report on the gains made even with the top quarter. When discussing the bottom, Jennifer always felt she hadn't done enough to make them better. That was Bernard's Green's goal: keep the heat on the lowest quartile.

Spotting Harry Latter's name, Dr. Green remarked, "Oh, isn't this the gentleman you recommended to me in August?"

"Yes, Bernard, that's he and you know it is." Jennifer was a stand-up principal, willing to accept the admonishment that she knew was about to come.

"He's the teacher about whom I pressed Willingham and here he is at the bottom of your list. How about that!

Because of your constant ravings about your staff and your reluctance to identify the bottom quarter since they're all so good, I'll have to assume that Mr. Latter is competent." Jennifer thought how skillful Dr. Green was. He was like a shoe salesman stuffing your feet into tight shoes and selling them to you because you really liked them at the time of purchase but refusing to take them back because you had taken them in spite of their tightness.

"No, not yet."

"You know my next question."

"Yes, and my answer is I'm working feverishly to make him a proficient teacher." She went on to describe Harry's three-and-a-half months at Clarksdale identifying each of Harry's failings and her subsequent actions to upgrade him. Green perused the summary data in Harry Latter's file.

"To be honest, Bernard, I don't know if he's going to make it in spite of my intensive work with him. I may have to come back to you and admit to having failed. Please don't drag Dennis Willingham into it. I basically strong-armed him into trusting my judgment in spite of his own expressed concerns."

"Don't try to protect him, Jennifer, he had a job to do and didn't do it. And I failed to do mine."

"Mr. Latter hasn't failed yet, Bernard, but, it's true, I'm losing confidence. I wanted to show him how the clinical cycle could help him to become competent. He doesn't seem to have the drive. He has to be spoon-fed. Though bright, he's not ambitious."

"He's lazy is what you're telling me."

"Yes, that's part of it but I think it's mostly caused by lack of confidence."

"Bullshit, Jennifer, get off that alibi. He's lazy without ambition, that's what you told me before putting icing on it. I'm not going to spend this whole hour on Mr. Latter. We need to discuss others as well as other matters. I'll have Emma call Eleanor to make an appointment for mid-January regarding your Mr. Latter. I'll expect a comprehensive report indicating his status at that time."

"Yes, of course," she responded.

The rest of the conference went smoothly. The entire session took 50 minutes.

By mid-December, Harry's improvement is snail-like. He is perplexed and uneasy. While continuing to work on classroom management, he prepares his instruction hastily. The discipline in his class is slow to improve. Self-motivation is missing from his teaching. His classroom presentations remain dreary and lackluster. He is too indolent and insecure to exert the effort needed to plan for independent and individualized student learning as delineated in Bloom's Taxonomy and in the district's curriculum and standards guide. He fears that by loosening the restraining leash he holds so tightly, the children will run wild; a repeat of his Whitewood problems.

Following the Christmas break Jennifer knows, the school year will be nearing the halfway point. She's becoming increasingly anxious about Harry's work and her need to spend an inordinate amount of time observing, prodding and assisting him as she thinks about her meeting with Dr. Green on the third Wednesday in January. She sits in Harry's class for stretches of time taking notes, which she dutifully shares with Harry. She uses every familiar supervisory technique she knows then searches out others. There are 15 to 30-minute observations and a series of brief drop-ins known as walk-throughs. She uses tabulation systems and gives Harry a couple of articles a week to read and apply to his instruction.

Harry realizes from his own classroom failings and candid exchanges with Jennifer that things are going poorly. When Harry changed school districts he lost his tenure. It takes 20 months of successful work following a transfer from one district to another for a tenured teacher to regain state approved tenure. This regulation gives the receiving school district time to make judicious determinations regarding incoming teachers. Unlike the termination of a tenured teacher, a school superintendent has broad discretion in deciding on the non-renewal of a non-tenured teacher's contract.

Jennifer designed, with Al Antonelli's permission, an in-service program tailored to Harry's needs. The Old River School District maintains a teacher professional growth program for its administrative and teaching staff. Children are dismissed one-and-a-half hours earlier than usual on Wednesdays at which time the staff is required to attend Old River's professional growth program. The program offerings are sophisticated and challenging and reflect school, district and state expectations. They are based on the assumption that teachers attending are competent and growing. Harry requires a more personalized and direct approach for his professional growth program.

Jennifer's individual program for Harry includes professional readings. He is responsible for submitting weekly reports to Jennifer on the articles assigned for that week and their implications for Harry's instruction.

Dorothy is scared by what Harry tells her. He is feeling the heat. What will happen to their budget and medical benefits if he is forced to leave teaching? Still, this dark overhanging cloud fails to inspire or alarm Harry enough to induce him to commit himself to what is necessary for him to get better. Jennifer, he realizes, has lots of paperwork including objective records that could be used to terminate him. They include summaries of what she observed during her supervisory visits including memos that suggest specific actions for Harry to take to become competent at his craft. There are additional notes from Jennifer taken when she stopped by his classroom unexpectedly. The notes serve as film from a camera that snapped stop-action shots of his instruction. Harry's work is not photogenic. The photos are not the kind of which Harry can be proud. When Jennifer confers with him she continues to be positive and supportive but always candid. Though feeling her disappointment and aware of the tight spot he's in he still senses a glimmer of hope.

Jennifer abhors using supervision as a stick rather than a carrot but she must have data with which to help Harry or to use if it comes to determining his future as a teacher. The purpose of supervision is for improvement. Coaching's purpose is not to be used as a hoe to weed out teachers. Jennifer is resolute in exercising every skill she possesses to bring Harry up, not down. His failure, if ever that came to pass, she told him when he came to Clarksdale, would be her failure as well. She wants desperately to succeed with him though that hope grows dimmer by the day as Harry seems to be giving up: quite unlike her work with other teachers who have grown and gained confidence from her tutelage.

Jennifer searches for signs of children learning in Harry's class. She hunts for signs of growth. She notes some continued effort to enforce class rules with Harry's frequent reminders regarding their class constitution responsibilities. But the kids are tired of his constant lecturing. Yes, he calls on kids for answers and he uses an improved reward system and addresses children by name. He meets the children at the door in the morning sans coffee mug and urges them to get to their work, work that is unimaginative and tedious. There are signs of some effort to improve but his teaching skills remain undeveloped.

Jennifer's scripted data are exact and clear. Harry's class is limping along with their insipid instructor stumbling ahead of, or is it behind, them. No matter how desperately Jennifer urges him to use Bloom's work he just can't or won't. He's like a juggler too tense to perform before his audience.

Harry seems despondent. Though he works hard to gain control of his class by following most of what Jennifer has suggested for classroom management, he misses the core of her message. He has to upgrade his teaching in tandem with classroom management. He is like a tiller of old working a team of two oxen. One ox is pulling: the other is lame. The lame ox holds the other back until the plowing finally comes to a halt.

The contrasting results between Grace and Harry's classes become more defined by the day. What else can Jennifer do? She planned a lesson and taught it in Harry's class assigning him the task of critiquing her work. He contributed next to nothing; he didn't know what he was looking for. She got permission from Dr. Green to hire a substitute to take Harry's class for a week while he team-taught with Grace. She had him report on Grace's lesson designs. Still, he seemed to be in a fog.

The accumulation of her work with Harry shows little positive growth. He is far from being knighted *Competent Teacher.* Harry is taking an excessive amount of her time while affecting her coaching efforts with others. January's meeting with Dr. Green is right around the corner. Unpleasant action is about to be taken.

Chapter 21: Man Overboard

One of Dr. Myers' assignments while enrolled in her doctoral program was to compile a list of traits that are common among exceptional teachers. She was assigned to observe skilled teachers in three selected schools: one elementary; one middle and one high school. Her specific task was to identify what qualities these successful teachers had in common then summarize her findings. She accepted this assignment eagerly.

She began by sorting and collecting easily identifiable behaviors and attributes. She expanded her list to include more sophisticated competencies as she became more attentive and observant. Following ten observations in each school she gathered and organized her notes then used them to pinpoint the traits common among these superior teachers. Perhaps I can make use of my old research with Harry, she thought. I'll provide him with the results from the study. It's succinct and simple to understand and it's compatible with the work I gave him in October.

Jennifer retrieved her paper from a dusty file, brushed it off and reviewed it. How does Harry measure up against this list? Is it different enough from the work she fashioned for him in the fall to be useful? There are overlapping concepts but, she wonders, if she gets this to Harry pronto, perhaps this paper, rife with simple adjectives, could be the key that widens his vision enough to get him on track. And, there are some new items in this list. The paper could be the nail that completes the building of a house rather than the last one in a coffin. Could her research possibly be the missing piece of the Harry Latter puzzle? She wonders if it will make a significant difference in Harry's work. She remains concerned, quite discouraged and only slightly hopeful. There are too many missing pieces to the puzzle.

Before Harry leaves school tomorrow Jennifer will give him the paper. She'll ask him to take it home, compare it to his own performance and do some soul searching. She'll ask him to jot down the items from the paper that apply to his teaching. Unlike the work she compiled for him earlier, this is real. It comes from observing outstanding and live teachers. She intends her message to be serious, clear and pointed. She has been shuffling Harry's cards for these past few months; it's time to deal and lay them on the table.

The next day Jennifer briefly reviews the following with Harry and gives him a copy with her directive for him to compare the qualities that he possesses with those identified in the paper:

During their classroom instruction the better teachers changed the pace of their instruction, varied the learning modes, acknowledged raised hands, advanced participation, praised independent learning and thoughtful responses, facilitated interaction among and between their students. They encouraged questions, promoted respect, motivated and challenged, re-directed mistakes, learned from their students, provided individual help, explained clearly, offered expertise as needed and reviewed lessons at the end of class. All were problem solvers, quiet but effective disciplinarians and well prepared. They organized group discussions and learning activities for their students, maintained accurate records of student growth. They clearly explained new concepts and information.

They were patient, supportive, knowledgeable, organized, punctual, demonstrative, caring, consistent, calm, understanding, warm, courteous, enthusiastic, fair, self-assured and confident. These teachers apparently like their work and their students.

These commonalities were observed in teachers from kindergarten through the twelfth grade.

Rather than accepting Jennifer's work as potentially helpful, Harry feels a noose tightening. He's concerned about Jennifer stepping up her observations; the frequency of her longer visits is nerve-racking. Sometime she stays for several minutes while at other times she's in the room for a half-hour checking kids' work and taking notes, which she shares with him after class. These are not supervision cycles like those she began with him earlier in the school year. And now he has a task that requires a kind of self-evaluation. He fears this kind of exercise can be dangerous and self-incriminating. Harry is always on the defensive and seldom considers that Jennifer is truly looking to help him.

Her classroom *pop-ins* are no longer announced beforehand. She seldom lets a day go by without speaking with him about his instruction. She is always constructive with her critiques but they often sail over his head. They are meant to be helpful; he finds them to be ominous.

Jennifer persisted with her attempts to have Harry apply what they discussed during their sessions. She was relentless in her determination to teach him Bloom's work until finally she wondered if Harry had developed a mental block regarding Bloom. He seemed intimidated by the Taxonomy ever since his arrival at Clarksdale.

As a kind of last resort she hoped her researched list would jolt him to action. She also wished that he would place a few of these easily defined practices into his skimpy repertoire. This is similar, Jennifer thought, to a beginning piano student flubbing basic scales.

"Once you've read the list carefully," she said, "tell me which items apply to your teaching." Those were the words that defined his chore.

He skimmed through the list before dinner. Unsettled by this assignment he doubted that the information would help. He quickly became conscious of how few items applied to him. He did find a few with which he could identify.

He noted that he *acknowledges raised hands* ever since his initial clinical cycle with Jennifer. He now *praises thoughtful responses* as noted in his recent modified reward system. Further, he wrote, that *he promotes respect* but the kids aren't yet where "they" should be. Harry also recorded that he is now *punctual and maintains accurate records*.

The areas that he cited were clearly results of Jennifer's coaching. She had not been able, however, to convince Harry that these efforts, to be effective, had to go hand-in-hand with instructional techniques such as those conveyed in the list. He was focused on the simple. His teaching was like one hand clapping; Jack without Jill; Lucy without Desi; Abbott without Costello; Rodgers without Hart.

Harry, finishing the assignment, could find no other teacher qualities that applied to him. He compared himself to the full list. He found only six of the thirty-nine mentioned in Jennifer's paper: another sleepless night.

Such nights were becoming more frequent as he recalled his last year at Whitewood, which seemed so distant a couple of months ago. Even his social life is different. He and Dorothy have pretty much lost touch with the Higgins' though Harry had occasionally run into Bill at the golf course before the colder weather set in. Their exchanges were only lukewarm. Bill usually asks, "How's it going?" to which Harry responds, "Okay." Harry sensed, when he first approached Bill about leaving Whitewood, that the friendship was irreparably damaged. Where the hell am I now he wondered.

In the morning, before school, he stopped to see his principal.

"Jennifer, I am doing a few of the things on your list. I've described how, and I hope you agree that I'm moving along in the right direction."

Before looking at Harry's findings she says, "Again, it's not my approval that's important, Harry. That would come with progress. I continue to be your partner although a very concerned one." She read what Harry had written. He must know how far from *exceptional* he is she reflected.

Jennifer had become increasingly concerned that Harry's class remained stuck on the first of Bloom's six steps required for learning. They were mired in the *knowledge* domain. The children did all the things listed in that domain. They recalled dates, events and places. They listed, defined and described and they tabulated, all among the lowest of the skills necessary for learning.

"Harry, look again at this list. How can I convince you? You're intelligent; you must know what you need to do; we've worked on your needs continually since August. I've gone over and over again what you must commit to. I'm now at a loss as to how to help you. We can't let your class fall apart or I would be terribly remiss in my own right."

Jennifer never forgot, in her personal dealings with parents, teachers or children that they were all human and, as such, they were all worthy of her respect. She practiced what Clarksdale stood for. She would make every effort not to rob Harry of his dignity. She was on a delicate tight-wire as she tried to balance sensitivity with reality. She was nearing a critical decision regarding Harry. She, at all costs, would be as sensitive as she could; a disheartening task at best.

It doesn't appear that Harry is capable of becoming a competent teacher. Will he show any sign of growth before Jennifer meets with her boss? If Harry could shine just a bit of light through his wall of bungling, failing and giving up; if he would demonstrate some real progress; if he would take a measure of responsibility Jennifer would be more than willing to show him the way. She considers how success is constructive and hopeful while failure is repugnant and destructive much like peace and war.

Can Harry respond? Does he want to? Is it too late? Though intelligent he seems to lack any intuit for teaching. His house of cards has a somewhat stronger base than when he first arrived but as he attempts to add an instruction card, the foundation is not strong enough to support it. Jennifer attempted from the beginning to help him build two houses jointly: one management and one instruction but Harry is too shaky to keep his one and only house of cards from collapsing.

Many bright young people learn the techniques of teaching; the what-to-do's and get A's throughout their education courses. Once in front of a classroom full of pupils, however, the technical knowledge alone, they find, doesn't necessarily breed success. There is an instinctive aspect to teaching that is very difficult to teach in education courses and more difficult to achieve. Some are unable to ever attain it yet manage to teach acceptably. It is or it isn't part of one's soul. Harry lacks that critical trait and is unable to overcome that deficiency with just technique, alone.

Jennifer is not a quitter. She is conscientious and determined to bring the best possible instruction to the students of Clarksdale. Her time to decide what recommendation she will bring to Bernard Green is nearing. Whatever that recommendation is, it will be backed with supportive data. She cannot, at this time, say with any degree of confidence that Harry will be a good teacher or even a competent one. She likes Harry and Dorothy and especially their children. The thought that she's fighting to keep out of any decision is what will happen to the family. She musn't allow her emotions to dictate what she knows she may soon face.

Tough work? "You are leaders," Dr. Green often tells Jennifer and her colleagues, "and employed to make exacting, tough and demanding decisions on behalf of the children. Solutions for the difficult problems you face are why you're paid comfortable salaries." The principals are garnering six-figures he reminds them. Their wages will never approach the seven-figure salary of a CEO nor will they receive any stock options. But they knew that long before accepting their administrative appointments.

Harry has precious little time to turn a one-eighty and begin to demonstrate growth. Jennifer has to be able to substantiate Harry's progress with a minimal amount of time to do so. Does she have time to legitimately recommend to Dr. Green that Harry has improved enough to remain at Clarksdale for the remainder of the year, at least? The sky is dark; there is no calm before the gathering storm for Harry. The storm is fast approaching. Jennifer is terribly concerned for Harry and his class. She has prided herself on the growth of her teachers, individually and as a group. Her success with the improvement of her staff and the satisfaction they've gained from their progress has given her confidence in her ability as an instructional leader.

Her teachers have welcomed Jennifer into their rooms knowing they will get better at what they do with Jennifer coaching them. They trust her wisdom and skill. They are comfortable with her input. She has proved herself to them. She regards Harry as *her* failure as much as it is his. Jennifer is now doing the heavy work. Her partner is practically inactive. The two-person team is falling apart. The mutual trust is fading. The schism is widening. They are beginning to function as antagonists, no longer allies.

Jennifer's frequent observations, her continuous pressure, her assignments, her critiques are misread by Harry. He sees Jennifer as a threat to his job and to his family. Jennifer's hope through her work with Harry has been to provide help and to throw a lifesaver to a man overboard.

Dr. Myers has a greater responsibility and it's to the children who are in danger of losing a precious year of learning. She could take the easier road and milk this issue throughout the year. It would be easier on her to wait until spring and recommend not renewing Harry's non-tenure contract for the following year than it will be to terminate him in January or February.

There will be the union with which to do battle for Harry if he asks for its help. He's entitled to union representation though he does not have tenure. There could be an attorney hired and loads of paperwork to produce and precise procedures to follow. She will be, as she was with the Cassidy's and their attorney, stuck in a quagmire of minutiae.

What principal would want to go through this kind of mêlée? Doesn't everyone know that a principal would never fire a competent teacher, she asks herself.

Chapter 22: Termination

It's the day before the Christmas break, late December, and two weeks following Jennifer's December evaluation conference with Superintendent Green. Jennifer waits in the hall for Harry's children to put on their boots, winter coats and mittens and waits for him to dismiss them before going to his room. She's uneasy. Harry is looking out the window when he hears Jennifer's familiar footsteps. He turns and she says, "Harry, please stop in to see me before you leave"

"Yes, ma'am, I'll stop by shortly." Harry's response, as most of his exchanges with Jennifer have been for the past few days, is formal, reserved and cool.

He joins her in the office, which has become Harry's second most familiar spot in the school. He politely refuses Jennifer's offer of coffee.

Jennifer has no easy way to inform Harry of her decision to recommend his termination especially at this time of year. However, much in their recent deliberations has led Harry to fear such a pronouncement. He won't be surprised she decides.

She is direct, honest and as sensitive as she can be under extremely trying circumstances. Armed with an abundance of data that are indisputable in establishing Harry's incompetence Jennifer begins.

"Harry, how deeply sorry I am to say what I must tell you. Harry, you have left me no alternative. You and I have failed our fifth-graders. Without immediate and dramatic improvement in your teaching, the only recourse left for me to take on behalf of our youngsters is to lay the groundwork for your dismissal." To hear that dreaded word come out of

Jennifer's mouth for the first time knocks the wind out of him.

"Jennifer, no!" is his reflex response. The words burst out from deep within him. "My wife, my kids, what will I tell them? What will I do? It's Christmas." Tears well up in his eyes. "Please give me more time. I'm trying to do what you tell me I should be doing."

"Harry, as I've so often told you, you're bright, sensitive and socially interesting in the company of adults. You just haven't demonstrated that you're cut out for teaching. This is a terrible moment for both of us. But Harry, you have many personal traits that will serve you well in another field. I've failed as your coach. I can't compound it by leaving these kids to die of thirst in an arid classroom. I've been in your room thirty-six times as of yesterday following one observation after another including our clinical work. There have been fifteen to thirty-minute observations and many walk-through visits. I've observed the same problems day after day. We've addressed these same failings since you've been here at Clarksdale.

"I've tried everything from collaborative examination of classroom data with specific follow-up suggestions. I've taught your class so *you* could observe *me*, I've paired you with Grace, I've urged you to work Bloom's Taxonomy into your instruction. Together we customized a personal in-service program that included a number of specific articles, a book on classroom management and a personal teaching guide, all so you would apply what you learned to the classroom. I've provided you with a list of qualities found among outstanding teachers; all to little avail. I can't allow this to go on."

"But, Jennifer, I'm trying to improve. I've only been here for four months. You've seen how I've incorporated ideas we hashed out. Right?"

"Harry, you've been here for nearly four months but you've been at this work for four years and we're still on step one when it comes to teaching kids how to become independent learners. On a scale of 10 we're a 1. This simply can't continue. You know that I have a scheduled meeting with Dr. Green in January to discuss your status. What am I to tell him after I show him all that's been done to help you succeed?"

"Can't you postpone the meeting, at least until February, please?" Harry pleads with tears now running down his cheeks. "I'll work so hard during Christmas break that you won't know me when we come back, please, Jennifer," he begs. I'll get started with Bloom this week. I'll work my tail off during the break. That would give me time to show you I can do it, please."

Jennifer couldn't, in good conscience, allow Harry to fumble through much longer.

"Harry. I'll ask Dr. Green to postpone our meeting for two weeks until the end of January but that's it. And your improvement must be dramatic and immediate. I'll be in your class more than ever."

"I know, I know, I'll do it, you'll see."

"I don't know, Harry. I remain very concerned about the children. They are losing all interest and worse, they are becoming discourteous. Your task is all-the-more-difficult because, now, you'll have to awaken them with some magic of your own making. They have a read on you and kids are excellent judges of good and not so good teachers. They are becoming lazy and unchallenged; habits that are difficult to break."

"I'll change that, you'll see."

"Harry, I don't know why, but I'll ask Dr. Green for a two-week postponement until the end of January."

Harry, dabbing at his eyes, leaves panic-stricken with this imminent threat hanging over his head, which is about to be placed in the restraining bar of a job-terminating guillotine. His commitment is strong but his confidence shaken as he heads home. He'll begin by using Jennifer's *Quality Teacher Traits* list to focus on his needs.

"You'll see," he repeats leaving Jennifer's office. "Merry Christmas," is his sincere parting statement.

He's uncertain how he'll introduce comprehension skills to his kids, the second step on the Taxonomy. He must generate a plan that will require his pupils to practice and demonstrate comprehension skills that will include, according to the Taxonomy, interpreting facts (which facts?), comparing (what to what?). Harry remains perplexed by the two skills. He's a quarterback who has been sacked and dazed. He is confused and disconsolate. Harry has no option but to get up and decide on the best play to call. His coach has taught him a variety of strategies for a variety of situations. Now, Harry has to come up with his own. His task is demoralizing and the Bloom playbook, he has always believed, is too complicated.

Bernard Green accedes to Jennifer's request but tells her that the end of January is his deadline and not to look for any further extensions.

The Christmas break is blessed with snow; a white Christmas. Abigail and Jonathan beg their dad to take them sledding. Harry obliges. What's one day he rationalizes. Dorothy's parents expect the Latter's to visit on Christmas Day. They live in Tremont, three hours away. When the Latter's take the kids to Tremont it's always for overnight. Gram and Gramps insist and six hours in the car in one day makes for a long and cranky ride home, especially if the weather is bad. Hey, there are still seven days of vacation left when we return he assures himself. He'll work on some extensive and thoughtful planning. Harry's personal behavior pattern is always the same: procrastination. The days dwindle down to a precious few. He drags his feet until the pressure of getting something done stresses him and extends his dallying to the last day of the Christmas vacation.

He ponders the thought of no longer being a teacher and weighs the advantages and the disadvantages of a profession that's taking such an inordinate amount of his time and sapping his energy while returning little in the way of success or riches. He recalls how, when he contemplated becoming a teacher, he was willing to trade the meager beginning teacher wage for lengthy time off. In addition to ample vacation time, he'd be out of class early in the afternoon leaving plenty of time for movies, golf, bowling and social activities. His commitment to the children never entered his mind.

A substantial portion of the general public shares Harry's earliest judgment of teaching and its easy life. With most of the population having sat in classrooms for thirteen years or more, conclusions have been drawn about teaching that perpetually and erroneously hang over the profession. Everyone's an expert on education and teaching because everyone attended school. Opinions are shaped by lack of knowledge. The public's assumptions about teachers were made while observing teachers from the students' side of the desks. It's akin to a private second-guessing a general because they both served in the same army.

Harry's dreams of time off as a teacher were delusional. He, first, had to attend summer school for two years to earn his state's required Master's degree. In addition to summer school he had to take graduate courses a couple of evenings a week while pursuing his degree. Correcting papers and creating lesson plans each night consumed most of his time.

The Latter's relied on Harry's paltry beginning salary to get them from bi-weekly to bi-weekly paydays. To make ends meet, Harry's subsequent summers were eaten up with part-time work after summer school sessions, He drove to work in their only car, a three-year-old Pontiac Grand Prix, they bought for one another as a wedding gift. Harry painted houses one summer and worked as a maintenance man in an apartment complex for two summers: so much for his dreams and misconceptions regarding a teacher's time off. Dorothy walked to the bus stop and worked as a clerk at Penney's where she earned a meager salary until she became pregnant.

Since leaving Whitewood to come to Clarksdale he's had to toil much harder and later into the evening to complete his schoolwork.

But now, though disenchanted and beleaguered, Harry had not allowed himself time to think of quitting. He decided he couldn't afford it. Second thoughts. What if Dorothy got a job. That would give me some breathing room to find some other kind of work. Ah, no, that won't do. The Christmas vacation days passed rapidly.

Harry's routine shows little improvement when school reconvenes. Yes, he is at the classroom door without fail to greet the children by name. They proceed to their desks and begin working in a reasonable amount of time though there is still a good deal of jostling before they settle down. Harry continues to use his reward system when children respond and uses their names when addressing them. But these low-level skills continue to be pointless without accompanying learning challenges. The students take as much advantage of him as they can. Harry's reluctance to call parents is a carryover from last year at Whitewood. He knows that parents have spread the word of his public embarrassment at that Champlain Board of Education meeting. Harry is paralyzed: unable to get out of his own way.

Following several more observations, Jennifer is beside herself and very troubled for the class. She concludes that Harry simply can't teach. She again confronts him with the bad news. By now Harry is numb. No one enjoys being in a threatening situation for an extended period of time and, at some point, there is usually a feeling of relief when the truth strikes.

Jennifer sadly informs Harry that she will recommend that Harry be relieved of his teaching position from Clarksdale and Old River.

Harry had braced himself for the inevitable.

"It's okay, Jennifer, he mumbles, "You're right. I hate to admit it and I'm sorry for you and personally I feel humiliated but relieved. I don't intend to fight your recommendation."

Non-tenured teachers in Old River, who are hired under terms of a written contract for the school year, must be notified by April 1st if their contracts will not be renewed. Terminating a teacher at the mid-year point is rare. They, like tenured, teachers must be given written reasons for termination or non-renewal if they so request. They can ask for a hearing before their Board of Education. Their chances, however, of having a superintendent's recommendation for termination or non-renewal overturned are about as good as winning Powerball and Harry knows it.

"I had begun to abhor getting up in the morning more than two years ago. I'm going to say it for the first time ever. I hate teaching!"

"It's been hell for you, Harry, I know. But you have a lot going for you personally in the adult world. You're simply misplaced as a teacher." There was an unnerving and awkward pause with neither able to speak consoling words.

Harry began to sob and hugged Jennifer then walked to the door.

"I'll call you tomorrow," he said as he struggled for breath, "to see what I have to do to finish up. There's no sense in prolonging the inevitable." Misty-eyed, Jennifer answered, "I'm so sorry for you, Harry, and for Dorothy and the kids, of course."

Jennifer's personal feelings were of sorrow for the Latter's. Her professional feelings were those of disappointment. Never did she want to use pieces of clinical supervision for anything other than to facilitate instruction and to improve a teacher's skills. Though she stopped using full clinical cycles with Harry almost two months earlier, she continued to collect objective data for him to see and discuss. She had to shed the coaching partnership and become supervisor. She used her reliable data-collecting tools to analyze the instruction in Harry's room but it was like using a monkey wrench as a hammer. Yet she was thankful that she had the data necessary to make her final judgment.

Constructive supervision to assist teachers to improve is as foreign as Swahili to many untrained principals and supervisors in America's schools. Jennifer guessed that Bill Higgins was inept as soon as she observed Harry in the classroom. When she realized how poor Harry's skills were, she acquired a copy of the evaluation program used in

Champlain and determined it to be an imperfect tool by which to assess and improve teacher performance.

The Champlain program didn't require a good deal of instructional knowledge by an evaluator nor was the word *improvement* included anywhere in the evaluation document. The program's checklist was its feature. Tenured teachers, who were to be assessed every third year, were measured according to a list of teacher standards developed by an ad hoc committee comprised of teachers, a principal and a union representative whose priority was to protect teachers.

The teacher's evaluator, principal or department-head, is required to observe, usually from between forty-five minutes and an hour twice during a teacher's evaluation year! They use the district's checklist in the classroom where teacher and student behaviors are verified as they are observed. If, of the 35 listed teacher proficiencies, the teacher accomplished 25 (approximately 70%), he/she would be judged competent for another three years and possibly might not see a principal or evaluator in the room for supervision purposes for that span of time. If a teacher were unable to demonstrate at least 25 skills on the checklist, that teacher would be scheduled for an additional observation. In most cases where similar *evaluation plans* exist, there is little assistance provided to the teacher to help him/her improve. Those supervising are often unable to help with instruction skills, not possessing them themselves. It's fending for oneself. Teachers have the observation checklist to guide them.

The *Champlain Program of Evaluation* was like bringing one's car to a mechanic after it breaks down rather than using preventive maintenance. How can teachers improve under such a bare-bones assessment program? How do principals offer any constructive and supportive assistance with such a limited framework? And what skill is required of a principal regarding instruction in such a fraudulent evaluation program? Items on the checklist simply indicate whether a skill is observable at the time of the tri-annual observation. There is no digging below the surface.

The checklists are divided into categories: *Classroom Management and Discipline, Instruction and Evaluation*

The items are worthy but are easily carried out by a crafty veteran teacher for a forty-five minute observation twice every three years, especially in the presence of a supervisor who is inexpert in the art of teaching. The supervisor, while in the classroom, will verify that the teacher has lesson objectives from which to deliver the lesson. One can conclude that a teacher only needs to control the classroom, engage the children, show lesson objectives, transfer from one lesson to the next and ask appropriate questions with the observer present.

Jennifer feared that an incalculable number of school districts use similar evaluation tools to measure teacher competence without providing vital instructional assistance. Professional growth plans are often assigned willy-nilly. It's demoralizing to ponder the fallout from such shabby programs. How will this nation extricate itself from these union dominated programs designed to protect all teachers *and their principals?* Jennifer fights her depressing conclusion about the general state of teacher evaluation and its failure, in too many school districts, to improve instruction. These failings are grounds for disparaging America's public schools.

She anticipates a sad and gloomy night. She has to prepare a thoughtful announcement for the Clarksdale parents for the day Harry is replaced and she has to plan what to say to the children. She'll inform Dr. Green of her decision and seek his go-ahead. She'll make an appointment to share all her data with him. As soon as she gets the nod from her superintendent, she'll meet with Dennis Willingham to screen applications and begin the hunt for an exceptional and capable teacher to replace Harry Latter. Before leaving the school, Jennifer calls Esther Benzinger.

"Esther, this is Jennifer Myers. How are you?" Following informal exchanges she asks if Esther is available to substitute for at least a month, possibly more. Esther Benzinger taught at Clarksdale for several years before leaving Old River to be married. She and Rob raised three children, each one-year older than the other. When Rob's engineering job was eliminated from the firm where he worked, Esther's father offered him employment with his insurance firm. Rob Benzinger accepted his father-in-law's offer and the Benzinger's came back to Old River. Esther was a fine teacher and a known quality. She was often called to substitute. She wasn't interested in returning to full-time teaching while her three kids were still in high school.

Jennifer was relieved when Esther said she'd sub for a month or two but that's all. Jennifer and Esther would meet the next day to plan for the transition.

Jennifer asked herself, did I do all I could to help Harry? I was so cock-sure we could, with his determination and cooperation, achieve success and a happy ending. I failed; he failed; we failed.

Chapter 23: Tenure

Tenure laws are relatively standard throughout the fifty states. The reason they exist is to protect teachers' jobs as soon as they have successfully completed a probationary period: 30-months in some states, 40-months in others. In many states a tenured teacher transferring from one school district to another is required to teach effectively for 20-months to regain tenure. Harry Latter falls into this category. Jennifer Myers' supervision and coaching skills represent the paragon of a well-prepared instructional expert. She earned her doctorate from a cutting edge university where the staff is comprised of specialists in the field of instruction, supervision and administration. Principals who possess credentials similar to Dr. Myers' are the jewels of public school education.

Until all graduate programs require rigorous training for potential principals in the disciplines of instruction and supervision, as some now do with a number of others preparing and determined to follow suit, our school administrators will lack the most critical skill necessary to improve teaching and to rid the profession of incompetents, tenured or not. Until superintendents are required by school boards to fill principal positions with instruction experts who are teachers of teachers, too many weak classroom educators will continue to haunt our schoolhouses and fail our young people.

With appropriate assistance from their coaches teachers could avoid the lethargy and so-called burnout that comes from lack of growth, motivation and support. Coaches must toil diligently to keep teachers well-oiled, finely-tuned and running at peak performance.

Dr. Myers accumulates supervisory documentation to support and assist every teacher at Clarksdale. Each teacher's file is filled with reviews, observations, summaries and suggestions, all aimed at improvement. That's the fundamental purpose of her work. If ever a tenured teacher, for any reason, were no longer teaching effectively, action plans and support systems would be quickly undertaken in support of that teacher. If all failed and termination became her last option, Dr. Myers would have amassed more than enough relevant data to recommend to Superintendent Green that dismissal proceedings should begin.

Incompetence is one of several acceptable reasons for dismissing a tenured teacher and is recognized as such by state statutes, boards of education and even unions. But the missing link is between the law's intent and its effectiveness. Dismissing tenured teachers for incompetence is as rare as snow in June. The problem is as much principal incompetence as it is teacher incompetence. Sadly, a large majority of principals lacks the skill, and in some circumstances, the time necessary to build a case for incompetence. Most have been trained as administrators with supervision but a tiny slice of the certification pie. Providing sufficient evidence of incompetence is where principals' difficulties begin and where the involved parties stake their opposing claims.

Without documentation describing what was done to help a deficient teacher, a principal would rarely, if ever, challenge an ineffective tenured teacher. Taking action to dismiss a teacher on tenure without compelling records, a principal would be red meat for union sharks whose aim is job security for all its paying members. The union would be right. The reproving principal wouldn't stand a chance of ridding his/her school of a weak teacher. Union reps, rubbing their hands, would immediately and aggressively ask where are the data to show what actions the principal took to help the teacher in question. Surely, they'd say, you couldn't have come to your conclusion on the basis of a mechanical checklist or just your opinion. Where are the facts? Facing the kind of documentation produced by a Jennifer Myers, the union balloon would be deflated and might become less confrontational and aggressive. It might even become compliant with the kind of evidence provided by a Jennifer Myers.

Reasons other than incompetence for initiating termination proceedings of a tenured teacher are: treason, insubordination, conviction of a felony, depravity or moral turpitude, failure to comply with reasonable orders, violation of a contract provision, failure to maintain the orderly discipline of students.

Initially, the rationale for establishing tenure was mistrust. Tenure evolved from early suspicions that principals might fire a teacher whom they didn't like for one reason or another or that boards of education would begin to release teachers who were moving up on the salary schedule. Teachers were fearful of losing jobs for arbitrary reasons. Those reasons remain chiseled in union stones today and continue to be used by unions to defend tenure. Tenure is one of the teachers' unions' holy commandments: Thou shall not fire a dues-paying member. Their second commandment is: Thou shall not pay teachers based on ability, only for years of service.

William, "call me Bill" Higgins couldn't begin to think of terminating or rating a teacher as poor. First he wouldn't know why someone is good or why someone is struggling. He is the kind of principal who gave rise to tenure laws in the first place. Ask any tenured teacher in Whitewood what Bill does when he supervises and they will look askance.

"Bill? He never comes to my room to supervise. He evaluates me once every three years. Other than that, he drops in to hand me my paycheck. Oh, he'll peek in occasionally, but sit in and take notes? Never. Why in the world would he?"

How many Bill Higgins' does America employ in its schools? Many teachers in many schools will proffer a similar response to that of the Whitewood teachers when asked about being supervised. "Oh, he knows what's going on just by walking through the halls." or, "When there's a problem with a parent or the superintendent he usually takes care of it himself or asks us about it. He's a really good guy. He even goes to the regional farm market early in the morning every couple of weeks to pick up wholesale stuff for us, fruit and produce kinds of things."

Principals like Bill Higgins wouldn't dare recommend the dismissal of a tenured teacher. His one and only option would be to terminate a teacher before that teacher gained tenure. Even then Bill Higgins would be on shaky ground; he is incapable of coaching *any* teacher. And his superintendent is unmindful of the sad situation at Whitewood. Alicia Morea also lacks instructional expertise having jumped through the same old certification hoops that other administrators, including Higgins, did before her.

As previously cited, Harry Latter lost his tenure when he left Champlain for Old River. He went to Old River bringing four years of classroom experience with him. Dr. Myers made her decision to terminate based on her exhaustive work with Harry taking into account that Harry Latter was no neophyte.

Still, Jennifer and Bernard Green were required to follow the state's regulations for terminating untenured teachers before firing Harry. Dismissal action can begin when a non-tenured teacher's incompetence is no longer tolerable or in the best interest of the children. Though legally an untenured teacher can challenge a school board's decision following its superintendent's recommendation, it is unlikely such a recommendation would be overturned. Harry knew, that with Jennifer's file, it was fruitless to fight. Harry looked at her overwhelming data as a tall building over which he could not hope to leap nor, at this point, did he any longer desire to do so.

Once a teacher attains tenure, however, the ball game changes. The little league field with its smaller dimensions becomes a major league ballpark and is much more of a challenge. The game conditions and rules are altered dramatically. Principals who do not supervise have little or no hope of releasing a tenure teacher no matter how poorly that teacher functions.

Recognizing that skilled teachers are golden, principals would rarely recommend terminating a satisfactory teacher. Even a principal without extensive data but looking to fire a teacher for lack of ability, might ask the teacher's union representative, "Why in the world would I initiate dismissal action against a competent teacher?" The logic would not persuade union officials; they demand proof. Without it, a principal is in a no-win situation. Though fully aware that poor teachers reflect badly on the principal and the school, the unskilled supervisor is paralyzed by his or her own inability to rid the school of incompetents.

It is highly unlikely that Jennifer Myers will ever have to terminate a tenured teacher for incompetence: not under her watchful eye. She would only recommend tenure for a skilled teacher. The teachers in her school have met her criteria for effective and productive instruction. Unfortunately, Clarksdale School is atypical among a multitude of tottering schools in our nation.

Objective data are the only means by which a coach should measure a teacher's work. For principals to effectively supervise they must understand the essentials of instruction; they must know how children learn, how to collect data, interpret them and use them to improve teacher performance. They need to know how to plan lessons and recognize learning when and where it does or doesn't occur. Mostly, they must have the skills to assist, support and work with their teachers. These essentials also require leadership at the top, a superintendent who knows what he/she needs when hiring a principal. The superintendent must hold the district supervisors accountable for constructive instructional work with the community's teachers. It is desirable for the superintendent to also have a comprehensive understanding of learning.

Can anyone expect productive schools without a coach able to assess skill, learning strategies and effective instruction in the classrooms? So Harry, a tenured teacher in

Champlain, came to Old River without the benefit of any meaningful help. Basically he was the victim of a weak principal who was the victim of a weak superintendent who was the victim of an uninformed board of education. Yet he was awarded tenure. How many taxpayers have any knowledge of the supervisory practices or lack thereof in their communities.

Too often one can see, on a local cable channel, a superintendent sitting at a table at a board of education meeting leaning back, hand supporting chin, smiling wryly, smugly and confidently but never uncomfortably because the board is interested in numbers, costs, safety, school maintenance and redistricting and he's a numbers expert; a good manager. Though the board might request a report about a program it is funding, curriculum information or test scores that reflect poorly on the schools, board members wouldn't ever think to ask the superintendent any questions about the status of supervision in the district. It simply wouldn't occur to them.

Chapter 24: Monitoring Student Standards

Another factor affecting teacher performance is how a teacher implements the curriculum. The curriculum's purpose is to ensure that all students gain basic skills necessary for intellectual growth and learning throughout life. Teachers like Harry Latter not only lack management skills and teaching ability, they often use the curriculum in helter-skelter fashion. Such handling of the curriculum can have a devastating effect on student learning. Monitoring the curriculum falls within the principals' jurisdiction. Some have neither the inclination nor the concern to add curriculum oversight to their supervision workload.

To assure that children gain proficiency by means of a curriculum that includes standards-based assessments, the principals in Old River must, in addition to coaching teaching skills, confirm that all teachers employ the curriculum guidelines in their daily plans. All students are expected to proficiently progress through Old River's K-12 common core curriculum.

Today, computer technology in some school districts offer principals instant curriculum feedback. Computer programs generate the built-in student standards for all grade levels and all areas of the curriculum. Access to this information helps the teacher and the principal to monitor student progress.

The following example for verifying a math standard comes from Old River's 4th grade math curriculum: *student demonstrates an understanding of math facts.* The principal and, or, the teacher accesses the math facts section of the curriculum to find the area of math currently being taught, learned and observed: *To learn fractions* is one of the identified skills culled from their search. The coach, while in the classroom to observe this learning objective, inspects the work of a student whose assignment is to shade in, with a red crayon, half of the square and three-fourths of the rectangle he/she was required to draw accurately with a ruler, and one-third of a pie drawn with a compass. The coach and teacher verify that the student's square has four equal sides and the rectangle has two equal horizontal sides longer than the other two symmetrical and perpendicular sides. The student's subsequent task is to write the fraction representing each of the above: ½, ¾ and ⅓. When the coach walks through the classroom to see this fraction lesson, he/she can readily see the instruction is generated from the math curriculum guide.

Some attentive, knowledgeable and active curriculum directors have long recognized the need for standards-based assessments.

They directed committees for eons to include such assessments for each K-12 curriculum area. The completed work, unfortunately, was often cumbersome, time-consuming and somewhat difficult to supervise. Teachers did not always use the guides for the purpose they were intended. The curriculum standards were unevenly employed. With school district standards now incorporated into a number of computer delivery systems, a principal and teacher can literally pull a skill or a standard from any curriculum area and determine if it's been presented, is being presented or will be presented.

District curriculum guides and standards represent what a school district requires of its students at each grade-level. The standards are accompanied by measures to determine strengths and weaknesses among the students and in the program itself. They help to confirm student progress and the effectiveness of the guides.

Lists of standards can be easily printed and forwarded to parents making it possible for them to follow their children's skill development. Parents and citizens with access to the Internet can, at the school's website, know precisely what is required and offered to the students in Old River and how some of their tax dollars are spent.

Chapter 25: Kids in Today's Pop Culture

Further complicating the skilled principals' efforts to supervise teachers are the insurmountable societal problems dropped at school for remediation and resolution. Schools are becoming treatment centers as they attempt to cope with a decaying society's contemporary problems: disrespect, drugs, crime, child abuse, and pregnancy (yes, even in grammar school). A few hours in front of a T.V. reveal and expose society's "pop culture" values: hedonism, narcissism, self-gratification, materialism, sexual promiscuity and idolatry and addictions of many kinds. Our *pop-culture* accepts this T.V. fare and now endorses what it outlawed only a few decades ago; the schools are recipients of the fallout.

The void in disadvantaged children's medical, physical, nutritional, familial and emotional needs, has become America's schools' to fill. Schools are saddled with moral and sexual issues while forbidden to offer proper solutions. How can schools define *proper* to the satisfaction of all?

Schools employ nurses, school psychologists, cafeteria personnel and social workers in their attempts to cope with the crises that society hasn't been able to manage: a society seemingly unable to control its youth. Our social order is out of control and the blame has been thrust onto the public schools.

Lacking enough hours, personnel and expertise to deal with these realities, schools are caught in a societal vise. They are faced with situations unheard of just a few years ago.

Nurse Samantha Miller recently asked Jenna Cohn, Clarksdale's social worker to contact seven-year-old Doria

Johson's mother. Miller suspected child abuse. Doria, a second-grader had bruises up and down both arms but refused to disclose how she got them. When Mrs. Cohn reached the home and knocked on the door, the woman who appeared at the door looked to be older than Doria's mother would have been. The lady was Doria's grandmother who appeared to be about thirty-five. When she learned why Jenna came to the apartment she slammed the door in her face.

A frightful segment of the public has washed its hands of its responsibility to its children. The effect is that the school curriculum is squeezed with programs intended to fill needs neglected by families and other societal institutions: needs that compete with time to do what rightfully is the schools' responsibility, teach the ABC's.

Schools have become providers of breakfast and free lunch to many needy children. Schoolteachers are expected to supervise eating habits and teach proper nutrition to kids who want pizza, hot dogs, soda, chips and dessert. Kids regularly discard what they don't want. Is the school expected to force children to eat what they dispose of? Ah, but it's become the school's job, not the parents', to teach good eating habits and proper nutrition. Waste, in the meantime, is rampant in America's school cafeterias. Force a child to eat and not waste good food and face a lawsuit!

Contemporary principals and teachers are confronted with challenges unimagined by their counterparts in the forties, fifties and early sixties when the most grievous student problems were chewing gum, pulling hair, losing homework, calling names and talking in class. The most often used words by teachers when asked about their work today are: *frustrated; discouraged.* They are slammed and second-guessed as they become further squeezed by new curriculum requirements, additions that belong more appropriately with family and clergy.

Impinging on present-day principals' most fundamental duty, *to improve classroom instruction*, are complicated and disturbing issues that demand judicious, delicate and often immediate responses. The principal who is a manager, as opposed to an instructional leader, uses these daily problems as expedient reasons for not providing classroom supervision. Supervision is relegated to the bottom of an inept principal's *to-do* list.

Today authority is challenged at every level and segment of society. These challenges have profoundly affected and shaped our culture and our schools. They have defied our long-established institutions and valued traditions. A societal tsnunami has destroyed scores of our time-honored values. We saw the wave coming in the rebellion of the 60's and its defiance of conventional laws and rules but were swallowed up before we were able to identify or escape its destructive path. Our judicial system, the police, the military, patriotism, organized religion, neighborhoods and families have been radically changed to the point of helplessness during this evolution of a society whose traditional rules have been regularly and inanely struck down by the courts.

Our changing society has made a mockery of regulations and discipline. What is right? What is wrong? Each person decides for himself or herself. The confusion spreads to the schools and is disruptive to teaching and learning. What will be challenged next by a student, a parent or a lawyer? Teachers are prohibited from opining on morality and, in some schools, even about patriotism in their classrooms. Condoms and how to use them are slowly but surely replacing the American flag and the Pledge of Allegiance in the classrooms of America.

Defining standards of right and wrong is disputed and even banned in many schools. The 60's opposition to long-standing and traditional rules, and that decade's defiance of authority and patriotism are now rooted in the schoolroom, contributing to student confusion and further impacting already overburdened schools.

Kids challenge the school, parents challenge the school, attorneys challenge the school and the public challenges the school. Schools have been extended beyond what was, in earlier times, reasonably expected of them. They are now burdened with *in loco parentis* responsibilities outside their capability and jurisdiction. Whatever actions school personnel take relating to any controversial issue, they risk criticism, litigation or attack by one malcontent or another. Numerous obstructions impede the public schools' primary mission, which is to teach the basics, civics and American History.

The schools educate students from many religions and many nations. Some come to school with no religion. City and suburban schools enroll students from China, Puerto Rico, South America, Mexico, Russia, Eastern Europe, Vietnam, Korea and Japan. Children are enrolled in America's schools from every continent save the Arctic and Antarctic. Many come to public school with limited or no English. Unbelievable as it may seem, some street kids, born in the United States who attend neighborhood schools are as alien to mainstream-America as are their foreign counter-parts.

Children bring their own mores, languages, cultures and backgrounds to the classroom while teachers are expected to be responsive to each student's mental, physical and emotional needs. Schools are required to teach the disturbed, the retarded and the severely handicapped, accept failing and delinquent students no longer wanted in private schools, feed impoverished children and, in many cases, provide after-school supervision. While making every effort to communicate with needy families, teachers and social workers are more than occasionally rebuked, insulted or ignored.

An innocent comment in school or a misinterpreted remark can trigger a disturbance or even an uproar that creates disorder. Schools operate within the narrowest of margins. When next Eleanor Haggerty answers the phone, a teacher or Jennifer Myers herself could conceivably be forced to spend several hours trying to resolve a contentious problem. These are the tangled issues that schools are expected to unravel and mend under the constant declarations that schools are failing our students. But, who really is failing our students?

As a new social problem is piled onto the one preceding it, each steals time from the three R's. School hours remain as they have for a hundred years. The school year is basically unchanged. With all the incredible societal changes, it is unfair to compare today's school results to those of the past whose main responsibilities were to teach and learn.

For the last forty-years home support for schools has continued to wane. America has found a convenient scapegoat in its public schools. Kids sense the schism between home and school and many use it to their advantage. Family and school are no longer the trusting partners they once were when both were committed to making Johnny a better student and a better citizen.

Today, many parents of troubled youngsters ease their guilt by blaming *the incompetents* at school for their own inability to raise their children or to restrict their out-of-control conduct. Occasionally an attorney is engaged to be sure the school is held responsible for the child's behavior. Parents who call on lawyers are plenty savvy when it comes to their rights but not usually as willing to accept their corresponding responsibilities.

One reason kids come to school is to learn American History yet some want to know why. Why should they have to learn about George Washington? What's he done for me? Who cares about The Declaration of Independence? "Man, we're living in a different world."

Fix our children; fix our problems is the hue and cry of uninvolved parents. Make certain our kids learn. We're holding you accountable. Serious and emerging national problems such as AIDS, addictions and pregnant teens are forced into the curriculum by legislators. When the blame for critical civil problems can be placed on the schools then society is able to travel its self-indulgent path guilt-free.

With split families, single teen-aged mothers, nameless fathers, fatherless homes, shaky relationships and unsafe neighborhoods, too many kids live without structure and, sadly, sometime without love. Nameless young fathers roam neighborhoods like Secretariat at stud. It's conceivable that one young man could father several children in less than a month without worry, responsibility or consequence for a pregnancy or a child born of that pregnancy. These young men, actually boys, reject any consideration of marriage, fatherhood or commitment. Love is not in their dictionary. Most youngsters bred from these encounters and conditions lack the discipline and motivation of classmates who live in stable and loving environments supported by two caring and interested parents. Their mothers are occasionally teenagers themselves and not mature enough to be mothers. Other family members are called to step in and help. The children come to school to be fed, watered, healed, taught and cared-for.

Early evening sitcoms offer sexual conquests as their main course. *Friends, Seinfeld, Everybody Loves Raymond* and *Two and a Half Men.* The latter, promotes sexual liaisons with several young women in bed with Mr. Sheen at the same time: the more, the funnier. There are so many of the same genre that have replaced *I Love Lucy, Mary Tyler Moore, The Andy Griffith Show, the Bob Newhart Show, Green Acres* and *The Carol Burnett Show.* The basic comedic theme of present day programs is jumping into bed with the opposite sex whether married or not. It seems that today's writers and producers, lacking creative or original ability, can only rely on themes of sexual triumphs or submissions to deliver humor to the homes of America. The entertainment industry's other concept of droll is to portray authority figures and parents as dim-witted adults.

Jerry Springer and Maury Povich and their tawdry, crude and disgusting shows are delivered to our children in time for their after-school snacks. T.V. courtroom scenes show disgraceful situations between and among warring spouses and neighbors. Even Oprah, goddess and idol of millions, frequently features sexual topics unfit for young consumption. MTV and rap/hip-hop (*music?)*

How many parents are aware of the kind of lyrics being poured into their children? The following is a *mild* sampling of the intro to a *50 Cent* lyrics *sung to*? *Rapped at* the kids of America daily:

"I'll take you to the candy shop
I'll let you lick the lollypop
Go 'head girl don't you stop
Keep goin 'til you hit the spot

You don't know who *50 Cent* is? You haven't read the rest of these lyrics or other similar rap garbage that endorses violence? There are two lengthy verses that follow, which make the above seem as tame as songs at a family gathering! They are available in full on the Internet. Do you want to be shocked at what children have access to? Research rap lyrics and then decide if performers like *50 Cent* are getting into school on your child's iPod while God is locked out of the schoolhouse by the United States Supreme Court.

These programs and this type of debauched lyrics and noise, defined as music, assault our children in the morning, afternoon, at dinner, throughout early evening and far into the night. Sex without love, as depicted by most of these offerings, is like going skinny-dipping: natural, fun, harmless, quickly forgotten AND meaningless.

Don Imus airs before school on TV and radio. He has made a career of referring to sex organs as playthings. Kids hear him scorn, disparage and mock those who follow a moral high ground. On their way to school, children are exposed to Imus' brilliantly clever but degrading humor. He legitimizes what he does by interviewing senators, representatives, mayors and even religious types.

Even a President of the United States and Catholic priests have lowered the bar to the point where our children have come to believe that nothing is sacred; nothing is off-limits.

Teachers seem to be the only ones being held to higher moral ground by our culture. They face children influenced by a *do what feels good and what gives you pleasure* nihilistic society. And teachers are expected to perform and produce with classrooms comprised of children swayed by an indifferent, self-satisfying and pleasure seeking adult culture.

Where are the slick-tongued politicians who have questions for everything but answers for very little? Where are the politicos who demand that schools succeed while paying no heed to the hindrances impeding the accomplishment of the schools' academic goals? Why aren't test scores improving, is the only question they want answered. Give me your vote, elect me, and I can go on ignoring the ills facing us. Keep me in power so I can up my perks and my salary and remain a TV icon. The political ego has become obsessed with power and recognition.

Within this jumble of conflicting ideas and morality the schools are expected to take on more responsibility while turning out competent students. Yet, in the face of outlandish expectations and under extremely trying circumstances our schools cannot abandon their mission to educate children. They must not use circumstances outside their control as an excuse for failure. Under the most trying and challenging of circumstances the schools MUST get better somehow, someway.

The somehow, someway and only way our students stand a chance is with the school principal coaching teachers or our schools will implode. Ignorant of the role the principal must play to make our schools better, legislators sputter unclear proposals, always delivered with additional dollars. Bills are passed and legislation enacted accompanied by some important senator's or representative's name forever tied to the law. In the end, without having produced long-lasting positive results such as Head Start, the programs usually, but unfortunately not always, fade away or are recycled with minor changes only to be resurrected and die again.

The many burdens carried by the schools, heavy as they may be, do not relieve them from their responsibility to teach children how to learn, to provide instruction to meet individual needs and to learn the 3 R's. But, for the schools to succeed it's incumbent upon our governments, at all levels, to place societal problems where they belong: with the clerics, with the police, with the courts, with the social institutions and especially with the families while requiring intensive and rigorous training for public school principals. Do our politicians have the guts and the will to hold families and institutions accountable for their responsibilities or will they continue to placate voters at the expense of our youth?

Dr. Jennifer Myers does not use the problems that have been laid at her door to excuse herself from what she was hired to do. But how much easier her task would be if these disgraceful societal problems could be eased from among her responsibilities. She is a specialist who labors and succeeds under improbable conditions. Though Clarksdale has a limited number of the kinds of dreadfulness listed above, there are enough difficult situations to ensure that a teacher of Harry Latter's ilk will not succeed.

Parents and families who support their schools, and, thankfully, they are countless, still raise concerns about public education. They are worried that the newer curricular requirements compromise their schools' efforts to teach the basic skills at all grade levels. They are sympathetic to the plight of their schools and the unbearable loads they carry. But they remain concerned.

One trusts that, by redirecting responsibilities that do not properly belong to the schools, quality instruction provided by quality teachers supervised by quality coaches can turn our schools around. The many outstanding and competent teachers gracing our nation's classrooms are hampered by society's intrusive demands. Capable teachers who oversee productive instruction will only get better with quality supervision. Capable coaches are the only ones who can positively impact teachers. Good teachers with outstanding principals can save our schools BUT society must retake ownership of *its* main responsibilities.

Many contemporary principals spend the bulk of their time trying to keep their schools from imploding in the face of the intolerable demands placed on them. The best among our principals who supervise instruction in the classrooms have a broad knowledge of what is happening in their front lines and the problems classroom teachers face. When asked how the children today differ from those of the past Jennifer's response is, "They don't it's the parents who are different."

There are many principals across America with Jennifer's skills but far too many without them. Where they exist, parents and children are receiving the best education that can be provided by skilled and underpaid public school educators under difficult and, in too many cases, impossible conditions.

To help schools become as effective as they can be, state and local boards must re-direct societal problems to parents and other institutions more qualified and able to respond to issues beyond the schools' mission, which is to turn out life-time-learners. They must appoint only principals who have been trained to supervise instruction.

Good education, in spite of all the negative cultural influences on the young, can then be delivered to our children and test scores, so important to the public, will rise.

Chapter 26: The Secret of Effective Schools

Few teachers today seek to become principals where once it was a desirable professional career goal to which outstanding teachers aspired. The demands of the job as regards time commitment, problems facing school leaders and the narrow gap between top teacher salaries and those paid to principals offer little incentive to trade the classroom for the principal's office. The hours are long with many evening meetings. There's the ominous risk of litigation looming around the next corner.

The job requires a strong, tactful, yet sensitive person, one who can stand up to frequent criticism and a variety of challenges. In many ways it has become a thankless job. Add the major responsibility of coaching teachers, monitoring the curriculum and managing a vibrant institution and one realizes the difficulty in finding top people willing to take on the job. This regretful condition must be corrected if America's public schools are to succeed.

Without skilled coaches, teacher and student progress is significantly limited; we must find ways to attract and train potential principals to coach teachers. If we accept the premise that, even, our better teachers require professional assistance to improve, surely the weaker teachers are in desperate need of coaching assistance. No one stands still on any job. One is either improving or regressing.

Those vitally interested in the educational condition of their schools unquestionably recognize that teachers are unlikely to improve without proficient coaches to guide them. The response to the public demand for good schools has to begin with better leadership from school principals. I assume that *all* teachers will improve their classroom skills with the assistance of expert instructional supervision; teachers will grow from insights gained from classroom observations.

From editors, talk radio hosts and every branch of the media comes the broad brush of rebuke painting a large red "F" across the breadth of America's public schools and its teachers for failing their students and the nation. All the while, the PRINCIPAL receives little attention and hardly any of the blame for the void in instruction.

Countless opinions and reports that focus on school failure target teachers as the cause. They are underscored as the key people in our schools and, of course, they are. Fortunately, the greater part of our teacher pool is comprised of competent teachers. Unfortunately, they are painted with the same brush as the less able. Teachers accused of turning out ill-equipped students continue to receive the bulk of the blame for failing schools. Principals have been off the hook far too long. It is high time to hold them accountable for upgrading their schools.

Any principal can watch teachers teach. In reality anyone can do that. But without understanding the psychology of learning and how teachers affect that learning, the principal is like Emeril's audience, interested but unskilled. To coach teachers and assist them with their craft, principals must have, like Emiril, specialized talents.

Instructional leadership remains the missing piece of America's education jigsaw. That piece is indispensable to complete an effective learning picture. Skilled principals are rare and valuable. It is only the likes of them that can lead us out of the ashes. Those paving the rocky road to school improvement are few in number. Can we be so dull-witted as to overlook and omit the person who occupies the principal's office when seeking effective school results?

When reading erudite tomes suggesting resolutions and listening to silver tongued gurus with tin recommendations for school improvement, one is hard-pressed to find any emphasis on the real solution to our school ills. *It's the Principal of the Thing!* Until we recognize that fact, our schools will remain mediocre, at best. The same urgent observations and shrill proposals of today are similar to those the nation read about and heard repeatedly some forty years ago. Principals were left out of the equation then, and we will fumble our way through another forty years of frustration with our schools unless the restructuring of the principal's job is recognized as a serious need and is begun immediately.

The principal must trade his/her outmoded gear for proficient tools to provide useful classroom intervention. It's time to fix the broken and antiquated learning plant. The principal must become the mechanic who can repair the damaged school engine, who can make it hum, who can re-tune it. BUT first, the mechanic must be schooled and re-trained to use the most modern tools and technology available. That's where federal and state funding must be re-directed.

For decades, school principals occupied an office of high importance in the school and the community. The position was esteemed by the public and competed for by the better teachers. For ages it was a managerial and public relations position. Hardly did students recognize the principal as anyone but the school disciplinarian from whom you kept your distance. Teachers seldom saw the principal in their classrooms. The principal of old was seen in the halls or in the office ensuring there was order and discipline. In far less complex times the teacher was in charge of the classroom.

Principals of yore and some current principals developed a budget, signed invoices, confirmed the delivery of school supplies, held staff meetings and completed all the required mundane, though necessary, managerial tasks related to the job. The principal was the school's director, organizer and boss, one who rarely dropped into the classroom while classes were in session. Principals hadn't been trained to supervise nor were they expected to. Yes, they knew who their good and weak teachers were; everyone knew including the kids and the parents but did they know why or could they help those who were less than good?

The principal's job was a reward, usually for having been a good teacher. Fairly often someone with community or political connections à la Bill Higgins became a principal. Past practices did little to produce instructional leaders who would be teachers of teachers.

Finding candidates with instructional expertise who are willing to become principals is like hailing a New York City cab when it's raining: problematical at best. The cure for ailing schools is obvious but we have ignored the obvious. Who else, but skilled principals can make our teachers better? Can we find them? Can we attract them? Can we hold them?

Chapter 27: Reflections

Jennifer Myers pondered Bernard Green's earliest days as superintendent in Old River and his pledge to train and convert Old River's principals into instructional supervisors. Throughout several interviews, while a candidate for the superintendent position in Old River, and questioned by several committees he stressed his conviction that the principal must be an instructional leader. He persuaded his interviewers that the principal was the means to improving teaching and learning. He assured the various interviewing committees that he was prepared to retrain principals and hold them responsible for identifying the components of good teaching and good learning in their schools and for coaching their teachers to improve. Dr. Green awakened those involved in the superintendent selection process to education's sleeping giants, the principals.

He assured the parent committee, the teacher committee, the administrator committee and the board of education that he would, with the board's support, develop a plan, with standards, that would turn out principals who could and would productively improve teachers' talents much like coaches in the arts and the athletic arenas do with their apprentices.

The Board Chairman asked, "How is this done elsewhere? Could we learn what others are doing?"

Green responded, "There are several ways to do the job. I'm not aware of any school districts that are known for such a comprehensive training commitment though I'm sure there are a few that have programs underway or even plans ready to be launched. But I believe school systems should tailor programs to fit their particular needs. If selected to become your superintendent I would determine, with the input of staff, what we'd need to bring our principals up to speed. I would conduct a needs assessment and bring my plan to you by mid-September for your approval.

"If this nation can be awakened to this desperate need, I believe a network will evolve among school districts working with similar ideas to communicate with and assist one another. Though situations will differ there are common standards that will be inherent in any program designed to develop instructional experts who can coach teachers effectively."

At each interview, Dr. Green stirred those questioning him with an exciting notion they had not previously considered. It was the notion of principals coaching teachers. He shed light on a topic that had not been lighted before. Dr. Bernard Green was unanimously selected in March to become Old River's ninth superintendent of schools. Beginning July 1st the Old River School System would be shaken to its roots.

During the first week in April and with the retiring superintendent's invitation, Dr. Green prepared for his coming superintendency in Old River by visiting Old River's twelve schools. He requested and received permission from the superintendent to take the district's assistant superintendent for instruction, Alonzo Antonelli, with him to briefly meet each principal at their respective schools; see them in their own bailiwicks. Soon thereafter, though it's not usually the protocol for an incoming new super to become active before his/her official beginning, he got permission to meet with each of the nine elementary, the two middle school principals and the high school principal to acquaint himself with the issues facing each of the twelve principals.

Though the principals had been introduced to Dr. Green at an administrative meeting where they had all gathered to say hello and welcome their soon–to-be boss, the occasion had been formal. Green had followed up that initial introduction with a quick tour with Al Antonelli. While driving from school to school with Antonelli, Dr. Green took the opportunity to become acquainted with Al, the administrator responsible for instruction throughout the district. Bernard Green picked Antonelli up at the administrative office.

"Al, I'm delighted that you're coming along to show me where the schools are and introduce me to the principals. As we ride, I'd like to get a handle on what you do. I'd prefer that you not offer opinions about the various principals. I want to get my own unbiased first impression of these folks and their operation. I would be pleased, however, for you to tell me all about yourself and your responsibilities."

"Thanks Dr. Green. I understand. I'm happy to make the introductions and to explain what I do in the district."

"Al, we'll be working as a team so from now on it's Bernie, O.K.?"

"Sure."

Antonelli informed Green that he supervised principals, oversaw district-wide departments, the athletic program and curriculum development and implementation. Mostly, with curriculum development, he laid out criteria for various curriculum committees and appointed chairpersons who reported to him on their committees' progress.

The principal introductions were brief. This time the principals and Bernard Green would be meeting in a more official setting. Green expected to gain some insight into each school's mood and tone while schools were still in session; always a reflection of the principal's relationship with staff and students. When entering a school, a professional educator can feel, taste and smell the ambiance and aura of that institution and its leader.

The two administrators visited three elementary schools each day for three days, two middle schools on the fourth day and the high school on the fifth day. Superintendent Green learned that Al Antonelli had a good handle on his job. He knew curriculum and spoke of the value and shortcomings of current work that was on the drawing board. Bernard was not as comfortable with Al's description of how he worked with the principals. Bernard concluded that there were no observable checks and balances on classroom supervision. The supervision, as Al explained it, fell short of the kind of supervision Dr. Green had in mind.

Bernard also observed during his time at the schools that Al was extremely friendly with ten of the twelve principals but more distant with the other two. He silently wondered why. Bernard wanted to know what Al looked for when evaluating principals and how he communicated his findings with them. Al said that he, with the present super, visited the schools together twice a year. In the fall they discussed the needs for the new school year based on issues of the past and in the spring they conferred about the results.

"How do you determine their successes and their failings?"

"I visit and look for what was agreed to in the fall. I take notes and talk with the principals about my findings. We agree or disagree. Before I leave, we usually see eye to eye until the next visit."

"How often have you visited, say, Jefferson School this year?

"I'm not sure, maybe three times."

"How do you know?"

"I check my calendar."

Both men were taking their own mental notes, sizing one another up over the span of a week. Bernard was planning to tighten Al's schedule. He was impressed with Al's knowledge of the curriculum but unsure of his effectiveness in evaluating the school principals. Al was unable to respond adequately to his question regarding the principals' supervisory practices. He judged Al to be bright and hardworking with potential to do the job he will be expected to do beginning in the fall.

Al was somewhat edgy following a few of Bernard's questions but not quite intimidated by them. He felt he had not satisfactorily answered all of Bernard's queries. He liked this man's openness but sensed the demands of his job were about to change if Dr. Green decided to keep him in his position.

Dr. Bernard Green was already into the planning stage of his commitment to the board of education.

On July 1st, his first day as superintendent, Bernard Green was in his office at 7 A.M. with an agenda to present to his executive team at their 8 A.M. meeting. The team was comprised of Al Antonelli, a director of pupil services, which included special education, a director of human resources, a director of finances and technology, a director of buildings and grounds and a testing consultant. Bernard Green expected his executive team to be committed to their tasks, honest and challenging.

There was coffee and tea for the group but no goodies. Prior to July 1st Bernard met with each of his executive team individually to learn what they do and how they mesh into the overall operation of the schools. In the past his predecessor sat at the head of a rectangular conference table. Dr. Green replaced that table with a round table for his executive team, a not so subtle message regarding his administrative style.

"Folks, please take careful note of what I expect. We are, as of this moment, a team. My anticipation is that we'll become a professional group designated to deliver the best instruction possible to the students of Old River. We will become a strong team. I expect you to confront me whenever you have something to question or suggest and, in turn, I'll challenge you regarding your contribution to this executive group. We are expected to lead and we'll operate accordingly.

"Whatever your title, it must connect to the children. They are the only reason we exist as a school system. Our challenge is to be certain that we carefully think of each move we make as a move to help the children. We will make every effort to improve what we do because that's what we'll demand of our teachers and our principals.

"Always the first priority with me as long as I'm here, will be to upgrade every teacher and every principal through supportive and insightful supervision. Each of you around this table will give daily consideration to how your job can support this thrust."

With his opening completed, Green sought his executive committee's reaction. Each nodded in agreement with one exception. The director of buildings and grounds was somewhat perplexed as to how his position could contribute to better teaching and supervision.

"Mike, you will contribute at this table with your ideas and input. They can surely extend beyond your job description. Your ideas should be as valid as anyone's here. Always remember that your work contributes to the education of the kids. Safe schools, well-maintained buildings, safe grounds, repairs, plowed surfaces, a comfortable environment all have a powerful effect on learning. But mostly, your ideas will help us around this table."

Bernard Green was serious and approachable. He set a tone of accomplishment. He was a determined and confident leader. One sensed a strong and resolute person in this new superintendent. If this first meeting were an indication, it appeared that these weekly executive meetings would be efficient, organized, stimulating, demanding and brief. Little time would be wasted. Green told his team that if the President's cabinet can complete its meetings in a couple hours, surely we should be able to. Written suggestions for the agenda were to be forwarded to Bernard's secretary at least a day before each scheduled meeting.

The priority at this initial meeting was to deliver a mission statement, *to improve teaching in concert with expert coaches*. The commitment would be shared with the principals and department heads at the opening administrative council meeting. It was clear to all that principals were going to have to become, if not already, instructional supervisors.

Dr. Green, before concluding, sought ideas for re-training principals and to determine which, if any, are recognized as classroom supervisors. Al said that Jennifer

Myers was a classroom supervisor: heads nodded and Bernard took note of Jennifer's name. Suggestions for getting principals upgraded were tossed around. The prevailing idea was to organize a workshop. Green asked Al Antonelli to draft a brief and succinct proposal for a training session and bring it to next week's meeting.

At their next gathering Al's work was discussed fully. Before the session was adjourned the executive team agreed on a format, which would be placed on the agenda for the administrative council meeting to solicit input from the principals concerning their preparation to supervise instruction. The basic layout was simple. There would be four afternoon administrative workshops during each semester of the school year. For four Wednesdays twice a year, the principals would be required to attend training sessions to get them ready for in-classroom supervision. In June, when administrators traditionally participate in a weeklong workshop, the topic will be supervision.

Dr. Green introduced the planned training program at the opening administrative meeting the last week in August. By then word had spread among the supervisory staff about what was coming. Not everyone was thrilled though not caught unawares. The local *Old River Observer* had covered the details and highlights of Dr. Green's appointment; the community had been informed. His mission statement, *to improve teaching with expert coaching,* had already taken hold.

Green used the same pitch about how everyone in the district was employed by Old River for the good of the children making it essential that principals assist their teachers to improve. He expounded on the need for the principal to be the key agent in public education to improve the delivery of instruction to children and to ensure that children become active learners in their education. He told them how critically important they are and how they will make a difference that will gain them and Old River's schools respect and admiration.

He offered his opinion as to why magnet and charter schools and voucher plans have become fashionable, but in his opinion, unnecessary if, "we, in this room and those like us across this nation, do our job." He opined that. "Our own schools should be magnets." He further stated that magnet and charter schools have had initial success because they attracted the best teachers who sought excitement and challenge in their work and principals who are enterprising, creative and productive though many lack the kind of coaching skills we will develop in Old River. "

The careful selection of principals to run magnet and charter schools was the most critical factor for ensuring successful programs. "This selection process proves my point about the principal and the key role he/she plays in establishing school success. The selection of outstanding teachers was the next most significant component for building successful programs. There is no good reason why communities should spend outlandish sums of money for special schools when a rigorous principal retraining program can revitalize and breathe new life into every school. As you become *effective* coaches, teachers must be taught the elements of *effective* instruction. We must all be on the same page."

Jennifer smiled as she reminisced about Bernard's first meetings in Old Orchard. Her smile lingered. Bernard Green had delivered on his promise. The Old River district is a rising star.

Chapter 28: Training Old River's Principals

Al Antonelli never stopped being impressed with Dr. Bernard Green. This man, from his first day as superintendent, pressed and stretched his *coaches,* a name Green favored for the principals. They were slowly but surely becoming skillful at coaching their teachers. Like Jennifer, Al frequently found himself recalling Green's rigorous early agenda. He admired Dr. Green's style, his optimism, his confidence and his tenacity. He remembered how Bernard Green took Old River by storm from day one.

Al recalled how intimidated he felt when Dr. Green told his executive team that Old River administrators were going to participate in a *coaching,* workshop beginning in mid-September. This man surely hit the road running. The idea was threatening. Al wasn't quite sure where he stood with his new boss.

Yet he was first to react to Dr. Green's training announcement. In retrospect he didn't know if he blurted out of insecurity or of wanting to impress his boss. Al, following a few seconds to gather his thoughts, suggested that Jennifer Myers be appointed the coaching workshop chairperson. She was already doing instructional work in Clarksdale's classrooms. She could help plan the training sessions' content, establish procedures for implementing the program and share some of her doctoral research briefs with her peers. The other executive committee members seconded Al's informal motion. Bernard agreed and asked Al to convene a meeting to include Al, Jennifer and himself. He wanted to know Jennifer's reaction before finalizing the recommendation.

The three met in Dr. Green's office to discuss the proposal. Expressing some initial hesitation Jennifer accepted. Once the leadership issue was settled the three talked about guidelines for the workshops.

"One thing is clear, we will design the seminars to meet our needs, not some other district's and you need to begin now," Bernard stated.

"To ensure proper focus our training will be called *Coaching for Instructional Improvement*," he added.

Following some further brainstorming they developed guidelines. Subsequent to the Board's acceptance of Bernard's proposal Al would describe the task and lay out the workshop schedule, with topics suggested by Jennifer, at the next administrative council meeting.

Bernard opened that meeting with two minor agenda items then looked to Al. "Al will describe the workshop parameters for your reaction." As planned, he turned the meeting over to him.

"Thanks, Dr. Green. I'll be brief. The purpose and importance of classroom supervision, or coaching, as we will frequently refer to supervision from now on, will be the subject of our first session. Coaching techniques will be presented and described at the second seminar. The third meeting will focus on teaching and learning patterns. At the fourth meeting Dr. Jordan Whittier, a rare kind of professor from State University, who is renown for his instructional expertise, will speak to us about the importance of observing active learning, with the accent on learning.

"Jennifer, as you know, will be the workshop leader and will guide us through our first three workshops. She will familiarize us with Goldhammer's Clinical Supervision model, Bloom's Taxonomy of Educational Objectives, Gardner's Multiple Intelligences theories and Madeline Hunter's mastery teaching assumptions. You will be expected to read the work of each of these pioneers between now and prior to our spring workshop." Following Al's outline of the plan he had asked for feedback and reactions before sharing the executive committee's thinking regarding the second semester.

The first question posed was, "Why Bloom?" Al turned to Jennifer.

"I recognize that Bloom's Taxonomy has been around for a very long time," she stated. "However I believe, if children demonstrate the skills identified in his Taxonomy, we can be assured they are learning by anyone's standard. Are there newer tools? Of course and we encourage you to pursue them to expand your expertise. For the purpose of developing a common understanding we're going to first emphasize Bloom. We simply can't go wrong working through his categories for learning."

There were a few additional questions and several more opinions offered about other aspects of the workshop activities during the spirited give and take that followed. Basically the principals knew that Dr. Green's agenda for this meeting was a reflection of the commitment he gave to the Board of Education when he was hired. Most expressed subdued approval while two principals voiced reluctant acknowledgement of the job expected of them. Bernard noted they were the same two who seemed indifferent to Al when he and Al visited the schools last spring.

Al spoke next, "During the spring sessions we'll learn all we can about active learning and will watch several videos of teachers working with their classes to encourage independent learning. The aim will be to understand the four researchers and the application of their theories to coaching teachers. We will then conduct three practice sessions with the various pieces of a supervision cycle, each preceded by a video demonstration. The initial year's training will conclude at the end of our June weeklong session. For the first four days of our annual June workshop we'll observe summer school teachers in the morning and conduct cycles with them in the afternoon with Jennifer and I and possibly Dr. Green observing and sharing objective feedback to assist with your clinical skills. Hopefully Bernard and I will be proficient enough to help you by then. On the last day of the June workshop we'll work on our supervision objectives for September."

Al recalled that he and Bernard met early the next day. Green asked Al to develop a system for monitoring and recording the principals' supervisory work for that current year, which would be adapted as principals progress during and after the workshops. Though this would precede their completed training, Bernard Green wanted Al to begin preparing for the following year.

"That will be *your* objective," he told Al.

Al began as soon as he and Bernard were finished. He created a matrix for himself with twelve columns, one for each principal and ten rows, one for each school month. His intent was to record each visit with a principal where they discussed and examined supervisory data. He would share the matrix with Bernard anytime his boss asked, to keep him advised about the progress he was making with his assigned objective.

Next he wrote several steps for the principals to record their coaching work with teachers. The principal would assign a number on a file folder for every teacher at his/her school. The principals would also create a matrix to record their supervision sessions with their teachers. Each time a principal did classroom coaching, all elements of that cycle would be summarized and filed in a numbered folder with the observation date entered on the matrix.

When Al visited a school to check the principal's work he could simply ask for number 8; that folder would be retrieved from the principal's file. Al and the principal could then analyze the merits of the classroom observation of teacher number 8. Initially, there would be many empty folders, especially at the middle and high schools but as time passed and principals' skills improved and department supervisors were retrained, folders would contain an accumulation of the coaching history for each teacher.

The first step in training principals to become coaches and teachers of teachers was to plan an approach that fit the district. There is no *only* way to retrain principals.

The content of the workshops had to be determined. Leaders and trainers had to be identified followed by a plan that fit the Old River schools.

"Some of you supervisors may already possess an expertise in classroom coaching," Bernard acknowledged to the principals at that initial meeting. "Jennifer, Al and I need to be skilled enough to provide individual assistance as necessary where you have gaps. Some may know little, others, a lot. We have to find the method that works best for you, our supervisors. But the essence and focus of our work must be on *teaching you principals the principles of teaching*; what constitutes teaching and learning and how to supervise these two classroom activities. The emerging science of teaching and learning must become a part of every principal's portfolio," he concluded.

Chapter 29: Practicum

Jennifer recollected vividly the noise, anticipation and conversation that filled the room where she was about to host the opening principal workshop. Bernard Green had placed his trust in her to initiate this extraordinary undertaking. She had been chosen to chair this groundbreaking event designed to mold Old River's staid principals into instructional leaders of teachers. This was the starting line for the commitment Bernard Green made when he was appointed to be the education leader in Old River.

"Good afternoon folks," she recalled him saying at that first workshop. "Today begins a new era for us and the Old River Public Schools. I need not reiterate what I've repeated often enough. We have a job to do, a daunting one but a necessary, critical and exciting one. The improvement of our teachers and our education here in Old River rests on the shoulders I see in front of me. Together we are going to make a difference! No parent, if we do our job, will easily leave any of Old River's schools for a magnet or charter school. Our community will not find the need to expend funds for vouchers to send *our* children elsewhere to educate them. We will establish a new level of proficiency beginning today, now." He turned to Al, "All yours, Al." Dr. Green took a seat with the others. He attended and participated in all the workshops.

Al contributed several supportive statements for the work ahead, reviewed the topics for each workshop and turned the meeting over to Jennifer.

"Thank-you. I feel more than a little humble standing here in front of you, my coworkers and friends. There is so much we can learn from one another. You each have your own administrative skills and strengths. Any one of you could run a workshop based on your own unique talent. I happen to have one that has been identified as important to the district at this time. So, I am honored and pleased to share my knowledge with you. Hopefully, you will find some of what I have planned, to be, not only interesting, but also useful.

"I have here a list for each of you that is filled with simple but forceful ideas related to teaching. It will help if we focus together on the teaching act. Though the ideas come from a variety of sources, I've taken the liberty of naming the list *Assumptions Concerning the Improvement of Teaching for Student Success.* The strength of the list is in its simplicity. I can't identify its source except to say that some of it appears to be from Goldhammer. It was among my notes and papers from some post-graduate class. I, some time ago, pasted it to one side of my desk as a reference and a reminder. Please take a few minutes to read the items and then, please keep it in a prominent place where you can frequently refer to it throughout the workshop and throughout the school year. I have found it to be indispensable. I've taken the liberty of inserting the word coach where possible." Jennifer handed out the paper.

Assumptions Concerning the Improvement of Teaching for Student Success

- Teachers will improve their classroom skills with the guidance of expert instructional coaches.
- Teaching is patterned behavior capable of being observed, identified, analyzed and improved.
- Patterned behaviors are identified when teachers' actions are recognized through repetition.
- When teaching patterns reflect good instruction, they need to be extended and enhanced.

- When teaching patterns reflect poor instruction, they need to be changed.
- Expert coaches are capable of recording and analyzing teachers' patterned behavior.
- Expert coaches are skilled in analyzing instructional patterns with their teachers.
- Expert coaches can assist teachers to recognize and shape student leaning patterns.
- Coaches and teachers, together, can select teaching patterns to be improved resulting in improved instruction.
- Teachers will develop lessons from data recorded during classroom observations.
- Teachers will recognize social and economic factors that affect children's learning.
- Teachers accept that schools are responsible for providing the best possible instruction for all their students.

Jennifer let the assumptions sink in before asking if there were a need for clarification.

"Does anyone disagree with any of these assumptions?" No one challenged the list. "Are they acceptable postulations from which we can work?" Again there were no challenges. "Good, then we can accept the list as a guideline for our workshops. Though wordier than the *Golden Rule*, they project a similar uncomplicated message. I have never strayed far from this checklist. I use it as a reminder when working with teachers."

Jennifer encouraged input by asking the participants to link the teaching assumptions to student learning. The workshop was underway and the conversion begun.

She conducted the three workshops for which she was responsible. She asked the members to recall children's learning, in their schools' classrooms, that can be identified in Bloom's Taxonomy. She challenged them to describe how instruction could be planned to support the learning process. She asked the principals to list numbers from 1 to 10 down the side of a page and identify one teaching pattern they could recall from each of ten teachers in their schools.

The second session consisted of demonstrating patterns that complemented active learning. She encouraged participation and discussion throughout her three sessions of the practicum. Her purpose, she repeated many times, was to increase awareness about what must take place in classrooms for learning to, not only occur, but to be meaningful.

At the third session she organized and connected the workshop components with the works of Goldhammer, Bloom, Hunter and Gardner.

At the fourth and last session of the fall offerings Jennifer introduced Jordan Whittier who spoke to the various instruction tenets he held dear. He spoke eloquently, logically and enthusiastically about Old River's embarkation on its pioneering voyage into the *deepness* of learning and teaching. *A Noble Effort* was the title of his remarks. He hoped the district would develop a public relations program to keep the city, county and even the state informed of its mission. He told the group that he planned to engage his university colleagues in a brainstorm session about how the university's graduate program could be modified to train potential principals in a new and cooperative way and work hand-in-hand with Old River. Jennifer closed this last session handing out a flyer that included a description of the components of a cycle of supervision, the framework for the second semester workshops.

Jennifer suggested several readings prior to the second semester. Again, she referred to the clinical concept for coaching teachers. This process like so many education reforms has been frequently modified since the appearance of Goldhammer's original work. However the basic steps and sequence of the process remain central in most adaptations. Several educators, who have contributed to the literature, are well known to educators. Acheson, Cogan and Gall have developed approaches based on techniques of observation. Madeline Hunter gave the movement a boost by defining and giving names to the standard practices employed by clinical supervisors. Many authors have contributed to, modified and advanced clinical supervision literature and practices since its introduction more than 40 years ago while maintaining, at least, its four basic steps.

Each workshop of the second semester, Jennifer recalled, was dedicated to one of the four stages of clinical supervision. She had brought videos for each step to illustrate the skills required to become successful coaches. She reminded the attendees repeatedly throughout the four sessions that the teacher and coach/principal were working as colleagues; not as supervisor and supervisee. Flashing a supervisor badge openly or subliminally was to be avoided and only used in those rare times when a teacher's incompetence was being challenged without hope of becoming competent, as was the case with Harry Latter.

Workshop for Pre-Observation Conference

At the first spring semester session principals reviewed the clinical coaching steps. Jennifer played a taped pre-observation session twice. The first was for the group to become familiar with how a conference is conducted, then showed it a second time for purposes of reinforcement and note-taking. She then asked the participants to identify the teacher's responsibility during the conference with the coach. It was obvious to the workshop group that coach and teacher were both committed to understanding the plan for the lesson to be observed.

Jennifer distributed printed copies of the lesson design from the tape they had just watched. She paired the principals and asked them to simulate what they had just seen. She and Al moved among the twosomes encouraging them to become comfortable with the exercise.

Workshop for Classroom Observation

Her approach with the following three workshops was similar. Jennifer asked the group to watch the teacher on the video teach the class. She had the group refer to the lesson design, which she had redistributed before showing the lesson. She assigned four of the participants to practice scripting the taped lesson. Jennifer cautioned against the temptation to opine. "Use only what you observe," she said. Four others were assigned to record student activities as quickly and as accurately as possible. Another four were to write verbatim, only the questions the teacher posed to the children. Jennifer used this format for each task listed in the lesson plan. The central office personnel were assigned to the various teams. Following the video lesson, she had each group analyze their assigned activity and prepare it as though they were going to sit with the teacher at the post-observation conference. This amounted to an exercise with manageable data for analysis.

Workshop for the Analysis of the Data and Preparation for the Post Conference

At the third seminar the group viewed a video showing the teacher comparing the observer's scripted notes with her own lesson plan to search for the congruency and how effective was the lesson. She looked for, and underlined, patterns from her teaching that could be improved and circled patterns that illustrated successful work with her class.

The video switched to the coach/principal who was analyzing the same data. The coach was checking patterns of teacher and student behavior that supported the lesson objectives. Are there any weak teacher patterns that must be addressed? Was there anything unexpected or unanticipated in the lesson? Does the teacher see any area for improvement? If yes, at that point the teacher and coach will prepare a plan for the next observation.

Al and Jennifer guided the principals as they compared their data with those collected by the coach on the tape. She reminded them that, in June, they would be conducting a full live cycle at summer school.

Workshop for the Post Conference

The final workshop video showed the teacher and coach examining their analysis of the data together. Because it is apparent that teacher and coach have a trusting relationship, they can scan the data without threat or anxiety. Their aim is to make progress. The teacher and coach work in harmony to clarify the lesson and its effect on the children. They substantiate their findings with patterns and decisions about what, if anything, the teacher will do differently for the next lesson. Once something is identified on which to work, the conference shifts to ideas for developing the next objective.

Unlike the previous pieces of the cycle, Jennifer and Al team the principals in pairs and assign one to be the teacher and the other, the coach. They focus on the information from the video. Al and Jennifer take notes on how the workshop coaches function at their *pretend* conference. This piece is added to give feedback to the coaches regarding their skills during the simulated conferences.

Jennifer summarized and reviewed, with the conferees, the steps in a clinical cycle. She reminded all that they would apply these skills for a full week at summer school. She and Al would observe their progress in all phases of their practicum.

Chapter 30: On-Site Training

The summer workshop for principals following Dr. Green's first year at the helm of the Old River School System was thorough and exacting. The principals practiced their skills and capped their early summer work by writing their objectives for coaching their teachers in the fall. They were treated to a video presentation of a coach working with a ballerina. They observed the coach and the dancer scrutinizing each tiny movement seeking perfection. The dancer hungered for input. The comparison between the video and what is expected of the principal as coach of a teacher's performance was discussed earnestly and at length. The workshop ended.

The principals' assignment was to select five teachers on their staff whom they would coach using these newly acquired skills. They were expected to summarize, in writing, each completed teaching cycle and file it in a folder with the teacher's number and name. Al Antonelli would supervise the progress in the elementary schools. Bernard Green, setting an example by leading, volunteered to work with the middle and high school principals. Jennifer would be released from Old River on occasion to help Al and Bernard to oversee the principals. Both, superintendent and assistant, would select random folders at the schools and evaluate the completed work. Additionally, they would invite Jennifer to review their own work periodically throughout the school year.

Dr. Green delivered his year-two objective to the board of education at its first September meeting. He delineated the skills the principals will have gained by the following June. His plan for the year was to have three in-service sessions for the principals to adjust their coaching skills as needed and to work with specific patterns related to individual teacher and student needs.

The secondary principals would, in June, with Dr. Myers' chairing another workshop, train their department heads and assistant principals to become coaches. The department heads' job description would be amended to be specific regarding their coaching responsibilities. The elementary principals would train the town-wide department heads of music, foreign language, physical education, art and special education.

The major drawback in the plan Dr. Green presented to his board was the many responsibilities required of the principals.

"You must be mindful of the tremendous obligation we are placing on our principals. We expect to demonstrate a noticeable improvement in teaching and learning. Ideally, to do this job efficiently and productively, we must find ways to provide more time for principals to supervise in the classrooms. I intend to explore options with Al and a principal team. We'll pick Jennifer's brain. She's furthest advanced and spends a goodly amount of time in the classrooms at Clarksdale. This, of course is the thorniest of our challenges.

"Because I believe with all my being that the concept we're committed to is the only way to improve schools, I would like to employ, with your permission, a non-certified half-time person with writing skills whose job it would be to meet with and keep the State Department of Education informed of every step we've taken and are about to take. I'm sure there is a highly skilled mother in town who would work part-time on such a project. In addition to keeping the State Department informed, that person would write a weekly column for the *Old River Observer* and prepare monthly letters to the parents for each school to send home with their students. We would be able to inform and educate parents about our venture. A newsletter would apprise them of the community cable channel coverage and make evident our commitment to instruction. Hopefully, more folks will pay attention to our undertaking and know that their tax dollars are supporting real learning for the students in their Old River schools.

"Further I intend to meet with the bureaucracy at the State Department in hopes of convincing them, with the work we've completed and the progress we intend to make, that change must take place in their department. I'll meet with Dr. Jordan Whittier at State University to learn what progress he's making with his colleagues. Our outreach must be dramatic and immediate. We absolutely need to drop a bomb that can shake the State.

"It may seem like an impossible task because so many public schools operated with horses and buggies from the turn of the last century into the 50's. Some years ago Old River traded its horse and buggy education for a Volkswagen. It's time, with our knowledge and with our technology, to zoom into this century in a Ferrari. Unless this nation wakes up and supports the fact that our schools can only be saved by expert instructional coaches in the persons of its principals, we may as well shut down."

Board member Charlene Chestford asked to be recognized. "Are, you telling us, Dr. Green, that you will need more personnel and more money to make your supervision work, which translates into beaucoup more dollars in tax revenue?"

"Yes and no. I don't anticipate a need for *beaucoup,* as you put it, dollars but for now Mrs. Chestford, we're asking for a small investment in a planned public information effort. It would be money well spent in my humble opinion but we will need additional money in the future to assist our principals with management work non-professionals could do. There are incredible and incalculable sums of money being wasted at the state and national level on education follies. I'm of the opinion that we could obtain a grant for a model program. Those billions of wasted dollars need to be redirected and redistributed to deliver and promote the coaching concept throughout this nation. That's a next step but we wouldn't come to you for additional funding without a specific plan on how to redistribute current state and federal finances."

Mrs. Chestford looked down at the pad in front of her and scribbled a few notes. The meeting was adjourned following a brief question and answer period.

During Dr. Green's second year as Old River's education leader, in an effort to ease the principals' burdens somewhat, Jennifer recalled, he changed administrative meeting times. He rescheduled his school-day meetings and moved them to Wednesday when children were released early for teacher in-service work. He reduced the number of required reports, streamlined and tightened his own meetings. He vowed to make his administrative council meetings more efficient and briefer. He knew this wouldn't make getting into the classrooms a whole lot easier but it would help and would demonstrate his sensitivity to and appreciation for the principals' hard work.

The principals, initially stumbling and struggling, began to get a handle on the cycle of supervision. The fact that Bernard Green told the teachers at their opening convocation kicking off the school year that he was grateful for the good work they do, he was convinced that, with a coach to team with, they would become even better at their profession. He informed them of what he expected from them and their principals. He explained that the principals were learning to become coaches and they, the teachers, would function as colleagues working with their principal/coaches to produce the best learners possible. The concept being introduced is *coaching for improvement*. They and the principals would blaze this new trail together. Dr. Green's vow was to ensure that all at the convocation would become better at their craft than they currently are. As expected, the teachers were leery and suspicious. Green concluded the convocation with, "Please have faith in the process. Give it a chance. You and your students are the ones who will benefit, trust me."

The Year of the Bi-cycle, as the teachers christened the clinical program, began a new era of teacher improvement in Old River. Principals had chosen the five teachers they would coach. Not surprisingly, they selected to work with the best and the average while omitting the least skilled. Green and his staff figured on that. Their primary intent was to have the *coaches* master the process. They rationalized that principals would hone their skills throughout the year and be better equipped to help the most needy later. If, however, Green or Antonelli became aware of any teacher in trouble, the situation would be addressed and a plan would be designed to deal with the problem expeditiously. Also they decided that the process would be better received if no one felt threatened by the methodology.

The principals had been trained to gather as much data as they could transcribe when observing in the classroom. This method would challenge their ability to collect all the lesson's activities. It would show the teachers how this approach could be helpful. From such all-inclusive data they, together with the teachers, should easily find patterns they'd choose to improve or work on.

During Al and Dr. Green's observations of the process, they began to rate the principals and their progress. As soon as a principal had established trust and could competently handle the range of data collected during an observation, he/she was ready to take the next step for which they had been trained.

A behavioral pattern (student or teacher), they explained to their staffs, is akin to recognizing a pattern in one's daily living: smoking, overeating, impatience, raising one's voice in anger. One would develop a plan to alter these negative patterns e.g. "I'll count to thirty before I raise my voice at my spouse."

Conversely, one might be kind, helpful and caring most of the time. A strategy could be employed to extend these traits. Basically, they explained, this is what we will do together once a pattern to be extended or improved is identified.

The *coaches* informed their *partners* that there are hundreds of patterns to be observed in a classroom. They made copies of teaching techniques that lend themselves to improvement or extension patterns. Every Old River teacher received the same simple list from which to begin the process.

Partial List of Patterns in the Classroom: Teachers and Students

Greetings: Does the teacher welcome students into the classroom?

Opening: How quickly are students engaged in learning?

Organization: How organized are the teacher and students?

Directions: How clear are lesson directions?

Lesson Objective (s): Is the lesson objective being followed? If not, why not? (There may be a good reason "why not") Is the lesson objective shared with the students before the class is taught?

Motivation: Does the teacher motivate the students?

Active Learning: Are students active participants in their learning?

Lecture: Is lecturing balanced?

Body Language: Is the teacher's body language supportive or contrary i.e. smiling, nodding, glaring, scowling, detached.

Questions: Do the questioning patterns support the lesson objective? Are the questions designed to stir the imagination and expand student thinking or do they elicit one-word responses?

Closure: Are lessons properly brought to an end? Is there a review of what was intended in this lesson? Is there an explanation or a question as to where this lesson leads?

Learning: Are the children being encouraged to take steps to learn on their own? How is that demonstrated?

Understanding: Do the children understand what they are doing? How does the teacher verify that?

Guidance: are children properly guided to learn on their own?

Support: Does the teacher provide support for the students in a positive manner?

From this small sampling, the teachers were asked to work on extending the list to include additional patterns. A list of pattern categories is virtually unending.

Educators, administrative and teaching, in Old River are on the same page. They are working with a similar agenda. They know where the system is heading. They are leading the way for the rest of the state.

Shouldn't federal, state and local spending for education be reexamined for the purpose of redistributing dollars to support similar efforts? Shouldn't the nation's education goal be to establish coaching programs such as the one implemented in Old River? Can the seeds be planted and the notion be spread throughout the land that the principal in our schools is the only one who can unlock the door to better learning thereby significantly improving public education?

Dollars for education must be rethought and redistributed at the national and state levels. It's time to transform cast-in-stone thinking from a stone-age education to the space age we inhabit. Can our schools proudly and confidently emerge from the ashes.

Lastly and most important, *can the public be awakened from its lethargy and its uninformed state to rise in protest to pressure local boards of education to establish supervisory standards for their principals that will result in quality teaching and LEARNING?* When teaching improves and the incompetents become competent or are weeded out, test scores will rise without the panic that accompanies their results today. We needn't fall prey to the myth that test scores are what identify good schools. An expert, able, committed and bold superintendent leading outstanding principals and teachers are what will set apart good schools: nothing else will work! Nothing!

Chapter 31: Testing Myths

Old River, like so many of America's cities and towns, has a more privileged section and a less advantaged one. Bridgehurst is the section of Old River that is populated, mostly by blue-collar workers, laborers and a number of welfare and underprivileged minority families. A significant number of the residents reside in housing projects, apartments or in two and three-story older houses while others own modest homes on stamp-sized lots with little space between them and their neighbors. The children from Bridgehurst exist devoid of many of the opportunities afforded their counterparts across town.

They attend neighborhood schools in the busy, commercial section of the municipality. Many youngsters lose interest in school at an early age. A number, who are unsupervised, roam the neighborhood in the evening and are often out fairly late into the night seeking and joining trouble. The destitute environment these children have embraced can often be traced directly to lack of a caring father. Single mothers, two of whom are barely out of their teens have children entering Jefferson Elementary School. One great-grandmother is bringing up two school-aged great-grandsons and a great-granddaughter. The mother abandoned her kids and the grandmother is an alcoholic. In two other cases, grandparents are raising their grandchildren and seeing them off to school each day.

The students from the more affluent backgrounds across town mostly reside in large, comfortable and expensive one-family homes with manicured lawns and pricey landscaping. The homes have two and three-car garages with plenty of space and privacy between residences.

The children's parents are usually well educated and successful as measured by any standard.

When children from these well-to-do environments attend public school, they attend with peers of similar backgrounds. Test scores at their schools have been significantly higher than those from across town for years. Influencing their test results is that these students have been exposed to a wide-range of experiences from the time they were born. They've traveled. They've visited other countries. They've seen wonders like the Grand Canyon and Old Faithful and they've been to Disney World. They've vacationed in Europe, Florida, Hawaii, Alaska, Bermuda, South America and the Caribbean among others. Many were read to while still in the womb. Many are able to read by the time they finish kindergarten. They take music and dancing lessons, their fathers coach Little League; they go to the library and dine in elegant restaurants. They are cognizant of the importance of school. Some have been programmed for Harvard, Yale, Stanford and the likes since infancy.

Now, dear reader, please answer the following one-item pass or fail test question. Which group of students will score higher on national, state and Old River tests? As long as the two neighborhoods remain as they are, the kids from the affluent side of Old River will, hands down, outscore their opposite number across town.

Student test scores are affected, in large part, by what children have experienced in their young lives and by the family environment in which they live. Travel, vacations, music lessons, theater, the arts, story hours and books, are all experiences that clearly influence their scores. Providing vouchers for parents or guardians to choose a different school for their disadvantaged children will not often plug the gaps no matter where the disadvantaged attend school.

Test results shape students' self-confidence positively or negatively, affect how they feel about themselves, and influence what others expect and think of them. Tests have an impact on pupils' attitudes toward school. Poor or failing scores re-enforce poor self-images.

One would assume that politicians at the local, state and national levels know all this. It's their business to know it. Yet, they adhere to the same age-old incorrect conclusion that the present inequities between two neighborhoods, as in Old River, or those that exist between urban and suburban school districts can be balanced with money and, more recently, with more intensive testing (NCLB). Money wrongly spent and testing wrongly administered will not balance the equation. The effort to eliminate the existing educational, societal and economic imbalance among neighborhoods or between urban and suburban schools without addressing the roots of their differences is not only negligent but borders on scandalous disregard.

Suburban school boards publicly express their concerns regarding declining test scores. Among their solutions is more time to teach what is being tested and/or redistricting minority and disadvantaged children. Seldom is the principal part of the solution. And rarely are the socio-economic conditions addressed.

Unfortunately, the givers of public monies ignore, in their solutions, the dissimilarities that exist between the classroom kids and the street kids for fear of being labeled bigoted. Some insightful Old River citizens facetiously opine that if kids in the two neighborhoods switched schools while everything else were left in place, including the teachers, poor test results would follow the students across town. Jefferson School under the able leadership of its instructional leader, Ron Comstock, is providing the best education possible within the conditions it controls.

Originally, when the Elementary Secondary Education Act (ESEA) was passed in 1965, its proponents' philosophy and beliefs were, and still are, that by giving school people more money for their disadvantaged populations schools would improve. The goal was to improve education for the poor, the minority and the handicapped. The handicapped gained a solid and deserved foothold in the schoolhouse when the Individuals with Disabilities Education Act (IDEA) was passed in 1975.

However, the poor and minority populations have not come close to closing the achievement gap.

Following several rewrites over a 40-year time span, ESEA has evolved into the current Bush administration's *No Child Left Behind* (NCLB) with its heavy emphasis on the use of testing to determine a school's success or failure. It uses the test hammer to force learning, a crude and uninspiring approach to school improvement. NCLB does, however, bring attention to the main issues confronting America's public schools: *accountability and testing, flexibility and local control, funding for what works,* and *expanded parental options* (vouchers). Yet the points of emphasis are akin to trying to blow bubbles without soap.

One of the program's headings is: PROMOTING TEACHER QUALITY AND SMALLER CLASSROOMS, both desirable aspirations. The word PRINCIPAL, however, is nowhere to be found among the sub-headings! The principal is missing! How does NCLB intend to improve teacher quality without addressing the role the principal must play in that effort?

Citing the need for smaller classrooms by NCLB is another noble aim. But, has anyone computed the cost of decreasing the size of classrooms even by as few as two students per class? With smaller classes, what teaching strategies would change? Teachers, without an instructional coach to help them grow professionally would continue to teach the way they always have. Is that the end we seek with smaller classrooms? A nationally renown Connecticut superintendent of schools of the 60's and 70's, Charles O. Richter, once remarked that, unless the union could show how smaller classes would be beneficial for children, he was fearful that the community would be buying, "mediocrity in a more intimate setting."

More testing of kids who are becoming indifferent to all the testing and preparation for testing is not the way to measure school success. Nor will more money spent on schools in the same old way do much, if anything, to improve instruction. First, the socio-economic structure of our schools, which are practically treatment-centers now, must be addressed. Expecting politicians to challenge the mess that our modern pop-culture has become is like looking for a canary to attack an eagle's nest.

Our leaders (if they exist) in the government and social institutions lack the courage to tackle the problems that are strangling, not only our scapegoat schools, but our country as well. Until they are able and willing to identify and define the problem, as any scientist can tell you, it cannot be solved. Mis-identification is useless as well.

Though lacking legal control of the socio-economic structure, schools continue to bear the responsibility for educating all pupils. Sadly, students from the less affluent environment, will continue to lag and will suffer the consequences of not reaching competency levels established by the *No Child Left Behind* government testing program under present familial conditions.

What magic can the schools these children attend call on to raise their test scores? It's like expecting a high school basketball team to compete at the collegiate level. It's a no-win proposition. What can be done, however, and what is within our control, is the commitment to raise the quality of instruction in *all schools*. If the best teaching possible is provided to pupils *via effective coaching*, test scores will improve proportionately.

However, until the family unit can function for the good of its children and society declares war on violence, explicit sex and greed; until the lies from Corporate America, politicians and special interest groups are recognized as contributing factors to our decline, there is little hope for our nation or its schools. Until attitudes, so critical for positive change, can be dramatically altered, we cannot expect our schools to save our youth.

It is illogical to believe that nation-wide behavior modification of the broken-down family unit can soon be realized. Sadly, this fact does not absolve the schools from its responsibility to educate every student. Attempts by school personnel to positively affect needy families are like trying to capture a battleship with a rowboat.

NCLB, like its ancestor programs, faces the same challenge to close the same gaps that continue to exist between disadvantaged and advantaged children as ESEA faced originally. Testing via NCLB is putting all the pressure on the schools and none on dysfunctional families.

Under NCLB guidelines, when a school is branded a failure, parents can shop for another school with government vouchers in hand while never having to assume any responsibility for their children's deficiencies. It is akin to the government providing credit cards to shop at another supermarket. Does the holder of the card know which store is better than the other? Is Stop and Shop a better market than Shaw's? Schools are charged with failure because children's test results are poor. Is it the chicken or the egg? Do we really know? The incongruity is absorbing but sad.

Testing is important but over-reliance on it is like using a spoon rather than a shovel to fill a ravine in student learning. Though testing gives significant and important feedback to teachers regarding classroom progress and individual student growth it does NOT provide techniques to improve learning. Schools' fear of the embarrassment and sanctions imposed for failure, is already is causing undue emphasis on math and reading instruction. More time spent using the same old teaching techniques for math and reading is likely to result in rote learning, drudgery and boredom. Kids might be trained to memorize math facts like our fifth-graders' memorized the capitals of the USA but is that learning?

Math and reading are critically important skills for students to acquire and use. Yes, we must upgrade instruction in those areas. But, schools that fail the government's imposed testing program will, unfortunately in many cases, simply increase time spent teaching reading and math while overlooking the quality of that instruction.

Many critics of NCLB worry about its effect on science and social studies. America's schools have been roundly and loudly criticized for not teaching American History and for failing students in science. Are we ready to trade less time for history and science for extended time teaching reading and math? Music and art are the soul of humankind. They play to our core and elevate our humanness. A number of schools are squeezing them out of or reducing their time from the curriculum to provide extra hours to prepare for tests. Are these the trade-offs we seek?

The emphasis on testing since the onset of NCLB, has produced some positive results. There are improved test scores in more than a few instances. It has spurred focus on special education students, a number of whom have improved their test scores under NCLB. The NCLB spotlight has, according to both its proponents and opponents, shed light on the nationwide need for holding schools accountable. It has resulted in identifying and adopting standards that have driven constructive curriculum development: both valuable plusses. It has raised awareness throughout the nation that many children are not learning. For those reasons alone NCLB has contributed appreciably to the improvement of education. It's the unbalanced emphasis on testing as the determiner of success that concerns its critics.

Many, who have brain-stormed the testing dilemma brought to the fore by NCLB, maintain that learning can't be defined by a series of tests; that it can't be determined by a measurement alone; that a student is more than a test score. They stridently voice unease that the national emphasis on testing is dominating classroom activity and suppressing teacher resourcefulness while lessening children's interest. It is critical that we not make numbers out of our children, they caution. How can drill after drill to prepare for tests keep children motivated much less interested especially those youngsters who are disadvantaged socially, emotionally or physically? The argument continues that standardized testing, as required by NCLB, does not validate success or failure. NCLB testing requirements have run amok, many believe, and are as out of control as a runaway horse bolting from a corral.

What punitive measures will the U.S. Department of Education impose on *failing* schools? What *supplemental services* will be provided? What happens if children continually fail the tests? How will they be helped? Will children, who are emerging as pre-teens, be kept in elementary school when they have begun to shave or develop into young women?

Standards are vital and valuable when aligned with the curriculum. Their purpose is for students to attain proficiency in all areas deemed important by the school district. While testing and NCLB can be credited with bringing attention to this necessary alignment, the need for testing and more testing can become pointless. Ironically, the very core of NCLB's testing objective, designed to put pressure on schools and teachers to improve, may be the very thing that undermines that lofty aim.

The answer to better schools is through the improvement of teaching. Adding more minutes to the reading and math curricula, when a teacher is ineffective, will not improve learning in these disciplines anymore than a cook, whose cakes are flat, is going to create a two tiered chocolate cake until he/she discovers the purpose of yeast. Poor teaching will not improve learning in reading and math simply by extending time and testing. Doing a task poorly repeatedly does not result in growth. Poor students will go only as far as their teachers can take them no matter their home conditions or their testing experiences.

Pressuring schools to improve teaching, as NCLB intends, via its testing hammer, is another in a long line of doomed federal efforts to improve schools. The concentration to improve schools has to be on the identification and development of expert coaches. That's where pressure needs to be applied. The best teaching possible will produce the best results. Testing is a necessary tool that is used by a teacher to gather important data. Testing does not teach. Teachers teach. We must make all of them as proficient as possible, then test scores will serve the purpose for which they were intended.

Chapter 32:
A Billion Here: A Billion There

Some years ago Everett Dirksen, United States Senator from Illinois shared an observation with his Senate colleagues. "A billion here and a billion there, and soon you're talking real money," he chided.

How much is a billion? Though the source for the following attempt to bring understanding to this complex concept could not be determined, an advertising agency once did the mathematics in an effort to put a billion into perspective. The results are fascinating: *A billion seconds ago it was 1959; a billion minutes ago Jesus was alive; a billion hours ago our ancestors were living in the Stone Age; A billion dollars ago was only 8 hours and 20 minutes ago at the rate Washington spends it!*" However long ago those conclusions were made is not certain but they are astounding.

Can we comprehend what a billion is? Can we even comprehend what a million is? If one were to count to a million one second at-a-time without stop, night and day, it would take 23 days to reach a million. To reach one billion doing a similar exercise would take 95 years.......*one* billion!

Now consider that from 1965 until 2004 the federal government invested more than 165 BILLION dollars for Title 1 of the ESEA alone, money designated specifically to improve education for the poor and disadvantaged. The gap between the more privileged and the disadvantaged in 2004 was wider than ever! The disparity is deplorable.

The *House Education & Workforce Committee*, John Bochner, Chairman, acknowledges in its Report Summary "that African American and Hispanic students continue to trail their more affluent counterparts in every grade level, in every subject. Today nearly 70% of inner-city fourth-graders cannot read at a basic level."

What a return on a $165 billion+ investment! What is fascinating in this report that embodies President Bush's education vision is the absence, still again, of the principal's role in improving our schools! Is everyone blind, deaf and dumb?

The President's comments, as listed here, are praiseworthy but empty in their promise. The parenthetic comments are mine:

"When states use federal dollars, they should be accountable for getting results. (ABSOLUTELY)

Parents should be empowered with data about the schools their children are attending, the qualification of the teachers teaching their children, and their children's academic progress. (HOW WILL THEY DETERMINE TEACHERS' QUALIFICATION?)

Programs should be streamlined and federal resources should be focused on helping students who are most in need of help. Dollars should flow to where they'll make the biggest impact for our children – not to bureaucracy. (FAMILIES MUST BECOME PARTNERS WITH THEIR SCHOOLS)

To meet higher expectations, teachers and local school officials (DOES THIS INCLUDE PRINCIPALS?) should have greater flexibility to decide how to address students' unique needs.

Parents want to choose the best possible education for their children." (OF COURSE THEY DO)

Major Provisions listed in the Conference Report are:

Enhancing Accountability Demanding Results
Unprecedented State & Local Flexibility
Streamlining Bureaucracy and Reducing Red Tape
Expanding Choices for Parents
Prohibiting National Testing
The President's Reading First Initiative
Promoting Teacher Quality and Smaller Classrooms
Dollars to the Classroom
Making Schools Safer
An Independent Benchmark
Promoting English Fluency
Protecting Home Schools
Rural Schools
School Prayer

Under each of the headings above are sentences and a few paragraphs that expand and attempt to clarify the main provisions of the President's words. HOWEVER, the word *principal* remains conspicuous by its absence throughout the provisions. Principal appears only once in the report. It's under the *Making Schools Safer* provision: "Would help ensure that teachers, *principals*, and other school professionals can undertake reasonable actions *to maintain order and discipline* in the classroom without the fear of being dragged into court or subjected to frivolous lawsuits."

Note the role of the principal. Is that what we expect in return for the salaries we pay our school leaders? There is little argument with the rest of the list. But how are these requirements going to be implemented and where is the supervisor to ensure that teachers will improve under the provision entitled *Promoting Teacher Quality and Smaller Classrooms?*

As far as promoting smaller classrooms is concerned has anyone who is planning to continue to burn a $165 billion more considered the cost of such an undertaking? In

Old River, Superintendent Bernard Green faced one of his few setbacks, an embarrassing one, when he brought a general proposal to his board to reduce class size in Old River's schools where 9,897 students are enrolled. The per-pupil cost is $9,998. One board member did a quick math calculation with simple figures and concluded that, to drop class size from 20 to 18 students, would require 10% more teachers and 10% more classrooms. With the average teacher salary over $60,000, Mr. Gronski's findings needed no further emphasis. The cost would be $600,000 in salaries alone without figuring the additional classrooms and their supplies.

Let's try counting to 1 million once more. Project these figures nationally (class sizes are more likely to be near 25 or higher than the 20 in Old River); the cost to reduce class size across this nation by as few as two students would be astronomical. Further, to reduce class size by two is unlikely to make even a small plunk in a lake as far as ripple effect on learning goes. And, would the reduction change teaching? Will the stand-up lecturer sit down to lecture?

It is time for this nation to put its foot down. Yes, *Enhance Accountability & Demand Results,* America. But do it by holding the superintendents accountable and responsible for training their principals to become qualified and active teacher coaches. It's the Principal of the Thing! Unless we wake up to that fact, in another four decades we will be trying to understand what a trillion is and how we wasted it by circumnavigating and ignoring the principals. If we get started now, it will take 2,000 centuries or 200,000 years to count to a trillion. Let's give that some serious consideration. We are about to burn billions more without forethought. More money, more testing, more rewards without a teacher of teachers accountable for upgrading the science of teaching will only lead to failure again.

Federal resources must be distributed differently. The disbursement of billions of dollars to 50 state departments of education must be done with the proviso that the states will monitor their school districts and forward proof of their progress toward the retraining and training of current principals and new principal candidates. Then we will turn the corner and head our nation in the right direction. There is no need to fund any other school programs. Get the principals up-to-speed with in-house training and require new certifying programs at state colleges. Put pressure on state departments of education to re-direct their resources from testing to supporting districts in their efforts to re-train. From a 2006 federal budget of 2.6 trillion dollars the education budget is 56 billion[4] a decrease of 1 percent from 2005. It would take 6,175 years (8181 A.D.) to count the Department of Education budget, one dollar at a time, from the year 2006! Let's use it differently; let's make it work

---

[4] **2006 Discretionary Budget Authority:** $56.0 billion: Department of Education (www.whitehouse.gov/omb/budget/fy2006/education.html)

Chapter 33: Remedies

It's time to rebuild America's monolithic and deteriorating enterprise: its public schools. It's essential that this task be undertaken eagerly, aggressively, with resolve and immediately. With national determination we put a man on the moon within a decade. Surely we can overhaul and renovate our education institution in that amount of time. The challenge is awesome but cannot be dismissed, avoided or postponed. How can our nation tackle such a monumental task?

Notions to Ponder

Just about everyone agrees that, to have productive and successful schools, our schools must employ skillful teachers. This cannot be realized by wishful thinking or with money alone. Our nation's principals must be held accountable to raise teacher competence to peak levels. Anything less is not acceptable.

1. The federal ESEA Title 1 Act of 1965 and its evolution over the decades into its most recent revision, the No Child Left Behind Act, was originally adopted to calm a bothered and dissatisfied segment of the public. It was enacted to close the gap between disadvantaged and middle class students. The millions upon millions of dollars Title 1 has spent since its beginning have failed to narrow that gap. Federal monies need to be *redistributed* to train and upgrade principals. The NCLB testing prescription for our

schools' disorders is not the answer. If teaching is poor to begin with, testing children will not improve the quality of their instruction. If someone gets heartburn from eating spicy foods, they don't recover by eating more of the same.

We must guard against the overuse of testing to determine school success or failure. Forceful pressure on schools to attain higher test scores may improve student test-taking skills but *will not make teaching better*; it will not produce better learners. Coaches employed in a number of professional lines of work warn that practicing errant skills is not only foolish, but actually impedes skill development. It reinforces weak habits. The same concept applies to teaching.

2. We must employ trained principals, the likes of Jennifer Myers, to ensure that teachers do become better at their craft. A teacher of teachers of Dr. Myers' caliber assigned to every school in America would unquestionably raise student achievement whether students attend rural, urban, suburban, elementary, middle or high school.

3. Public schools must compete. One need only become familiar with what magnet schools have to offer to realize why many are successful. It's because those responsible for initially staffing them recruited only exceptional principals and teachers. Magnet school staffs represent creative, committed and talented professionals. We must meet those same conditions in all our schools. Our schools must fulfill the conditions that exist in the first generation of magnet schools.

4. There are two other critical and overlooked factors affecting the education of a host of public school children: their home-life and family conditions work against their success in the mainstream of society. Welfare monies must be distributed differently. Un-

employed but healthy and able parents who collect welfare checks should be made to work with their children at school to earn their checks. They must connect, become involved and cooperate with their neighborhood school and its social worker. Many children, minority and white living in hardship or without a nurturing parent have little hope and less desire for success in school. They believe school is not for them. Such a situation might be changed if parents are required to become involved with their children at the schoolhouse.

Many needy White, Afro-American and Hispanic children from socially decaying neighborhoods choose to rebel. Their rebellion is projected through their uniform of the day: a cap with visor askew or other diverse headwear, macho sleeveless tees, baggy and sagging pants, tattoos, pierced body parts and outlandishly expensive sneakers. Their intent is to project a gangsta-tough look. They are committed to a counter-culture life-style and see no use for schooling. They remain cynical, confrontational and contemptuous regarding society's authority. While in the schoolhouse they are incorrigible. A teacher attempting to discipline them risks insult, profanity or, in rare cases, physical threat. Unfortunately their security comes from their gang relationships, which substitute for family. The most critical factor for forecasting success in school is the quality of children's family life.

A possible start to begin to change this deplorable situation might be for our citizenry to consider President Bush's *Marriage Initiative*. Though voluntary, it might help many wallowing individuals to understand the benefits of marriage. The President's proposal provides information on the value of marriage in one's life, including, and most important, its value in children's lives. The initiative includes pre-marriage counseling, fatherhood training, information provided to teen-aged girls to prevent pregnancy. It addresses child-support payments. These actions could easily be tied to welfare programs and be offered in neighborhood schools.

Financial assistance to families could become part of new community welfare efforts to provide parenting skills for those who need them. Parents must be taught the negative impact sitting in front of TV for hours has on their youngsters and further, they must come to understand their responsibility for controlling their children's night-time activities; they need to recognize the importance of the school and its worth for their children's future success.

The welfare system should require fathers to own up to their responsibility of raising their offspring. Out of wedlock births are paralyzing, not only our schools, but our entire social system as well.

When does it become the responsibility of the parent(s) and not the state to work in partnership with the schools on behalf of their children? Poverty and lack of parental accountability form a formidable barrier that schools cannot cross without changes in the social conditions that cause these deplorable no-win situations. Struggling families have to be re-directed, trained and shown that work and commitment to family can lead to better lives for their children at home and school.

Where are the members of the clergy?

5. The prescription for doctoring ailing schools, for far too many years, has been to medicate with large doses of money, most recently accompanied by more testing while the doctor doesn't bother to find the cause of the patient's illness or if the "money prescription" works; the patient continues to ail and no one knows why. Continuing to spend in the same old way is pointless. Money spent on education without quality control or responsibility can be no more ef-

fective than it would be in an addicted gambler's wallet.

Currently, in-service workshops are among the most popular efforts to improve teaching. These programs usually motivate teachers to expand their repertoire. Unfortunately, their impact is fleeting and, without a principal's endorsement and attention, they are not usually practical or effective over the long run.

6. Whether in the city, on the farm or in the suburbs, teachers within the same state must acquire the same endorsement to be certified. They must all jump through the same hoop. That being the case, we should expect *all* teachers, with appropriate supervision, to be effective whether they teach in a city or small town.

7. We must use the annual billions of dollars spent, and to a great extent, wasted on public education in bold new ways. The U.S. Department of Education must be empowered to redistribute the money it now expends on Title 1's failures. A redistribution of federal dollars must be tied to exacting requirements for training principals who then must be directed to spend considerably more time in classrooms teaching teachers.

   New ideas, recommendations and requirements to improve schools have come to the schools over the decades tied to bundles of national, state and local funding. Initially new programs created by bureaucrats hit schools like surging streams, but without leadership to ensure their success, they usually slow to a trickle before evaporating and leaving dusty and fading trails of dried up dollars dropping like dead leaves.

8. Some of the state and federal funds should be *redirected* to provide administrative assistance for middle and elementary schools. The emphasis is on *redirected, not added.* Managers could be hired to provide time for both, the principal and assistant to do classroom coaching.

   There is a sprinkling of school systems in our nation that has made a commitment to increase supervision in their elementary schools by appointing school managers to provide more time for the principal to work with teachers. The managers tackle some of the grunt work required of elementary principals. They handle a number if non-instructional matters. They are assigned to schools through graduate programs by their graduate advisors much as student teachers are assigned to schools.

   Creative superintendents should be able to design and propose inexpensive solutions to find ways to relieve principals from mundane tasks that restrict their time to supervise. One school district created an additional teaching position for each of its elementary schools and introduced a principal training job. It appointed *teacher coordinators,* one for each school, to work with the principal and the teachers to help coordinate the curriculum. Some programs will work in one district but not necessarily in another.

9. The kind of work that was done in Old River with its principal in-service program, including the workshops and the training week in the summer school, would require very little funding. The method for training would be up to the states and local school districts but would require that coaches acquire knowledge about how students learn and how teachers can be helped to positively affect student learning.

10. Schools of Education must be taken to task. Certain of their education programs are in need of adjustment

and upgrading. Also, they need to create ways to attract and challenge quality students. Currently, education majors generally have lower SAT scores than students at other colleges. If teacher preparatory colleges are to be productive institutions they must revise their offerings. The road to certification needs to be rigorous. Students should be schooled in the science of teaching and the psychology of learning and how to inspire student learning. Teacher salaries that begin in the $40,000's range need to be publicized to attract better students to the teaching profession.

Are schools of education allowing weak teacher candidates like Harry Latter to attain certification without demonstrating proof of teaching ability? Are poorer teacher candidates being hired by the cities because the better teachers opt for the suburbs? These questions have to be addressed frankly and bluntly if our preparing institutions are to retool for the purpose of certifying successful and productive graduates.

11. It's also time for the fifty state departments of education to trade their obsession with testing for a monitoring system to oversee that school districts have appropriate supervision programs in place. They need to assume the responsibility for providing help to initiate and facilitate training rather than sit back, wait for test results, post them and declare which schools are failing. The state department bureaucrats need to shape up and get serious about their role in the improvement of instruction.

12. Following the training of its principals, Old River continued its move forward. It designed an in-service program for teacher development along the lines of its administrative workshops. It ran for two school years and helped teachers know what was expected of them. Everyone in Old River is working with the same recipe.

Similar programs should be encouraged and endorsed by The United States Department of Education and state departments of education should provide resources to assist local districts to make such training programs operational.

13. Superintendents of schools, with support from their state departments of education and through their boards of education, must be accountable for organizing and establishing training sessions to prepare their principals to become instructional leaders.

14. All boards of education across this nation should have a supervision policy, a policy that specifically requires supervisory competency by its school principals, department heads and other supervisors. The adopted policy should list the specifics of the policy's intent.

    The Old River Board policy explicitly holds Superintendent Green accountable for managing its coaching program. The district's principals are answerable to Bernard Green through his assistant superintendent for instruction. The Old River Board of Education is secure in knowing their superintendent has instant access to the status of the supervision program.

15. To attract outstanding principal candidates, salary incentives should be adjusted. The price to upgrade supervision in our schools must include raising principal salaries to accomplish the education job expected of them. It will cost no more than what has been wastefully spent on government programs like Title 1 over the past 4 decades.

    Federal spending for K-12 improvement from 1965 through 2002 totaled $165 billion ($321 billion in 2002 dollars). Add to that, $4,184,161,348 spent for NCLB since its inception in 2002. Those monies were and are designated for school improvement. The government projects an NCLB budget of $97,144,765,294 through 2014! The bulk of that *is for personnel*! Of that sum, $19,839,448,838 is earmarked for school improvement. Obviously there is money enough to redistribute to attract competent principals. (For those who have forgotten, the number before the three commas represents billions!) It takes a long time to count to a billion!

16. The cream of our principal crop must be expected to use, not just the newest, but also the best supervisory tools to become more expert at their craft. They will add the newer and efficient instruments, like technology, to their *Improving Teacher Toolboxes* and continue to hone their coaching skills.

17. The principal's job description needs to stress that improving instruction is the principal's priority. The job description or position guide must hold principals to a lofty standard. It must specify the skills required to coach teachers and include the principal's curriculum responsibility.

18. It's imperative that potential school leaders be identified, encouraged, enlisted and trained to become instructional leaders. The state certifying boards could turn this responsibility over to the school districts. The days of the school manager must go the way of the typewriter.

19. Federal dollars earmarked for improving education must be dispensed, tightly controlled and validated. Principals will be targeted, monitored and evaluated under strict and specific guidelines to guarantee their qualification to affect better instruction in the classrooms of America.

As schools succeed, vouchers will become a thing of the past as will the need for magnet and charter schools. Neighborhood schools will deliver the excellence parents seek and deserve because their principals will be teachers of teachers and their teachers will be, not only certified, but qualified teachers of children.

It's time, America! <u>It's the *Principal* of the Thing!</u> There is no other way.